State, Civil Society and Right to Education

State, Civil Society and Right to Education

Jeebanlata Salam

RAWAT PUBLICATIONS
Jaipur • New Delhi • Bangalore • Hyderabad • Guwahati • Kolkata

ISBN 978-81-316-0466-3

Published by
Prem Rawat for **Rawat Publications**
Satyam Apts, Sector 3, Jawahar Nagar, Jaipur 302 004 (India)
Phone: 0141 265 1748 / 7006 Fax: 0141 265 1748
E-mail: info@rawatbooks.com
Website: www.rawatbooks.com

New Delhi Office
4858/24, Ansari Road, Daryaganj, New Delhi 110 002
Phone: 011 2326 3290

Also at *Bangalore, Hyderabad, Guwahati* and *Kolkata*

Typeset by Rawat Computers, Jaipur
Printed at Chaman Enterprises, New Delhi

In memory of
those children killed in violence.

Contents

Abbreviations

AIDS	:	Acquired Immune Deficiency Syndrome
AMCO	:	All Manipur Christian Organisation
AMESTA	:	All Manipur Elementary Teachers Association
AMUCO	:	All Manipur United Clubs Organisation
AMSU	:	All Manipur Students Union
AFSPA	:	Armed Forces Special Powers Act (1958)
B.Ed	:	Bachelor of Education
BJP	:	Bharatiya Janata Party
CABE	:	Central Advisory Board of Education
COHR	:	Coordination for Human Rights
CSCHR	:	Civil Society Coalition on Human Rights
CSOs	:	Civil Society Organisations
DESAM	:	Democratic Students' Alliance of Manipur
DIET	:	District Institute of Educational Training
ECCE	:	Early Childhood Care and Education
EFA	:	Education for All
EGS	:	Education Guarantee Scheme
FORCES	:	Forum for Child Care and Crèche Services
GoI	:	Government of India
HRA	:	Human Rights Alert
ICDS	:	Integrated Child Development Services
K.G.	:	Kindergarten
KYKL	:	Kanglei Yawol Kunna Lup

LFS	:	Little Flower School
MCLM	:	Manipur Chanura Leishem Marup
MDWF	:	Manipur Democratic Women Front
MoU	:	Memorandum of Understanding
NAFRE	:	National Alliance on the Fundamental Right to Education
NCF	:	National Curriculum Framework
NEP	:	National Education Policy
NGOs	:	Non-Governmental Organisations
NSCN(M)	:	National Socialist Council of Nagaland (Muiva)
OB	:	Operation Blackboard
OSS	:	Operation Summer Storm
POA	:	Programme of Action
POTA	:	Prevention of Terrorist Activities Act
PREPARK	:	People Revolutionary Party of Kangleipak
PROBE	:	Primary Report on Basic Education
RTI	:	Right to Information (Act)
PTA	:	Parent Teacher Association
SAYO	:	Southern Angamai Youth Organisation
SPSS	:	Statistical Package for Social Sciences
SSA	:	Sarva Shiksha Abhigyan
STDs	:	Sexually Transmitted Diseases
UCM	:	United Committee Manipur
UNC	:	United Naga Council
VEC	:	Village Education Committee

Preface

Making the right to education a fully realised and realistic goal remains profoundly challenging, carrying heavy consequences for India's millions of children, who experience diverse forms of social exclusion. Such children have been victim to multiple forms of silent and loud emergencies, such as hunger, poverty, destitution, illiteracy, armed conflict and displacement, etc., meaning they are systematically deprived of quality education, while some have not even set foot inside a school.

Since independence, India has formed a number of education commissions and committees that are well equipped to provide education with a mass character. Of late, India became a signatory to the Education for All (EFA) declaration, the Dakar Framework for Action and the Millennium Development Goals, while civil society actors play a watchdog role and campaign for bringing such children into the ambit of basic education. Strangely enough, despite such developments, such children remain in a poor position at the bottom of the heap. As such, millions of children, who are perfectly capable and eager to learn, remain illiterate, with profound consequences for their future lives.

Therefore, under all these circumstances, realising the right to education for all children is not a straightforward task and remains profoundly challenging for a society as hierarchical as India's. Furthermore, the right to education for all and its realisation goes well beyond the territory of education policies and projects alone. The present research study has attempted to delve into some of the contending issues and complexities by examining the socio-economic and political reality of a people. A book of this kind, which is both empirical and academic, has its limitations in terms of its scope, essentially focusing on the school community, children and parents living in the state of Manipur, a politically volatile region, situated in the north-easternmost part of India.

Nonetheless, the emerging issues and problems raised in the book provide insight regarding the complexities and contradictions that have been largely marginalised in popular educational discourse, both among academics and in education policy. It is these contradictions and paradoxes that have prompted me to reflect and engage in the present research study. Such critical reflection and engagement would not have taken root had I not been a member of the Indian Social Institute, New Delhi, where various civil society groups come together to discuss educational issues, including the controversial Free and Compulsory Education Bill, 2004, which was finally translated into the present Act, The Right of Children to Free and Compulsory Education Act, 2009, popularly known as Right to Education.

It was during this routine engagement with the Indian Social Institute that I produced a short, critical write up (Education Policies and Praxis: A Reference to Free and Compulsory Education Bill, Legal News and Views, Indian Social Institute, 2004) on the Free and Compulsory Education Bill proposed by the National Democratic Alliance (NDA) of the BJP-led government. The paper was distributed among Catholic schools in Delhi and various civil society groups. As the Bill was brought to the attention of the public, various academics, researchers, social activists and teachers from various parts of India began to reflect critically on the issue during seminars, workshops and discussions, a trend that gradually gained a nation-wide momentum, culminating in national seminars, held mostly during the period 2003–04. The contributors came out strongly against the historical shift of education, which went from being present in the Directive Principles of State Policy to becoming a Fundamental Right. The proposal to make education a Fundamental Right was unsuccessful when debated back in 1950 for if elementary education as a fundamental right is to be translated into action, it would be profoundly challenging for a country in which millions are deprived of even basic amenities like food and shelter. Secondly, making education a Fundamental Right also pushes responsibility on parents for educating their children and, in case schools remain non-functional, it is the responsibility of parents to report to the court. This issue alone makes it extremely difficult and challenging to realise the right to education for all children, since making the educational right workable for children from poor and disadvantaged backgrounds requires these parents to be socially empowered. This provides reason enough in explaining that translating the right to education into an achievable goal requires societal reforms, not just reforms in the education sector alone. This observation is relevant not only for a particular region but for the country as a whole. As a matter of fact, it is relevant to examine such an issue even for the state of Kerala, which claims to have achieved a 100 per cent literacy rate. In reality, the truth is that, even in Kerala, there are some children who have not yet seen the door of a school. As such, it is clear that the present study, focusing on Manipur state, sheds light upon regional challenges, which are part of a nation-wide phenomenon, leaving much scope for further study of other regions.

Despite the great significance of a study of this kind for all regions in India, I chose the state of Manipur, not solely because I am a native of this state, but precisely because the state suffers from longstanding violent conflict, which presents unique and pressing issues in the field of education. Like universal adult suffrage, land reform measures, and democratic decentralisation, etc., the Right to Education Act has tremendous potential for social transformation. Today, we are living in a knowledge-based society and education has become an important resource. At the heart of the Right to Education lies the idea of bringing educationally excluded children into the mainstream education system. However, like other measures mentioned above, this Act has not lived up to expectation and I have endeavoured to explore why.

Engaging in research of this kind is a journey, reflective of the complex paradoxical times we live in and I am truly grateful to my country, India, which, vast in diversity, showers upon us immense possibilities for exploration and discovery. First, I would like to express my eternal gratitude to Professor Avijit Pathak, who has been of great inspiration, for providing me with constant nurture in order to improve the present research study and for encouraging me to publish the book.

I am indeed grateful to all those researchers, academicians, teachers, lawyers and social activists who have shared a common platform with me during the course of our engagement in dialogues and discussions on the present issue. Their company, engagement and solidarity gave me tremendous hope regarding the immense possibilities of bringing about change, despite the extremely challenging political environment of our times.

I am truly indebted to all those toiling parents, who despite being busy with daily work, interacted with me, engaging with me passionately on the issue of my research and also to the school community of

Don Bosco, Bethel and Phoijing Junior High School. I am thankful to all the staff members of Bosco Mangaal for giving me sufficient time to learn about Bosco Mangaal despite their busy schedule.

I remain ever grateful to Kameshwar Chaudhary of Ambedkar University, Lucknow, Avinash Kumar Singh, Yosephine Yazali of NUEPA, New Delhi, Tiplut Nongbri, Geetha B. Nambissan of Jawaharlal Nehru University, New Delhi for their constant intellectual engagement, enthusiasm, friendly and cheerful dialogue with me in the area of my research whenever I find an opportunity to be with them.

I extend my thanks to Sachin Sharma, Shilpi, Satyendra, Ambreen, Aqsa Agha, Rajesh, Avinash Mishra, Jai Parkash, Sachdev Tanuja, Nishant, Shashi Bhushan, Sucharita Khuntia, Rekha Konsam and Shanti for their moral encouragement. I am especially thankful to Levish Leivon Kom for closely reading the final manuscript.

Words are not enough to express my gratitude to Premita, Rishikanta, Premlata and Jhaljit for their company during visits to the field sites. They endured all kinds of discomforts with dogged perseverance, while I often dragged them to the sites of enquiry. I am also profusely thankful to sister Anandi, uncle Damu Singh, Che Ibemhal and Etei Surjit Singh for providing me a constant source of strength and unconditional support during the course of my field study.

Time and again, I remember my mother who could not continue her journey of life in this world. I shared the details of my research studies with her almost until her last days. If not for her incessant encouragement and faith in me to undertake this research, I am sure, this noble contribution and engagement may simply have not been possible. It is almost impossible to delink my existence in this world from the presence of my late father in me. He has been my eternal source of inspiration, courage and strength as a doting father, a true friend and a great teacher.

I remain ever indebted to all those who have made this noble contribution possible.

CHAPTER 1

Introduction: Sociological Relevance and Modes of Enquiry

In recent years, various national and international educational strategies have been devised, with the aim of improving access to and rates of completion of basic education by 2015, with interim goals of eliminating gender disparities in education across India by 2005,[1] along with the achievement of Universal Elementary Education by 2007.[2] With the passing of the 86th amendment to the Constitution of India in 2002, the Government of India declared elementary education a fundamental right, a landmark development further supported by a recent revival among civil society movements with the same goal. However, despite such developments, various socio-cultural issues stand alongside those of political, economic and governance, together presenting huge challenges in the Indian context. A sound sociological understanding of such challenges is of crucial importance in order to examine the complexities, problems and possibilities of ensuring children's right to education, both by state and civil society sectors. The present study attempts to delve into some of these formidable challenges in ensuring access to quality and equitable education, both by the state and the civil society.

The right to education, rooted in the universality of human rights, asserts that meaningful educational participation by all children is possible only when all children can access to a schooling system of equal opportunity. The concept of equal opportunity is, however, profoundly challenging, since it embodies the notion of egalitarianism – the idea that everyone ought to receive education as a right, not merely by chance or charity. In this context, the state has the primary responsibility to fulfil its duty, to ensure all people possess rights. Therefore, the state must provide conditions that enable all children to access equitable quality education, as well as ensuring a reasonable standard of living for all. The remarkable shift in the nature of the state's function is, therefore, a profound one in the history of the relationship between the state and its children. This, in turn, forces the state to be highly responsive in translating its policies and commitments into legislation, against which citizens have legal recourse. At this point, it is important to revisit issues such as rights, equality and social justice vis-à-vis the state, since these treaties are intertwined. In an interesting debate on the issue of social justice[3] that is inextricably bound up with the welfare state. Like John Rawls, Young (*Rethinking Social Justice: A Conceptual Analysis by Sharon Gewirtz*, p. 49) illustrates a well-articulated argument as to how the provision of opportunities can be enabling, rather than focusing on distribution. Therefore, for Young, opportunity is neither a thing to be possessed nor a thing to be distributed in terms of rights and duties and the social and economic goods accruing from social cooperation. Instead, the primary issue is the creation of equal opportunities for all. Further, Young Quotes Kathleen Lynch who has neatly outlined the argument that equality of opportunity is dependent upon the existence of equal formal rights, equality of access and equality of participation, to ensure equal outcome for different strata of society in order to prevent disadvantage. This may not necessarily force poor parents to feel the need to send their children to carefully selected, expensive private schools.

In a similar vein, sociologists believe that ascribed factors of individuals should not affect an individual's life chances of vertical mobility and that only those inequalities resulting from individual's talents and efforts can be regarded as fair and just. As such, schooling has become more and more closely related to adult status and modern societies treat schools as an important transit route, through which equality of opportunity could be achieved, in order to prevent any kind of handicap or disadvantage due to the low income of one's family. Bearing in mind this sociological argument regarding equality of opportunity vis-à-vis education, equality of educational opportunity would then mean the provision of equal opportunities by schools for all children, regardless of status and income, so that all can earn income and status in ways that sociologists would argue are legitimate or justified. This argument emphasises the role of the welfare state, which became much more pronounced after the Second World War. A welfare state[4] plays an interventionist role for the overall well-being of its members, by safeguarding minimum standards of income, nutrition, health, education, housing, etc. The assurance of such benefits is treated as a matter of political right. In this context, school expansion has been associated with the extension of citizenship rights (Peters, 1996), for which the vision of equality of educational opportunity was envisioned. Skills, training, certification and political socialisation as contributing factors for rational allocation of resources, social mobility, social integration and social control are seen as important roles of a welfare state. As such, by undertaking educational reforms in favour of the poor masses and the traditionally excluded social groups, schooling is, therefore, viewed as a key component among the actions to be undertaken by the welfare state.

However, in contemporary times, the idea of the welfare state has become a threatening concept for the state itself. In the course of its own making and history, particularly in recent times, the philosophy of the welfare state has taken a huge backseat, since it has failed to confront fundamental problems of silent and loud emergencies[5] such as widespread poverty, hunger, morbidity, malnutrition, illiteracy, conflict, violence, natural disasters and other calamities faced by its people. The fundamental argument is that if the state fails to act upon a high level of silent and loud emergencies experienced by children living under certain socio-political and economic conditions, it imposes unfair educational disadvantage and deprivations on such children. Secondly, if the state is fully equipped to provide an equitable quality education to all citizens within a democratic political culture, the state becomes an arena in which various powerful social groups continuously seek to make their own vision of education and its role in society the predominant one. This amply explains the reason why education policies and practices of the state are often driven by the ideology and/or political expediency of powerful social groups, whose vision of education is often fundamentally opposed to the agenda of educating the poor masses. In reality, this is reflected by India's extremely weak educational infrastructure, which leaves millions of people illiterates, who, given the opportunity, would be perfectly capable of becoming educated citizens.

With repeated state failure to generate mass schooling for all, mass education is left to philanthropic organisations, voluntary associations and other civil society actors. The entry of such civil society organisations into the public sphere suggests that civil society is capable of organising itself independently of the state in response to the crisis of welfare services, including the inadequate provision of quality schooling. For instance, in India, such organisations render valuable supplementary educational services by extending educational facilities to deprived children. For example, various Christian organisations and Rama Krishna missions render excellent educational services in remote far-flung areas, such as isolated tribal regions and undeveloped rural areas of the country, where even state agencies do not dream of venturing for the implementation of development projects.

It is in reaction to such state apathy and the state's failure to address people's basic concerns that there started a mushrooming growth of various civil society sectors in different parts of India in the late 1970s. Furthermore, the growth of civil society increased by leaps and bounds in the 1990s. It should be noted that, despite possessing a common dream of addressing issues of welfare, the aims and objectives of various civil society sectors follow different courses of activism. For instance, some sectors work closely with the state, while others, such as various Christian organisations, NGOs and private schools, work independently in the field of education, and others engage as critics of state policy and practice. The diverse range of interests represented by such popular civil society movements is vast, and a great strength in responding to the diversified needs and aspirations of the people. Thus, in the area of education, civil society groups have demonstrated that they are capable of presenting a considerable challenge to state policies, by developing a common position around specific education policies, through projecting a collective voice.

As such, the importance of the resurgence of civil society organisations in their various forms, particularly in post-independent India, should not be understated. The emergence of civil society during this period has helped to delineate the upsurge of popular movements against the state. Thus, civil society can also be creatively conceptualised as a meaningful space, where like-minded individuals pursue self-defined ends in an associational form, in response to the state's failure to provide welfare services to its people. Numerous civil society sectors have emerged that are willing to take up the challenges of development through grassroots activism. From this point of view, the formation of civil society movements need not necessarily aim to topple the inherently failed state. It is in this context that the present study examines civil society's contributions to education and mass literacy campaigns in the state of Manipur.

The failure of the state in the education sector has not only paved the way for such civil society organisations to establish private schools, but has also simultaneously empowered them. The development of many private schools, such as Catholic missionary schools, has acted as a model for future developments, with a strong impact on producing more individual private schools, charging high fees, traditionally attended by children from urban and semi-urban affluent families. Such private schools have become very successful in terms of offering a 'whole package', defined in terms of the general feel-good atmosphere of the school, discipline and morality, habits of cleanliness, school uniforms, emphasis on English language, speech pattern, teacher accountability, management, weekly tests, thorough examination systems, homework assignments, performance, class consciousness and so forth. Such a 'whole package', which is severely lacking in government schools, is highly attractive for majority parents, since it provides highly-prized essentials for the future of their children in this era of fierce competition.

The freedom that parents exercise while choosing schools is, no doubt, considered a legitimate right, as parents are the best judges of the needs of their children. However, the increasing phenomenon of parental freedom in choosing schools has further empowered private schools, leaving government schools virtually impoverished and to be attended only by those children whose parents are either subsistent survivors or intermittent income earners, most of whom are daily wage earners. Government schools are indeed bleak and rarely provide a happy experience for such children and parents. Therefore, there is a constant fear that the future prospects of children studying in government schools are likely to disappear into a void. Furthermore, the shift of focus towards differential levels of educational efficacy among private schools has proved immensely attractive not only for affluent and middle class parents, but also, dangerously so, for policy makers such as politicians and bureaucrats, whose ruthless snatching of funding and government school resources allocated for children remains unquestioned.

When elementary education is made a fundamental right, the focus shifts to self-assertion, that is why it is rightfully argued that transformation of the educational right to a fundamental entitlement requires a great deal of assertion. However, many poor parents typically experience a distinct lack of voice and assertion, owing mainly to their everyday engagement in a struggle for survival. A significant proportion of households are under the burden of severe economic constraints, which bring about a sense of helplessness and despair that greatly undermines both parents' and children's participation in school life. The difficult situation of such parents denies them the opportunity to form PTAs, the fundamental basis of developing the much needed, social capital (among parents) that can collectively contest the views of the policy makers and implementers and hold the unresponsive system to account for the sake of their children.

When state accountability fails, school children of poor households are the hardest hit, since the stripping of reasonable school facilities denies them even the very limited opportunities that are available for their social mobility through schooling. This also defeats the hopes and dreams of parents and eventually children themselves, for whom schooling is regarded as a key to higher income and status, which is particularly crucial for social mobility, often meaning the difference between lifelong entrapment in poverty and a decent standard of living. Hence, a more meaningful debate could be one that centres on rights, obligations and the duties of the state.

Deprivation of schooling facilities becomes all the more aggravated when the lives of such children are often critically constrained by insurgent violence, ethnic conflict, armed emergencies, displacement, state tyranny and so forth, where the writ of the state has ceased to exist, because during such educational emergencies, schooling facilities are often periodically destroyed or destabilised. This has encouraged the private tuition system to flourish at a fast speed, which only children of affluent families can afford. The situation further deteriorates the public school system, with the strongest impact on children of poor families, who cannot opt for any alternative schooling, except the failed government school. Secondly, every violent incident forces civilians to come to a standstill, since such incidents are treated with repressive state forces, followed by curfews, destruction of property, mass strikes and *bandhs*, etc., for a particular time, generally called by non-state actors. Closure of public institutions including *keithels* (market places) uproots poor households from day-to-day economic engagement, greatly diminishing their economic capacity to earn a livelihood that partly supports their children's schooling. Thus, the cumulative losses caused by violence and failure of government schools for poor students are irreversible.

In the foregoing discussion, the educational developments and literacy profile of Manipur is particularly interesting. Beginning from a position well below the national average, 0.9 per cent literacy rate in 1901, the present literacy rate of the state is 68.87 per cent, set against the all-India average literacy rate of 65.37 per cent (Census of India,

1991 and 2001). However, despite the impressive literacy achievements and overwhelming support for children's education from parents and the community at large, issues of educational equity, quality and access for disadvantaged children remain critical. The scenario needs to be explored in the light of state intervention and the role of various civil society actors in the field of education.

The present study attempts to explore how elementary education as a fundamental entitlement can be exercised in the state of Manipur, where there are constant violations of multiple forms of fundamental human rights, including violence in public space, which critically constrains one's access to schooling. Facilitating the right to education as a basic entitlement can be a step forward in ensuring equity, access and quality in terms of accountability to the agreed duties of the state and concerned civil society sectors, both of which call for inculcation of a new set of values in order to achieve this goal. Furthermore, Manipur has been marginalised as far as educational research is concerned and perhaps no research study has been done to explore how the participatory rights-based approach to education can be achieved. It is against this background, the present research study attempts to explore the role of different agencies, such as the state and non-state organisations, in the area of education undertaken by the Christian missionaries, one private school and an NGO, by choosing Imphal district as the main site of enquiry.

Main Site of Enquiry: Imphal District

Located at the heart of the valley of Manipur, Imphal is the state capital of Manipur. The Imphal valley is bound to the north and the west by Senapati district, to the east by Ukhrul district and to the south by the districts of Thoubal and Bishnupur. The district has eight sub-divisions, with administrative units of various levels, such as the Community Development Block, the Zila Parishad (district council), the Gram Panchayat (village council) and the Pradhan (village head). For administrative purposes, Imphal district is divided into east and west. Imphal east was carved out in the year 1997. Imphal valley is also a mosaic of different communities such as the Meiteis, the Scheduled Tribes and the Scheduled Castes who are the original inhabitants, while the Meitei Pangals (Muslims), the Nepalis, the Jains, the Sikhs and the Bengalis are immigrants to the region. The valley is well connected to all important parts of the state through road networks.

Imphal district has also been the hub of learning and the centre of the growth of educational institutions since early times. It was in this valley that the growth and inception of the modern formal education system took root during the British occupation of Manipur. Among all the districts in the state, Imphal valley continues to be the most advanced district in terms of educational growth, with many famous colleges and schools located in the district. The district is also found to have the largest number of non-governmental organisations (NGOs) operating in the field of school education. Non-governmental agencies such as Christian missionaries, the International Society for Krishna Consciousness (ISKCON), the Madrasas, Shree Digambar Jain Society, individual private-run schools, All Manipur Students Union (AMSU), Democratic Students Association (DESAM) and the Teachers Association are the main civil society actors that traditionally address the educational concerns of the region. Among these, the work of the missionaries and private individuals in school expansion have been commendable, while other bodies like DESAM and the Teachers' Association play roles in examination-related reforms, fee hikes and making education a zone free from outside interference, including violence, conflict and corruption, etc. Apart from these factors, it is the presence of these many non-state actors in Imphal valley that has prompted me to choose Imphal as the main site of field enquiry for the present research study.

In Imphal west district, I studied one government school, Phoijing Junior High School and one private school, Bethel, both located on the border with Imphal Bishnupur district. I examined Don Bosco School and an NGO, Bosco Mangaal from Chingmeirong area, located in Imphal east district, while I chose Keisampat and Phoijing wards from Imphal west district for the purpose of interacting with parents. The main subjects of the study are, thus, school authorities, teachers, NGO programme managers, social animators, parents and children. While interacting with such groups and individuals, I adopted various research methods, including purposive sampling methods for individual interviews and direct close, face-to-face interaction, as well as participant observation methods. The data methods used are both exploratory and descriptive, using both qualitative and quantitative methods of collection of information.

My first encounter of collecting information in the field was among households of Phoijing *leikai* (ward), a rural area of Imphal west district. I gathered information and case studies by interviewing parents of varied economic backgrounds, such as rickshaw pullers, construction workers, brick makers, farmers, vegetable sellers, casual workers and salaried employees. In the process of daily and continued encounters with these informants, I gained deeper knowledge and insights of previously unexplored issues, especially with regard to the area of this research.

Being a native and an insider, I gained easy access to almost all parents that I approached, both male and female, most of whom treated me like their own daughter or sister. Being a woman did not hamper my interaction with male members while attempting in-depth, face-to-face interaction with them. Interestingly enough, both males and females were quite receptive and open to my approach to them, unlike my previous experience in other regions of India, like Rajasthan, where both men and women are reluctant to interact with outsiders and women, often covering their faces with a veil, which can be an obstacle to free and open interaction. This suggests that the dynamics of gender relations is also closely related to the social structure of a particular society. Coming to the journey of the present study, to cite an interesting case, my first interaction was with a household for whom I had purchased some fish, in order to foster an atmosphere of comfort and friendliness. I requested the mother to prepare the fish for lunch and visited other neighbouring households in the meantime. The eldest son, Rishikanta, 19 years old boy, accompanied me when visiting the surrounding areas and helped me to identify other potential respondents. In this way, I utilised a probability sampling method, by identifying households with children studying at primary and elementary stages. The selection of the sample respondents, such as parents and households, was done with the help of Rishikanta, since households have a fair knowledge about the schooling status of children in their neighbourhoods. I ensured that the children included in my research were under the care of immediate parents, rather than other kin groups, since the purpose was to understand the level of parental participation in children's schooling, their perceptions about school education and their concerns of the present education scenario in the state, etc. In this way, the probability sampling method was of immense help in identifying suitable households.

After interacting with three households in the neighbourhood, I returned to the first household for lunch, though quite late in the afternoon. There, the husband of the land-lady had returned from his construction work, and spoke to me fondly, appreciating the taste of the fish and asking me to join him for lunch, while other members looked on smilingly. After lunch I helped to clean the floor and washed the utensils with the nearby pond water. Placing myself in the respondents' own setting was an easy and successful method of gaining their confidence, which proved to be quite fruitful in getting as much information as I had wished to collect. Then, the land-lady spread a reed mat near the *tulsi* plant (basil), where I was sitting along with other family members (grandmother, her daughters-in-law and their children), who were keenly listening to our conversation. In an attempt to sustain the enthusiasm of the respondents during long hours of interaction, I arranged snacks from nearby tea stalls, while the family of the respondents provided tea. In this way, the journey of investigation in the rural Imphal west continued for many days. Despite my passionate engagement with the parents, I felt a sense of guilt for taking away a major chunk of their time, which could otherwise have been used to engage in activities valuable to their livelihoods.

To my pleasant surprise, a majority of parents took keen interest in my approach and interaction with them. Most of them hardly bothered about the purpose of such a study; rather they felt a sigh of relief in sharing their long suppressed grievances about the Manipur's education system caught in the clutches of political turmoil and corruption. Yet, it should be noted that 'well-to-do', salaried households were reluctant to share any information, doubting my background and fearing me to be an agent of an insurgent group, despite repeated clarifications about my identity. As such, a few rich parents were unwilling to partake in interaction, regardless of my efforts. In most cases, however, I encountered ready cooperation from both male and female interviewees, even more so if they were found to be related to me through affine and/or consanguine association.

It was an exciting experience to interact with parents of both upper and low strata social groups. However, interviewing female parents was a little difficult, since most women go to market for trading, starting in the early afternoon until sunset. Therefore, in such a case, the attempt to balance the representation of both the sexes was possible only if I could begin my field investigation in the early hours and end in the late evening. As such, most interaction with male respondents took place during late afternoon.

In attempting to collect uninterrupted information from the site, however, the difficulty was that of transport since the area does not have a good public transport system. For this reason, a number of times, my niece, who is familiar with the area, would lead me towards correct routes. In order to reach my target households, we found a short-cut of 1.5 km through the agricultural fields.

Occasionally, in-depth, face-to-face interaction with households lasted as late as 7.30 pm or 8 pm in the night. Again, the difficulty is that, in Manipur, electricity is only available on alternate days, for two short hours, so the darkness spreads after sunset. As such, I had to walk in the dark along the river bank to reach my niece's home in the evenings. On our way back home, we braved barking dogs and haunting places. Most importantly, in the state of Manipur, it is never safe to step out of one's home after sunset, due to the presence of heavily armed security forces.

The entire journey of investigation in the area was quite challenging. Yet, I chose the sleepy, rural *leikai* of Imphal west with the purpose of gaining an understanding of how parents in rural areas of Imphal perceive the educational situation in the state and their struggles to partake in the schooling of their children during difficult times. Most importantly, it was a delightful experience to hear the nuanced life experience of these parents through close and direct interaction, besides gaining insights into their lives through non-participant observation. For instance, I would find some households engaging in cooking, gardening, weaving, even incense making, during the course of our conversations, while children and other family members looked on, keenly listening to our conversation.

Later, I concentrated my investigation on urban areas of Imphal west district where the socio-political environment and overall terrain is in sharp contrast with that of rural Imphal west. Being much more developed, with good transport facilities, I had an altogether different experience. I was able to reach the places and target informants despite long travel of 16 km per day.

In urban Imphal west, the centre of my enquiry was Keisampat *leikai.* Its location is at the epicentre of the capital of Imphal. All routes of travel to important places in Manipur start from this epicentre, since it is an important bus station, providing good transport facilities. It is also the most happening place for all kinds of trade and commerce of small-scale industries. What's more, important government offices are also located near and around Keisampat *leikai*.

However, locating households and identifying target parents was not as easy as my experience in the rural Phoijing area of Imphal west.

This was due to the fact that, in urban Imphal, most houses are separated from each other by high concrete walls and tall iron gates, unlike those in rural houses, where bamboo fences, hedges and bamboo wickets are used to ward off stray cattle. Yet, in urban Imphal, one advantage was that I could easily access both men and women, since most of them were found engaged in self-employment ventures, as the area is a hub-bub of trade and commerce. That way, I could, without any hesitation, approach them and start conversing with them.

Most women I interacted with were low middle class traders. My interaction with females occurred at their workplace, while interaction with male respondents took place at home, since most of them were salaried employees. In-depth, face-to-face interaction with the women respondents took more time than with any other parent respondents, since I sometimes had to stop interacting because the respondent had to attend to either customers or to their own work engagements. For example, while interacting with a female cook working in a canteen, she had to immediately stop to relight the fire or when eatables were becoming overfried or overcooked, though I found her an interesting and enthusiastic respondent, who was completely involved in the issue of discussion. Another such case is of a female respondent who runs a fast-food stall, where she sells delicious *bora* (pakore) and *shengju* (a kind of mixed green vegetable salad). On reaching her stall, located right in front of her home, she was alone with her elderly mother-in-law, who was in her late 70s. In the middle of our informal talk, I could see a group of young, unmarried girls and middle-aged women beginning to occupy the tables kept there for customers. Despite such interruptions, casual, informal talk and chat with these women traders was most fruitful and satisfying. Here, in urban Imphal too, I had the privilege to utilise probability sampling method besides utilising observation method.

The idea of interacting and having casual chat with rickshaw pullers as parents, though appealing, was somewhat difficult, since they did not want to lose a day's wage. However, I did manage to interact with a few of them, though they looked tired and completely drained. During the interaction, I had tea with them to start the conversation in a cheerful way. Such a friendly and cheerful approach effectively removed all obstacles in the way of gaining their perspective on issues and encouraging them to participate.

However, interaction with these parents could not stretch beyond late evening hours, since I had to travel back for another 16 km by public transport, for which facilities are not available after late evening hours. Moreover, as the area is an important location in Imphal capital, I often encountered disturbances, such as occasional economic *bandhs* (blockades of markets, roadways, vehicles, etc.), strikes and sit-in protests by various civil society organisations, relating to various social issues including school education. Sometimes, in the middle of the road, I found myself suddenly caught up by protest demonstrations of school teachers in large numbers. No doubt, such disruptions hampered my engagement in my routine schedule of interaction with my target respondents. It also curtailed my free movement within Imphal town, diverting my routes, sometimes forcing me to cancel already scheduled interactions with the target population, or compelled me to take longer routes to reach the actual field site. However, my experience with the teachers in protest demonstrations helped me in enriching my understanding of the perennial political crisis of the state and its impact on school education. In a situation such as this, I was bound to brave all possible dangers of uncertain political violence in Imphal during the journey of field investigation. No doubt, the rich experience I, as a researcher, gained during such emergency times, in fact, enhanced my field enquiry. Despite all odds and hurdles, the experience did indeed prove to be enriching for the present research study.

In this way, I gathered data and information from 40 parents of Imphal district, in both urban and rural areas. In my daily engagement, I came to understand that, in fact, all parents – the poor and the rich – are deeply conscious about the crisis of the present schooling system. Their vision of educating a child and the meaning it could hold for society is a profound one, if one deeply reflects upon it.

Other respondents I interacted with in this study included school teachers, educationists, Catholic missionary fathers, NGO workers, programme managers and students. Government school teachers at Phoijing Junior High School were the first among the teachers I interacted with. They were encouraging and cooperative. While interacting with these teachers, I could talk to them only during office hours, from 9.30 am to 2.30 pm. It was during these hours that I could engage in informal chat, talk, observe and study the school setting and its environment. My interaction with these teachers went far beyond any structured schedule, since the nature of engagement and informal interaction simply could not be guided by any structured schedule. Most of our interactions consisted more of deep conversation, informal chat, and serious engagement on school education, in which the process was largely substantiated and enriched through my observation of the school. Their understanding of my research study made it easy for me, as a researcher, to access to school premises and even join classroom interaction with students.

The teachers were knowledgeable, intelligent, dedicated and sensible. Most appeared to be somewhat happy to realise that the school they are teaching in is one of the few surviving functional government schools, at a time when other government schools are almost failed. Throughout my interaction with them, the teachers were quite encouraging and cooperative, articulate and expressive about their deep grievances against the state authorities, who are responsible for the sorry state of their school, while some openly condemned the insurgents, who, in connivance with the bureaucrats, secretly redirect school resources into their own pockets. I gained ready permission to interact and be with the students during classroom teaching. During such moments, I had the opportunity to engage as a participant observer, as I was mingling and sitting among the students in the last row of the classroom. To be in the classroom, it was necessary for one to show a good spirit and remain self-motivated, if one was willing to examine classroom interaction in a discouraging environment of this kind. In the dusty and dingy room, with waste paper littered around, broken walls and windows were constantly disturbing. To breathe freely and concentrate in such a classroom environment, I had to constantly cover my nose with a handkerchief, without letting the teacher and the students notice. The students initially looked at me with suspicion and curiosity, having noticed someone quite new among them. Later, when I had joined them for a few days, they slowly forgot the idea that I was sitting next to them. Finally, I was like one of them.

After classroom observation, I interacted with students of class VIII. On the first visit, the students were a bit hesitant to open up and interact. On the second day's visit, I shared eatables with twenty children for interaction. In fact, it was the effort of the female cook during mid-day meals that helped me to break the ice with these students. Steadily, meaningful interaction could be conducted, especially after visiting them often. Finally, with the assistance of the cook, I could successfully communicate with them, not just about the issues related to their schooling, but also about their innermost personal problems faced by them at home and in the larger community. It was a moving experience, on noticing that some of the students were anaemic due to the lack of appropriate food.

On the contrary, students in Bethel and Don Bosco schools were not only articulate and interactive, but also inquisitive about my purpose of visiting them and conversed on particular issues, such as education, as a matter of right for them as children. In fact, a few students of Don Bosco School enquired about how and in what ways my research would benefit them in the future. They were intelligent and capable of discussing a wide range of issues, including political violence and human rights issues in Afghanistan, Palestine and consequently brought their observations to their own home state. Students in both the schools listened to my conversations very keenly and participated readily.

Despite difficult entry to Bethel school, once I was permitted to be inside the school premise, I could start my in-depth study. However, not much time was allotted to interact with the students by the secretary of Bethel school, since the school authorities feared that the interaction might disrupt their routine academic engagement. Hence, my interaction with these students lasted for only one hour every day. Among the staff teachers, the principal, the secretary and the female teachers were quite welcoming and cooperative. The teachers, being in a private school, were not that ready to speak freely on certain issues, such as their unhappy and negative experiences of the school, reasons for not forming PTAs in the school, the school fee structure and salary structure, etc.

The administration staffs of Bethel school were quite supportive and extended all possible help, by opening thick registers and records of past years on the status of children's participation in school. However, despite daily visits to the school, it was difficult to make an appointment with the secretary, who was found actively engaged in supervising administration, as well as academic and construction work. It was yet compelling for me, as a researcher, to engage the secretary in sharing his journey and discussing the possible factors of establishing an enterprising school such as Bethel, which apparently seems to function unhindered by unwanted elements such as extortion and threats from the local, violent insurgents. The secretary of Bethel school, Mr Tomba Singh was quite forthcoming in my approach to him and showed enthusiasm in sharing his enriching journey of establishing the school. After repeated attempts to make an appointment with him, I finally managed to interact with him at great length.

The interview focused mostly on the journey of establishing Bethel school, as a response to the failure of the state to provide a functional school in his own village, where many talented children are deprived of basic schooling facilities. With immense self-motivation and constant encouragement from friends, kin groups and other like-minded people, he started Bethel school without a roof. Today, the school, despite its rough and humble journey, has become one of the most successful and sought after schools in the locality for providing schooling facilities to hundreds of children from near and far. His entire experience in the journey of establishing the school informs one that, in every community, there are individuals who are quite selfless in nature and can provide immense possibilities to society.

After my examination of the Bethel school was complete, I shifted my focus to Don Bosco School, located in Imphal east district. Don Bosco is situated at a distance of 2 km north of Keisampat *leikai*. Visiting Don Bosco School was rather a difficult experience, since there is no direct bus service link and one is forced to use either rickshaws or public tempos (large auto-rickshaws). These tempos were not readily available, since the station of these tempos is located on the right side of Kangla gate. Kangla stands at a distance of some 100 metres from Keisampat where the main bus station is situated. The area in and around Kangla is quite crowded with traffic. Unexpected events can envelop the area and stop the traffic at any time. By being aware of such uncertainties, I made sure to reach Don Bosco School in the early morning hours every day, before the area between Keisampat and Kangla became crowded.

On the first day of my visit to Don Bosco School, before entering the school and its residential complex, I looked around and observed the surrounding areas. I noticed a church of the Virgin Mary, which was rich in its architecture. Right beside the church, there were some school children playing basketball. My purpose of visit on the first day was rather to observe and study the environment, its setting and the people, particularly the Catholic Church and the engagement of Catholic Fathers in various preoccupations.

As I was standing near the church of the Virgin Mary, a Catholic Father approached me, and inquired about my purpose of visit. It was a great opportunity, since the Father took me straight to another Father M.C. George, who was then the director of Don Bosco School. Father George was extremely busy, engaging in routine paper work, but shared his experience enthusiastically, though our interaction was short. Father George readily accepted my research on Don Bosco School and extended all possible cooperation and made arrangements so that I could meet with the head teacher. Through interaction with Father George, I also learnt about Bosco Mangaal and its education services in the state.

Though it was difficult to get an appointment with the school's head teacher, Mr Indu Bushan (since he was engaged, almost all of the time, either in academic related work or attending to guests and parents), once my introduction was formalised, I could easily access the school premises for the remaining days and started my in-depth research. More than any other teacher in the schools mentioned above, making an appointment with the teachers of Don Bosco was not an easy task, though my experience with them was indeed enlightening. The time spent with each of the interviewee teachers was that of quality over quantity. These teachers, as I experienced, adopt the most humanistic approach in their everyday dialogue with their students. Besides being knowledgeable and possessing the art of teaching skills in their respective disciplines, they were skillfully trained in dealing with students of different temperaments, psychological attributes and calibres of different kinds. Even the teaching methods they employ are far beyond conventional ones that are usually confined to the '3 Rs', i.e., arithmetic, reading and writing. After all, these teachers consider themselves to be serious professionals in teaching and are highly dedicated to their vocation. What's more, they seemed quite pleased to convey such positive reflections of themselves, so that the future generations may look up to them as role models.

Though my focus was prioritised, interaction with these teachers went beyond my research domain. Even their gestures, behaviour and their keen interest in the conversation were quite fascinating and, as such, I never felt bored or exhausted. Sometimes, in the middle of such interaction, the focus even shifted from deep, serious issues to light, cheerful jokes.

The approach to my study of Bosco Mangaal was a little different. First, it was Father M.C. George who prompted me to visit Bosco

Mangaal. On the first day itself, without being equipped with any study method, I approached the programme manager. The structure and functions of Bosco Mangaal, being in its early stage of establishment, are not complex to study. It was a delightful experience to learn about Bosco Mangaal, since not a single other NGO in the state is working solely in the area of children's education. In addition, the Bosco Mangaal focuses completely on educating children of destitute families of all communities. My main aim in studying Bosco Mangaal was to understand its modus operandi and the course of its far-reaching, successful journey. Despite her hectic schedule, the programme manager interacted with great patience and responded well to my intense queries. I visited Bosco Mangaal for days at a time. During these visits, I became familiar and comfortable with the staff, social animators and administrators. Occasionally, I had the opportunity to interact with staff members to extract information, even by sharing food with them. After every visit, I made systematic documentation to identify irregularities and doubts to clear up in my next visit.

After having clarified their mission, I visited literacy centres to interact with the teachers and the students. In the absence of a public transport system in these villages, the animators took me to literacy centres by motorbike. The narrow roadways on the river banks leading to literacy centres could only be navigated by these means. This was a rare opportunity for me to visit the empirical sites of enquiry. Visiting the literacy centres was an extremely enriching and satisfying experience. Through the visit, I was exposed to alternative forms of teaching/learning methods, which despite making use of modest and limited facilities were exciting and rewarding for the children.

After selecting the right samples for interaction and observation, observing the subjects of my research and interacting with the target population in close, direct, face-to-face interaction on a continued basis with an objective approach, demanded rigorousness, discipline, determination, courage, patience, empathy, flexibility, enthusiasm, alertness, adventurousness, passion, insightfulness and, above all, unshaken faith in myself as a researcher. By possessing these traits, it is possible for a researcher to effortlessly win the hearts of the respondents, arouse immense interest and gather an ocean of knowledge and information from them as crucial informants. In this way, the research was completed after in-depth interaction with 40 households, 30 teachers (10 from each school), 60 students (20 from each school), the cook, Oja Tomba, the secretary of Bethel school, Father M.C. George, the director of Don Bosco School, one programme manager and two animators from Bosco Mangaal. As such, the data set used in the present study has the strength of 136 interviewees. I accept the limitations of my data, with the obvious problems of attempting to form generalisations based on a small sample, since the study is of limited range. However, the study confirms and strengthens a number of generally held perceptions, which have not been sufficiently tested on an empirical basis to date. In addition, some of the narrations found in Chapters 4, 5 and 6 are the author's own translations otherwise unstated.

In an investigative study of this kind, a researcher cannot simply investigate by following the structured yardsticks of interaction; rather she must enter into intensive interaction with the informers, besides being a keen observer of the field setting. During such informal chats and casual conversation, a researcher must incorporate both objective and subjective criteria. Incorporating subjective issues are important, since the research issue deals with human values and social issues, which can sometimes be quite delicate. Therefore, subjective issues have a strong relevance in a sociological investigation of this kind. As the famous sociologist, Max Weber would argue, the human world is concerned with mental phenomenon, values and empathic understanding. These values remain objective so long as the investigation renders intelligible analysis. Yet, it is equally important to firmly remain ethically neutral, to ensure the outcome of research is as objective as possible. Durkheim proposes treating research issues as social facts because facts are external, existing over and above the individual researcher. In my present research, I have incorporated both the methods of Max Weber and Durkheim, as I consider their methodology relevant to the present study.

To begin with, Chapter 2 explores the dynamics of state, civil society interface, both theoretically and empirically. It also examines a body of debates, by situating education within the appropriate theoretical paradigms. It seeks to explore these debates and depicts how the state wields considerable power in providing, regulating and controlling the curriculum and pedagogy of school education, which are heavily in favour of the dominant culture that essentially excludes the culture of disadvantaged social groups. Yet, the culture of this politics of exclusion need not completely militate against the educational rights of disadvantaged children if there is active involvement from strong civil society movements at the grassroots. In the light of such an argument, the chapter seeks to explore the dynamics of state-civil society interface in education, both of which call for the inculcation of a new set of values, in order to make children's right to education an achievable goal.

According to the argument that the educational rights agenda must be understood in the light of socio-economic and political realities of the people, Chapter 3 examines the socio-political, economic and educational circumstances of the people of Manipur and, in particular, Imphal district, as the main empirical site for the present study. I anticipate that this broad sketch will provide an understanding of the interlocking relationships between education, the dynamics of the social fabric of Manipuri society and the volatile socio-political challenges within the state.

It is in relation to these challenges that the issue of the right to education is examined in Chapter 4. Besides the anxiety ridden parents' aspirations and educational vision for their children, it also examines their shock, frustration and critical reflections about the educational crisis that largely fails to nurture the youth of the region. Parental school choice, familial economic status, children's educational destinations and educational emergencies faced by school community are some of the crucial issues addressed in the chapter.

Chapter 5 investigates the importance of how the state organises educational policies and practices in most situations, in terms of provisioning of school, funding and regulation in pedagogy and curriculum choice and points to the failure of state policy in providing equitable, quality schooling to disadvantaged children. In addition, the chapter captures the quantum of violence in the state and its critical impact on learning opportunities for disadvantaged children in particular.

Chapter 6 examines the success stories of civil society institutions (each with its own unique trajectory), in providing quality education to children. However, the chapter critically highlights the self-limiting goals of civil society organisations, which often shift their vision and interests to systematically exclude disadvantaged children from their education agenda, further suggesting that civil society institutions are not free from the structural logic of social stratification.

Finally, reflecting upon the findings of the study, Chapter 7 underlines the importance of breaking the historical mistrust between state and civil society, by generating dialogue based on faith. The chapter further explores the various societal reforms that we need to achieve in order to realise a radical education project such as educational right for all children.

Notes

1. The World Conference on Education For All (EFA) held at Jomtein, Thailand in 1990 called upon all member countries, including India, to make concerted efforts to achieve EFA by 2000. Goal No. 2 of The World Education Forum, popularly known as the Dakar Declaration, 2000, aims to ensure that, by 2015, all children of primary going age group complete primary schooling of an acceptable quality. In the year 2000, the Millennium Development Goals pledged to eliminate gender disparities in primary education and secondary education as a critical step to eliminate extreme poverty (Year 2000 Assessment, Education For All, India, 2000 and EFA Global Monitoring Report, UNESCO. Paris, 2002).
2. State Education Ministers' Resolution on 'The Implication of the Proposal to Make Elementary Education a Fundamental Right', Government of India, 1998.
3. Social justice is closely related to the concept of equality of educational opportunity and is more usefully understood when it deals with how everyone should be treated in a society that is believed to be good. This suggests two things: the distributional and the relational dimensions of social justice. John Rawls' classical contribution to social justice takes the form of a distributional approach, which concerns how goods are distributed. According to this, a good society distributes resources to its members in a fair manner and the subject matter of justice is the way that major social institutions distribute fundamental rights and duties and determine the distribution of advantages from social cooperation. Reducing social justice to merely distribution of rights and duties and the social and economic goods accruing from social cooperation is severely limiting. As an extension to Rawls' conception of social justice, Sharon Gewirtz, argues for social justice from relational aspects, by suggesting that it is about the nature and ordering of social relations, the formal and informal rules governing how members of society treat each other both at macro and micro levels. It necessarily entails practices and procedures governing the organisation of political, economic and social institutions, including family. Young's argument is that opportunity itself is more of 'doing' rather than 'having' and that opportunity entails to the concept of enabling rather than possession (Peters, 1996). Coming to the central focus, equality of educational opportunity is accompanied with equality of outcomes. This takes both weak and strong liberal views of justice. Conceptually, this is the essence of the right to education agenda, where every school going child should be

given the same opportunity of objective school conditions to prevent disadvantage of equal success, or more precisely, to achieve equal outcomes. At the national policy level, it is the Kothari Commission Report (1964–66) that endorses a similar kind of approach to school education for all children.

4. Rooted in Western European tradition of social democracy, the idea of welfare state became much more pronounced after the Second World War. The concept can be traced to the developments that took place in Britain in the 19th Century. It is identified with a number of state interventions in social and economic affairs to alleviate mass poverty. After 'the system of poor' was rationalised and placed under state control, many welfare programmes became a rational concern. Consequently, upon these developments, it was in 1870 that the Education Act brought primary education under the realm of state responsibility. In USA, educational reform based on compensatory programmes was considered to be the most efficient mechanism for breaking the vicious cycle of poverty among the poor. The intense debates among its advocates such as R.H. Tawney, Adam Smith, Jeremy Bentham, John Rawls and T.H. Marshall, all project the welfare state to be a system that helps the poor more than any other known system (Barry, 2002).
5. 'The Right to be a Child', 1994. New Delhi: UNICEF.

CHAPTER 2

Exploring the Dynamics of State-Civil Society Interface

Translating the right to education into a reality calls for accountability from the state as per its proposed constitutional duties, as well as strong willingness within the civil society to intervene during violations of rights. The rights approach, however, places major responsibility on the state,[1] requiring it to do everything possible to ensure children's basic entitlement to education. Despite these arguments, massive educational deprivation among children remains a crucial issue in regions where stubborn social norms such as casteism, patriarchy, fundamentalism, conflict and violence, to mention just a few, are rampant. Equally significant is the exclusivist strategy of state policy, through their control over school curriculum, the content of school textbooks and pedagogy, as well as through ideologically-driven policies and reforms, misallocation and appropriation of budgetary allocations, non-implementation of educational incentives and facilities, and transmission losses in the federal state, local level linkages, etc. These are some of the ground realities posing major stumbling blocks in making the right to education for children a realistic goal. Yet, such factors need not completely militate against the efforts to achieve education for all if there is involvement from strong civil society movements at the grassroots. The possibilities and challenges for meaningful engagement of civil society actors in education are also largely conditioned by the prevalent social, political and cultural contexts in which these are invited to participate.

Education as an Arena of Celebration of the Dominant Class Ideology: An Antithesis to the Rights Agenda of Education

Some children are fortunate enough to be born into a particular class/caste, by virtue of which they can access good schooling facilities and participate meaningfully in modern society. On the contrary, some children do not even have the opportunity to see the door of a school. As such, it is clear that the educational system is far from free of the structural logic of social stratification. In other words, education cannot be treated in isolation or remain neutral from class factors as it helps to 'reproduce' or maintain class interests. This provides the basic logic of the Marxian proposition regarding the role of education, as opposed to the structural-functional model of education, which posits it as an agent of social change, which can create greater social equality.

The Marxian model emphasises the importance of structures, particularly class, within society, examining tensions between dominant and disadvantaged groups within society in order to understand how relationships of power and control are established and perpetuated through education. Marxists such as Bowls and Gintis, while referring to the American education system, argue that education helps to maintain the existing social order in varying degrees: firstly, by legitimising class structure because one's economic success often depends on the acquisition of education/skills; and secondly, by preparing young people for their place in a class-dominated, capitalist society. Hence, education is believed to promote success for some children at the cost of other children, who are identified as failures. Structural Marxist, Louis Althuser examines education and its functions along the lines of Bowls and Gintis.

Like Bowls and Gintis, Althuser observes that education performs the role of reproduction and thus reinforces the capitalist relations of production, which is full of exploitation and oppression. Interestingly, education, for Althuser, is an integral part of the capitalist state, having two apparatuses – the Repressive State Apparatus and the Ideological State Apparatus. Repressive State Apparatus is identified with the state and its various elements such as police, armies, commandos, legal systems, while religion, the education system, family, trade unions, media, art, culture, etc., are forms of Ideological State Apparatus. Althuser further argues that the Repressive State Apparatus alone is incapable of maintaining its dominance in society and, thereby, necessitates the use of other subtle forms of repression through Ideological State Apparatus. As such, the education system is seen as a part of state apparatus that is even more important than the political domain in disseminating the ruling ideology among its members. Althuser does not deny the role of other agencies in indoctrinating the ruling ideology, for example, the press, by cramming every citizen with daily doses of nationalism, chauvinism, liberalism and so forth (Blackage and Hunt, 2001). Yet, the impact of education on children, in the most formative period of one's life, is extremely powerful. According to Althuser, schools are the active agencies of preparing a class of wage labourers and capitalists, by fostering modesty, resignation and submissiveness, while instilling cynicism, contempt, arrogance and self-importance for the future capitalists and managers. Schooling is thus channelled to meet the requirements of a repressive and exploitative capitalist state.

For Pierre Bourdieu, schools play the role of cultural reproduction. While highlighting the cultural reproduction of the dominant class ideology in schooling systems, Bourdieu highlights how education performs the role of eliminating children of the lower strata from the schooling process. The essence of his argument is that school culture is more appropriate and essentially similar with the culture of children of middle class parents. Children coming from upper strata are successful performers and their dominant class position is justified by their educational success, while the underprivileged position of the lower class is justified by their educational failure. According to Bourdieu, unlike lower strata parents, middle class parents possess cultural capital, or what he calls '*habitus*', the disposition to socialise, act, think or feel in a particular way. What's more, they are able to endow their children with appropriate cultural capital that would give them a greater likelihood of success at school, while working class children without access to such cultural resources are less likely to be successful in the educational system. Hence, the education system produces and reproduces class inequalities.

Bourdieu's observation can further be substantiated with Bernstein's argument that various linguistic codes used in schools produce differential impacts on the performance of children coming from different backgrounds. He argues that middle class children are more familiar with more elaborate code and that they are the ones who perform better in schools, since there is no fundamental difference between their home language and the language used in schools, while children from the lower echelons of society use more restricted code[2] and may experience difficulty in school, which may lead to less success in the education system. Therefore, for the Marxists, the education system is not free from class interest and its articulation. The works of such Marxist thinkers find ample relevance in many of the education research studies conducted in India, few of which are addressed later in the foregoing chapter.

Structural-functionalists also treat education as an integral subsystem of society and, therefore, cannot be understood independently. However, the main point of departure is that the functionalist, being heavily influenced by theory of organic analogy, draws a logical analysis of the concept 'society' as a whole and the mechanisms that operate to maintain its continuity. 'Society', as the functionalists suggest, is a social system made up of different institutions such as religion, law, culture and education system. Each of these systems requires a minimal degree of integration between the parts and the integration is based on value consensus. It is the value consensus, which integrates the various parts of society. What is, therefore, particularly distinctive about the functionalists' approach is its emphasis on maintenance of equilibrium, based on a homeostatic model of a self-regulating and sustaining process. Emile Durkheim, for instance, seeks to understand education as a *social fact* that is both causal and functional in nature. To understand education as a social fact, from the point of causal relationship, is to examine the way in which education serves the needs of the social organism. Durkheim further argues that education can fit into a particular society and that, in this sense, education is a means to an end – the end being determined by society. Therefore, education is, above all, a social means to a social end – the means by which a society guarantees its own survival. The teacher as a member of the adult family, is a critical link in cultural transmission of a society through education. Implicit in this, what is observed is that the specific feature of educational structures and their cultural contents have a strong functional relationship with the needs of society, defined by the members of society. Thus, for each society, education acts as the means by which it secures in children the essential conditions of its own existence. To quote Durkheim's definition of education,

> Education is the influence exercised by adult generations on those that are not yet ready for social life. Its object is to arouse and to develop in the child a certain number of physical, intellectual, and moral states that are demanded of him by both the political society as a whole and the special mileux for which he is specifically destined. (Durkheim, 1957: 28)

Therefore, for Durkheim, it is through education that an egoistic, unprepared child can legitimately be transformed into a social being in his own society. Further, Durkheim argues, if the society is to continue, it also requires some specialisation, for division of labour is necessary to maintain an orderly society. Educational changes are, accordingly, a reflection of more basic changes in social structure and a particular form of education is demanded to suit the need of these changes. Education fulfils society's needs in these respects. For Durkheim, by creating the new generation for society in this process, education does the function of laying down the conditions for society to perpetuate itself, in which the process itself is *sui generis*. Durkheim further argues that society can survive only if there exists among its members a sufficient degree of homogeneity. Education perpetuates and reinforces this homogeneity, by fixing in the child, from the beginning, the essential similarities which collective life demands.

Durkheim's main point of contention is that children are subjected to the school regime, for schools transmit both general values providing the necessary homogeneity for social survival and the specific skills demanded by society. Durkheim's observation essentially reflects 'social determinism of education', or the idea that society perpetuates itself through education, playing such a vital role in the life of individuals to the extent that human beings are no longer social beings without it. Therefore, Durkheim's stress on the functional importance of education for society underlies deeper meaning, wherein education is not just a matter of allowing an individual to develop in accordance with his nature, but disclosing whatever hidden capacities lie there only waiting to be revealed. It is through education that a new being is created and nurtured. Thus, for Durkheim, education has basic essential roles to perpetuate for the continuity of collective life, such as the specialisation of labour and prevention of its members from facing societal crisis such as anomie and pathological social situations.

Another functionalist, Talcott Parsons, has examined the positive roles of education in society, with reference to American society. Parsons argues that American schools instil two major values in a child – value of achievement and value of equality of opportunity. Every society, in Parsons' view, possesses these common cultures of schools performing important functions in society as a whole. To Parsons, individual children are born with ascriptive statuses and it is primarily due to education that differentiation among children begins through acquired roles. Children enter school relatively homogeneous in terms of their ascriptive status such as family and societal background. Schools constitute what is called 'contest' or 'competition', where the students as contestants find themselves in a setting of equal opportunity. Later, through the process of differential performance in schools, children start acquiring status by means of grades and qualifications, which provide the fundamental criteria for the assignment of future statuses and new roles in society. The child becomes achievement-oriented and the process is sanctioned by his academic success and the fulfilment of educational obligations. Through role performance and achievement, differentiation in status develops. According to Parsons, sharing this value orientation is crucial in maintaining solidarity in society. Secondly, as Parsons argues, industrial societies require high achievement orientations among individuals, which necessitates differential rewards for differential achievement – a principle, which has been established in American schools. Thus, Parsons argues that the education system is an important mechanism for the selection of individuals for their future roles in society and the transmission of society's value consensus through generations. In this way, education helps to maintain society as a well co-coordinated whole.

The proposition advanced by the functionalist paradigm has begun to wane as its limitations have become apparent, since the model has stressed too much on the factors of social cohesion and order, at the expense of conflict and division present in every known society. Stressing stability and order also implies that divisions or inequalities of society based on factors such as class, caste, race, gender, etc., are greatly minimised, despite their overarching presence in society, which is especially the case in a highly hierarchical society such as India. Therefore, crucial issues of power, inequality, struggle and tensions, arising out of conflicts of interest between the dominant and the disadvantaged groups within society, are real manifestations. Education, as one of the most powerful and socially valued attributes, is perceived to be under the control of a few dominant groups. For instance, while education remains an inalienable part of the state apparatus, the state remains a continuous arena in which different groups seek to make their vision of education and its role in society predominant. Caste, class and gender considerations are also built into the structures and practices of the state and provide ample content for conflict inside and outside of education.

Thus, in the words of Panini, the membership of a caste implies that a person becomes part of a social network, which controls insider's information about social opportunities (Srinivas, 1962). In the process, education becomes a site, in which conflicts over differential power relations of contending social groups concerning the means and ends of schooling are at play. This is partly the reason why educational policies and reforms in India are often driven by the ideology and political expediency of powerful social groups, whose self-interest is fundamentally opposed to educating disadvantaged social groups. Educational deprivation of these social groups is further reinforced by a power structure of closely-knit economic, political and bureaucratic forces. This is reflected in the disproportionately low-level participation of disadvantaged social groups in education,[3] such as Scheduled Castes (SCs), Scheduled Tribes (STs) and female children.

It is also observed that, among girls, those from economically and educationally backward communities have a distinctly disadvantageous position. This is severe among SC communities because, besides being female, girls from these communities also share the social stigma of her community in the form of 'untouchability' (Mishra, 2000). Systematic exclusion of these social groups from equal opportunities to participate in basic education reinforces diverse kinds of deprivation, by further inhibiting the limited options that are there for their vertical social mobility. Expansion of basic education is, therefore, an essential requirement for the rapid elimination of gross inequalities, in as much as the strongest impact education has on the economy, governance and a host of factors including social stratification (Apple, 1982). Hence, the deprivation of education to the young generation of such social groups is, in some ways, more dangerous than the deprivation of food and other basic social securities (Ghathia, 2000), because reduction of exclusion in other areas of social security is less likely to be reversed if accompanied by education.

The irrelevance and controversial nature of today's school curriculum and pedagogical and educational policies for disadvantaged social groups remains a much debated issue. The exclusivist policy of the state builds up a massive categorising force to the extent of identifying the disadvantaged groups as the 'other' or the 'excluded'. Research studies reveal the link between overall failure of schools and the social life experiences of these social groups and the consequential devastating effects on their lives. When schools pay little attention to the practical needs of the disadvantaged children and almost none to their cultural needs such as language, culture, etc., the curriculum policy appears to treat these differences as 'cultural deficit'[4] that essentially belongs to the subaltern culture and thereby compels the excluded children to face 'dead time'[5] in school. The exclusion of socio-cultural and historical reality in the content of the curriculum and pedagogy[6] fails to give meaning to their lives amidst the humiliation and alienating experiences faced at the hands of their own classmates and teachers, most of whom belong to the culturally dominant group. The 'unwanted' school experience leads to their overall failure to participate fully in school life and their withdrawal from school, while they are the ones who are most in need of schooling. The systematic silence about the culture of the weaker communities in school practice, is thus a manifestation of how school and its processes are dominated by urban middle class culture, which may be considered a colonial hangover, since most early educational expansion was confined to the upper and middle class urbanites (Singh, 1986). Hence, the major flaws of today's overall school practices, which are devoid of secular and democratic forces, are largely reflected through the under-representation and misrepresentation of the culture of the marginalised communities in formal systems of learning. This signifies the contempt and the neglect of these communities as subaltern, primitive, illiterate and unlettered folk.

The 'official knowledge' imbibed through the curriculum is, thus, socially constructed and the medium through which it is communicated to children is also linked to relations of power and dominance, which bear upon the education of disadvantaged children. Less privileged social groups are the obvious victims, since these children experience school processes without any tangible continuity with their social-cultural milieu at home. In this context, school's subjectivity towards what is to be taught constitutes socially constructed knowledge, whereas knowledge is neither a static entity, nor it is independent of the one who possesses it. Instead, it becomes a social invention, heavily biased in favour of a few powerful and significant social groups, articulated through school curricular and other pedagogical forms. Thus, the forms of knowledge that make up the school curriculum are related to the interest of particular class or professional groups because school curriculum is a product of pressure from certain groups with various vested interests (Kumar, 1991). In turn, this strategy acts as a powerful force, indoctrinating a value system that easily falls in line with the established pattern of education, set up within the frame of reference of these powerful social groups.

Therefore, the more crucial issue is, if education is an important route by which children learn about themselves, their place in society and what life might hold for them in the future, the messages contained within textbooks are of considerable importance. This raises serious concerns regarding whose knowledge and interpretations of knowledge will prevail as a final outcome (ibid.). This is also related to the overall educational outcomes, including achievement in school performance, as Bernstein aptly observes that children using 'elaborated code' at home are better performers, while children using 'restricted code' are poor performers in school. The argument is that acceptance and appreciation of language and culture of disadvantaged groups, say tribal children, by schools will enable them to develop a positive sense of identity or self-worth and, thereby, it leads to higher educational achievement, while the denial of one's culture and mother tongue in formal systems of schooling disconnects them from any tangible continuity with school and school processes. This is seen to be particularly significant for tribes, since language remains an irrefutable distinguishing trait (Mandelbaum, 1972) for many tribal groups and their self-identification. However, empirical studies capture the harsh realities that tribal children currently face in school education that is reflected in their high rates of attrition, such as poor enrolment, low retention and high dropout rates. The policy of instructing in the medium of children's respective mother tongues in the classroom is not given any practical relevance and when followed (in very few states), it is implemented in an erratic manner. Silencing and evading some of these aspects in the education of disadvantaged children is a major infringement on their cultural rights. On the contrary, when education is made a fundamental right for these children, educational strategies must aim to remove all obstacles that come in the way of empowering these social groups. The practice of living mode of exclusion such as language and culture in education could be seen as reflecting a lack of respect for the culture and the heritage of these children and perceived as a deliberate treatment of their culture as inferior, primitive or uncivilised, though culture should be respected as its own entity.

Depriving these children of their right to education is an outright denial of equal opportunity by inhibiting their access to other forms of opportunity. In this profound sense, the right to education cannot be merely equated with making children acquire the skills of reading, writing and arithmetic or providing them with information or knowledge. Instead, it should mean empowering them to be confident individuals, who can make maximum use of their innate and acquired capacities: individuals who can engage and critically reflect about themselves and about the world they engage in and individuals who can transform themselves and the world. In this sense, education has the power to liberate the self. The enormous task of education is therefore not merely to develop individuals to be adjusted to their present circumstantial existence, but also individuals who can be active agents of social change for a better world.

Another observation is that the present situation of the educational system is characterised by the powerful global wave of privatisation that takes away disproportionately large amounts from the limited public budget, since private institutions also receive financial assistance from the state. These are educational projects that drastically distance themselves from the basic fundamentals of the education for all (EFA) strategy and are thus an antithesis to the EFA goal. An agenda of this kind is a negation of the EFA programme, since mass literacy is not possible without formal educational facilities, while even the existing public schooling system that is characterised by weak infrastructure facilities needs to be revamped vigorously. The formal education system needs to utilise public resources judiciously. In other words, if education for all is to be realised, it is of major importance that school supply factors be strengthened and properly utilised.

However, on the contrary, in the face of neo-liberal forces and structural adjustment programmes, the reduction spending in sectors such as education is a real problem. The handiwork of neo-liberalism is to pass the cost of educational services to clients through private enterprises, based on the premise that the consumer is the best judge of his or her own needs and wants. The entry of a powerful global wave of privatisation in the education sector simultaneously contributes to the impoverishment of government schools. Research studies and survey reports (Bhatty, 1998; PROBE, 1998; Sen and Dreze, 1998; Verghese, 1995) show that the proportion of publicly funded schools hardly meets the basic requirements of school facilities, where the majority children hail from economically backward social groups. Arun C. Mehta (2004) provides incredible information about India's educational status at primary and elementary stages. The report indicates a disproportionately high number of SCs (87.52%) and STs (71.84%) being enrolled at primary stage in government schools, while the number of government school buildings that needed minor and major repairs was high.

Considering these findings, it can be argued that a large number of SC/ST children attend schools that operate without teaching or learning material aids. It remains an irrefutable fact that children from impoverished families are the ones who encounter an impoverished school environment and patterns of persistent inequality in terms of poor quality teaching, a limited range and depth of learning and limited opportunities. The existence of impoverished, dysfunctional government schools along with good quality private schools over a period of time is a form of social apartheid (Dreze and Sen, 1998). Differential access to schools accentuates inequalities in social and economic opportunities, thereby providing a breeding ground for a fractured society. As such, this type of education agenda is in sharp contrast to any effort to ensure the educational right for all children. Therefore, the argument is that schooling facilities cannot be sharply differentiated, while attempting to make educational right for all children an achievable goal.

Furthermore, strengthening of school infrastructure, facilities and resources depends upon the level of overall infrastructural development in the particular region concerned, for example, road connectivity, commuting facilities, drinking water and electricity supply, postal service facilities, health care systems and even the relatively peaceful existence of people. This observation further suggests that guaranteeing the right to education for children is an obligation of the state, simply because markets, voluntary organisations or charitable institutions are not sufficient enough to perform the momentous task of implementing the educational right, since guaranteeing the same right entails guaranteeing other correlated rights.

The educational emergency experienced by children in conflict zones, as in the case of Kashmir and parts of the north-eastern region, poses another big challenge in making the educational right for these children a realistic goal. It will be useful here to outline the case of the most recent incident in the state of Manipur, Operation Summer Storm (OSS), conducted by the Indian army to root out insurgents from Keibul Lamjao, a National Park, located at Loktak Lake. During the operation, besides displacing thousands of villagers, schoolgoing children near and around the region were prevented from going to school. *The Sangai Express*, a local newspaper, reported that during the nine-day operation, schools located in Nongmaikhong and Khordak, near the Keibul Lamjao Park, were shut down, withholding the regular functioning of schools and denying the right to education to more than 1,168 children in the area. These children belong to the four government schools operating near and around the park. The operation created panic among parents and children about whether the situation would necessitate the repetition of an academic year. This incident demonstrates that the conflict zone(s) of India are far from safe havens for children of school age.

Militarisation during the OSS displaced communities including teachers, students and parents who were compelled to take shelter in safer places. The operation also stripped parents of their engagement in their respective livelihood occupations. Due to the incessant fighting and heavy guns and mortars, the villagers were unable to plant rice and were prevented from fishing, which forms the main source of their income. Guidelines for continuing education in times of emergency and post-emergency have not been drawn up either by the state or the civil society sector. This is despite the fact that the Indian state became a party to the UN Convention on the Rights of Child in 1992, wherein Article 28.1 states that state parties must recognise the right of the child to education with a view to achieving this right progressively and on the basis of equal opportunity, directing the state with unbridled power to intervene as and when children's educational right is violated.

State and Education Reconsidered

Given the above discourse, it would be futile to attempt to separate education from the realm of operation of the state apparatus vis-à-vis its role in overall development policy. The notion of 'state', therefore, becomes important for understanding its role in education, even more so at the present time, when education has increasingly become a state function. From the Marxist perspective, the state as an institution is of crucial importance, in which its main function is to maintain and defend class domination, the bourgeois class or in other terms, the ruling class. For Marx, the state is a committee of executives, who manage the common affairs of the whole bourgeoisie (Marx and Engels, 1968). Hence, the role of the state is determined by its location in capitalist relations and all modern states serve to strengthen the domination of the bourgeoisie over the proletariat. Therefore, for Marxists, educational institutions, being part of this superstructure, are seen as being designed by the state so as to facilitate the monopoly and domination of the ruling class, who have control over the infrastructure of society. Following this proposition, Antonio Gramsci argues that education systems and schools in particular are privileged instruments for the socialisation of hegemonic culture.[7] The Marxian model thus emphasises the exploitative aspects of state action, by viewing the state as a part of the ideological hegemony of the dominant classes, along with coercive state apparatus (Peters and Marshall, 1996).

Against the Marxist discourse on education, as an instrument used by the state to oppress and suppress the dominated masses, the liberal pluralists argue that the state is constituted not only by one dominant class but rather groups of elites with competing interest and, as such, power is diffused and balanced and no particular class is able to weigh too heavily upon the state. Therefore, the state remains subjected to a multitude of conflicting interests and pressures and the state is the only mirror, which society holds up to itself (Milliband, 1976: 5). From this perspective, state policy is a collective consensus of public opinion, imposed upon the political arena by those competing groups. As such, the state becomes an arbitrator of those competing voices and aspirations. Therefore, the state is a collective creation of its individual members, providing a set of common social goods, including education. However, the voices of those competing groups need not necessarily represent all sections of society, since they belong to the elites wielding state power as a distinct and separate entity. Furthermore, when public policy is defined and implemented, tensions, contradictions, agreements and disagreements among various competing groups are played out, sometimes requiring the state to use repressive forces to contain these contradictions, so that laws are obeyed and transgressors are punished. As Max Weber puts it, the state has a monopoly over the legitimate use of violence within its defined territory.

While highlighting the role of modern state, Weber views the monopoly of the state as inevitable and compulsory for effective administration (Thio, 1986). However, Weber views the notion of domination as central to his analysis, examining the state and its function beyond the notion of exploitation and domination and proposing that the state be seen as a set of comprehensive institutions, varying from those responsible for law and order, to those linked to social policy and education (Peters and Marshall, 1996). Therefore, reducing the role of the state to a proposition of domination and exploitation is to downplay other important state functions, especially when one attempts to examine the context of the function of a welfare state, where the need for multiple roles of the state arises. Education, in this context, remains an inseparable entity of the overall development task undertaken by the welfare state.

The Welfare State and Education: Constitutional Landmarks

In the immediate aftermath of India's independence, the Constitution of India provided the framework of state policy through its Fundamental Rights and Directive Principles, within which provisions are made for securing the welfare of its citizens.[8] The right to education, which is implicit in the right to life,[9] guaranteed by Article 21, can thus be construed in the light of the Directive Principles in part IV of the Constitution. Article 45 of the Constitution mandates that the state shall endeavour to provide, within a period of ten years from the commencement of the Constitution, for free and compulsory education for all children, until they reach fourteen years of age. In other words, every child in India has the right to free education until he/she reaches 14 years of age. Thereafter, his/her right to education is subject to the limits of their economic capacity and the development of the state (Saikia Committee Report).

The urgency and compulsion as stated in the Constitution was established way back in 1950,[10] within a time limit. After the 50s, various education commissions and policies were framed in an attempt to give education a mass character. The Kothari Education Commission, constituted in 1964–66, is of special significance, since it strongly recommended a common school system, in which the main aim is to promote equality of educational opportunity through the provision of equitable quality education for all types of schools – private, private-aided and government. The Commission set the goal of achieving Universal Elementary Education (UEE) by 1986. The NEP 1986 is the most comprehensive and relevant education policy India has devised so far to achieve UEE by 2000. The Ramamurthi Committee was set up in 1990, leading to the formulation of the Programme of Action (POA) 1992. In the same year, India ratified the UN Convention on Rights of the Child, by which, it inter alia, committed itself to remove children from work activities that interfere with their schooling and make primary education free and compulsory. The Convention also stresses the child's right to special protection including education in situations of armed and conflict emergencies, displacement, etc. In the historic judgment, in

Unnikrishnan versus the State of Andhra Pradesh, 1993, the Supreme Court of India not only asserted the right to free education for all citizens until the age of 14 years, but as a fundamental entitlement, being derived from the right to life. In this judgment, right to education is read in conjunction with Article 21, i.e., right to life and liberty. The domestic education policy developments were strengthened when India signed a number of international treaties, including the Jomtein Conference 1990, in which the main aim was to achieve EFA in 2000.

As such, soon after independence, there were large-scale reform policies set in action as step towards achieving social justice by introducing parliamentary democracy. The Indian state, being a conditioned state, was, however, not indigenous in its social formation[11] and had been an expression of pervasive elite domination. Today, political power continues to be under the control of the privileged groups.[12] Being an interventionist developing state, it continues to control a substantial portion of resources of a poor economy and many of society's free floating resources are controlled by bureaucrats and politicians (Kohli, 1987), leaving a huge proportion of the population in an inescapable vicious cycle of poverty and helplessness. The elite dominated democracy in an inherited administrative colonial structure failed to bring a vibrant democracy that has further strengthened the existing social inequalities and human suffering, along the lines of region, caste, class, tribe, gender, etc.

The increasing crisis of deprivation, disenchantment and various forms of human rights violation faced by the people at the hands of the state, which began in the mid-60s and 70s, clearly indicate deeper symptoms of crisis in human governance. When the colonial government came to an end, there were heightened expectations on the basis of the new promises made by the state, but these were radically altered with periods of drift and inaction, producing a growing hiatus between promises and performance and consequently between the government and people, resulting in massive discontent, unrest and violence (Kothari, 1976). One such incidence was the imposition of state emergencies in the mid-70s, during which violations of human rights, particularly of civil liberties, took place on a large scale. It was during this period that many began to challenge the actions of the state, giving rise to various grassroot-based movements yearning for social change. The late 70s witnessed the growth of various voluntary agencies and civil society actors as strong forces in reaction to disillusionment regarding the state's failure to address the persistence of silent emergencies and loud emergencies. Numerous voluntary agencies were created by activists to take up the challenges of development, through concerted grassroots activism. Because of their involvement at the grassroots, these sectors emerged highly effective in strengthening and building indigenous capacity, addressing concerns for equity and democracy and in promoting respect for societal diversity.

The involvement of civil society organisations in various social sectors became much more pronounced and underwent massive transformation in the 1990s in response to India's new economic policy, as it moved from a closed planned economy to liberalisation and private competition. This represented a break from the past policies based on state intervention to new policies of self-reliance and economic independence. Though the new policy opened up new opportunities and avenues, it raised serious concerns regarding the prospect of a reduced role for the welfare state in addressing poverty and social welfare. The emerging scenario of state withdrawal forced the non-state sectors to face new challenges of radically different economic policies and apathetic state policies in the face of pervasive human crisis, such as mass poverty, morbidity, mass illiteracy, discrimination, exploitation and injustice of various kinds. These new developments are repugnant to the Directive Principles of State Policy and the main thrust of good governance to be pursued by the state, in which the mandate is based on the philosophy of liberal democracy as enshrined in the Constitution of India.

After the 1990s, the policies pursued by the Indian state, however, were not only in total contrast, but also a clear violation of the basic principles of ordering the economic system and political decisions that ought to be based on the constitutional mandate. The new developments not only pushed the political masters and the bureaucrats into moral confusion, they also facilitated them to make hay while the sun of liberalisation policy started shining. The huge concentration of economic resources and political power in the hands of a miniscule number of people caused a wide chasm and disjunction between the power and the people, in which the new developments steadily paved the way for powerful private corporate sectors (whose interest is in sharp contrast to public interest) to increasingly occupy the space vacated by the unresponsive state. Representatives of state machinery thus became far removed from the masses. In reaction to the non-responsive state, there was further mushrooming growth of various civil society sectors. Some of these sectors work closely with the state and some independently, while others act as critics of state policy and practice. The range of interests represented by the popular movements of the civil society sector is a great strength in responding to the diversity of needs and aspirations of the people, but also capable of voicing a considerable challenge to the development of a common position around a specific education policy, through a collective voice.

State and Civil Society

Following on from the above discussion, the concept and scope of civil society is as complex as the nature of society and state. Historically, the concept was a part of a western intellectual tradition that developed between the 17th and 19th century, along with various forms of social formations in western society. In the old European tradition, civil society was coterminous with the state, that to be a member of civil society was to be a citizen of the state and thus, citizens are obligated to act without engaging in harmful acts to other citizens. This notion of civil society vis-à-vis the state points to the concept of civil society-state developed by Locke and Hobbes. For both the philosophers, the state of nature can be abolished with the emergence of civil society, which is the same as the state of grace and good government. The concept of state-civil society developed by these philosophers remained unchallenged until late 18th century.

The notion of civil society became quite popular in 19th century Europe. During this period many political thinkers ranging from Thomas Paine and Hegel to Gramsci contributed to the notion of civil society as a domain almost parallel to but separate from the state. For example, in his conception of state-civil society, Paine argues that civil society existed before the emergence of the state, and the sociability of civil society predisposes that individuals are capable of regulating themselves and live in solidarity based on reciprocal self-interest and a shared sense of mutual help. The state is deemed a necessarily evil, since it crushes popular aspirations, while terming civil society an unqualified good (Keane, 1988). Paine was insightful in pointing the out despotic constitutional monarchy of Britain and the Bourbon absolutism of France and concluded that states everywhere subjugate and barbarise their subjects. Political controversies surrounding the failures of the Keynesian welfare state policies played another important role in stimulating the state and civil society schema. This new development in the political and economic domain was reflected in the changing economic realities, such as the rise of private property, market competition and the emergence of the bourgeoisie and proletariat classes.

For Marx, civil society emerged when the relationship between classes was based on property that had already grown beyond the ancient and medieval communal society. Marx thus located civil society in the realm of economic relations, which he deemed the decisive element, while defining the state in the realm of political order. Accordingly, he argues that civil society develops only within the middle class and the social organisation that evolves directly out of production and commerce, which always forms the basis of the state and the superstructure. In another sense, civil society develops in the capitalist mode of production as a corruption of the instrumental relationship between the propertied classes and hence is a product of capitalism. Marx further argues that the state, being in the realm of the political order, defends private property by entering into ultimate alignment with the ruling class. Therefore, for Marx, the poor and the unprivileged are excluded from the encirclement of civil society. As such, Marx is critical of civil society from the point of view of the poor, who are not as corrupt as civil society. For Marx, civil society while displaying many features of civility and democracy is essentially an arena of class oppression, which failed to live up to its promise of creating an individual space, where freedom and self-determination could find a Meaning. Therefore, civil society had to be organised through deep rooted democratic transformation, which has to be revolutionary in nature. Then only is it possible to civilise the civil society.

In striking contrast to Paine and Marx, Hegel's understanding of civil society is based on the assumption that civil society is a historically produced sphere of the ethical life positioned between the male dominated patriarchal household and the universal state. For Hegel, family is a private sphere based on love and trust, while civil society moves closer to the state. Hence, both civil society and state are spheres of public activities. Furthermore, for Hegel, civil society is a mosaic of private individuals, classes, groups and institutions, whose transactions are regulated by civil law and, as such, civil society is not directly dependent on the state. Hence, creation of civil society is an outcome of a long and complex process of historical transformation.

The creation of civil society is the achievement of the modern world (as quoted in John Kean's edited book, *Civil Society and the State: New European Perspectives,* p. 50). Hegel further argues that modern civil society is incapable of resolving its own crisis and problems and hence its civility cannot remain civil unless it is politically regulated by the higher surveillance of the state. In this argument, Hegel sees the state as ethically superior and capable of regulating and controlling the institutions of civil society by articulating universal interest. As such, civil society remains subservient to the state.

Interestingly, Antonio Gramsci, in contrast to Hegel, views state as an apparatus, an instrument that does not represent universal interest for all, but particular interest. In order to command legitimacy over civil society by the state, the state uses different forms of control. Civil society is the sphere where the state operates to enforce intangible, invisible and subtle forms of power, through mass media, educational institutions, religious organisations, voluntary sectors, etc., and it is through these mediums that the mind and the psyche of individuals are controlled. Thus, for Gramsci, civil society belongs to a super-structural sphere. Secondly, Gramsci justifies the fact that the state does not require other methods of coercive forces such as prisons, judicial systems, armies, etc., except in times of crisis and so long as the apparatus of ideological hegemony can manage. Gramsci further argues that state manipulates public opinion through the institutions of civil society, partly because the leaders of these institutions share common values and partly because of direct state involvement in these institutions. In other words, Gramsci would argue it is in civil society that the state would find acceptance for its policies and programmes. Gramsci's attempt to abolish the state-civil society schema was shaped by the Marxian goal of a communist society without class divisions. Gramsci, specifically referring to the western bourgeoisie system, anticipated that civil society comprises a variety of institutions, which function to produce or to transform the dominant bourgeoisie sense of reality that tends to be shaped by the dominated class. This would ultimately lead to a future society without a state, which Gramsci referred to as the regulated society, or sometimes synonymously used as the civil society. Thus, civil society in the Gramscian sense constitutes an active and positive stage of historical development. The Gramscian engagement on the civil society-state relationship was greatly shaped by the new political and economic developments in Italy during the First World War, at which time, the dominant class ceased to be the ruling class.

It is in the face of such complexities that the notion of civil society and its treatment vis-à-vis the state remains fraught with difficulties across regions, social formations and time and space. However, the reworking of controversies surrounding the state-civil society relationship has produced new dimensions, as various civil society movements have grown out of popular movements across the globe, such as the black and civil rights movement, feminist movements, youth movements and peace movements in Western Europe, while some of these movements have roots in the movements of the English Revolution of 1642, the American War of Independence in 1776 and The French Revolution of 1789. These movements and their core messages are spread across the globe with huge support from all territorial boundaries and social class. In the 90s, civil society movements across the globe became a new mantra encompassing a wide range of social issues asserted by individuals and social groups of various kinds. Such movements have gained vast prominence, particularly in relation to resistance against state actions.

Thus, despite confusions and fluidities in the understanding of the concept, advocates of civil society refer to issues related to citizenship rights. As argued by many advocates, the emergence of civil society is related to the relatively weak performance of the state in providing basic social securities, or its overriding misuse of power, where people counterpose themselves against state power and, in the process, either replace it or reform it. Therefore, it has inherent linkages with democracy and citizenship rights. Civil society institutions/organisations[13] are thus considered to be crucial in enabling citizens to participate in the wider social, political, economic and cultural life of their communities and nations. They can also act as important mediators between the state and the community they represent. Hence, as put forth by Prasad, Neera Chandhok and others, the important roles played by civil society include promoting good governance, strengthening democracy, enabling citizen participation, providing a social safety valve and community building roles. Thus, in our present times, the resurgence of civil society in various forms is synonymous with popular movements in reaction to the institutional crisis and governance of the state. There is, therefore, a growing consensus that through the initiatives of civil society organisations, issues of public concern can effectively be addressed by providing a platform and space for all.[14] Civil society thus symbolises a condition necessary for the existence of a democratic mentality, both within and outside the state that are fundamentally opposed to anti democratic and anti secular forces.

State, Civil Society and Education Revisited

While arguing that the state is held responsible for providing school education to all children, all sections of society have to play a role to achieve the same goal. This forms one of the most important responses on the part of civil society sector, particularly at a time when parents, communities, NGOs and other private bodies are increasingly called upon to share in providing educational services, which were previously considered the responsibility of the state (Wazir, 2000).

Right to education and its enforcement, therefore, need not rest with a single institution such as the state; rather it should be a shared responsibility. This calls for a paradigm shift in the regulation and management of schools, with shared responsibility on the part of civil society. This is an important development, which necessitates the building of partnerships with various forms of civil society organisations, such as religious organisations, private bodies, community-based organisations, non-governmental organisations, etc., in order to bring a number of children into schooling, who would otherwise remain beyond its reach.

In conformity with the policy outlines of achieving educational right for all children, the Government of India initiated the latest education policy, the Sarva Shiksha Abhiyan (SSA), a policy for universal elementary education to be achieved by 2010, with special focus on SCs, STs, girls and other disadvantaged children. It is an attempt to deliver quality education through the provision of community owned quality education. The Indian state's effort to make education a judiciable right has, in turn, brought many civil society sectors into active partnership in the programmes of education for all in India.[15]

Interestingly, the experience of strong civil society movements in education in various parts of India shows that civil society organisations have led the way in demonstrating a strong demand for education that highlights the obligation on the state to act upon such demands. The famous Lok Jhumbish programme that began in the 1980s in Rajasthan is an evident of such a movement, which applied micro and school mapping strategies through a participatory appraisal method. The uniqueness of the programme lies in its decentralised participatory approach with involvement of civil society sectors, including the Village Education Committee, nominated by the community themselves. Another important project taken up by the state is the Shiksa Karmi project (the barefoot teacher) that was initiated in the 1990s. This was implemented to overcome the problem of teacher absenteeism, by employing local educational workers in the absence of primary school teachers. The project aims at achieving the universalisation and qualitative improvement of primary education in remote and socio-economically backward villages, through community support and local ownership, in order to meet the educational needs of the deprived sections of society in such areas.

The case of the famous Education Guarantee Scheme of Madhya Pradesh shows that educational developments in the state are mostly due to state initiatives, in which civil society actors play partnership roles. The experience of the Education Guarantee Scheme shows the involvement of various stakeholders, such as the local communities, panchayats and the state government in the effort to universalise elementary education. The model shows the unique rights-based participatory approach in demanding schools in villages, where such facilities are not available. Other such major educational projects undertaken are the Bihar Education Project, and the Total Literacy Campaign of Kerala to name a few. The outcomes of these projects in all these regions have shown varying response in educational progress in respective states. For example, in Rajasthan state, the trend of literacy progress in the period of 1991–2001 is indeed fascinating. The literacy increase between 1991 and 2001 was by a difference of 22.48 per cent. The increase in literacy was due to the phenomenal expansion of educational facilities in the state, by involving various civil society organisations in education and literacy campaigns.

While highlighting the successful educational experience of Rajasthan, the role of NGOs in enlarging the network of agencies and individuals for implementing basic education has been greatly appraised. NGOs also bring flexibility and innovation into basic education programmes. Social mobilisation, facilitating the formation of VECs, establishing networks between PRIs, assisting in supervision, training and evaluation, assisting resource units in the planning and modification of curriculum with relevance to children's social background, providing training in local communication skill to educators and participating in review of and evaluation of activities on a continuing basis are the major areas that the NGO sector has been involved. These roles are identified as crucial in meeting the educational needs of children of socially and economically backward sections of society. NGOs that strongly participate in education in other parts of India include Digantar and Vihaan in Rajasthan, the M.V. Foundation in Andhra Pradesh, CREDA in Uttar Pradesh, Mobility India, APSA, REDS and Rastrothana Parishad in Karnataka, Pratham, India, etc. These NGOs serve with innovative experimentation in different models with grassroots communities for and with whom they work, by devising the best methods for addressing short- and long-term issues of inequality in educational participation. Equally important is the role played by Christian organisations in the education sector. Kerala and parts of the north-eastern states of India depict impressive literacy attainments and overall educational progress. Much of this success has been attributed to the pioneering works of the missionaries in these regions. It was also noticed that, in the mid-19th century, in the Travancore region of Kerala, 65 per cent of the Christians were literate, while among Hindus and Muslims, literacy rates were 53 per cent and 35 per cent respectively (Dreze and Sen, 1998). The education activities of the missionaries, however, were not so successful in northern parts of India and almost negligible in the case of Rajasthan or Uttar Pradesh.

Despite the important contributions played by civil society organisations in education, the role of the state in educational services continues to be crucial, since mass education cannot be dependent on charitable or private organisations or market institutions, more so when education is made fundamental as a matter of right in as much as the educational right of children and its fulfilment depends on the democratic functioning of various institutions of the state within society. Therefore, its realisation depends on how various sections of society assert their educational right and the state, as an important association of institutions, fulfils the same as a duty bearer. In light of the given argument, the next chapter attempts to examine the dynamics of the social fabric of Manipuri society and its volatile socio-political challenges, in order to explore significant linkages between these factors and the educational right of children.

Notes

1. The genesis of the concept 'right to education' is traced to the age of enlightenment in Europe. Education was considered so vitally important for human life that it was conceived as a natural right for any human being. In a broader sense, in the 19th century, educational rights were pursued to defend and advance the ideas of freedom of science, research and teaching against the dominance of the Church. The Right to Education, with a corresponding state duty, was prescribed for the first time by Article 121 of the Constitution of the Soviet Union and, thereafter, the Right to Education was recognised as a prominent human right in various international treaties. The Right to Education as a second generation right can be completely achieved by positive state action (Hodgson Douglas, 1998).
2. Restricted code is the language containing many unstated assumptions, which speakers are expected to know. It is a speech form that is tied to the cultural setting of lower classes and more suitable for communication about practical experience than for discussing more abstract ideas. In contrast, the meanings of elaborated code can be individualised to suit the needs of particular situations and are less bound to particular context and hence the child from such a background can easily generalise and express ideas. Elaborated code essentially belongs to the culture of the middle class (Giddens, 1998: 426).
3. The Census of India 2001 indicates the literacy rates for the Scheduled Castes and Scheduled Tribes to be as low as 54.69 per cent and 47.10 per cent as against to that of 64.44 per cent for the general population. The corresponding female literacy figures among these social groups are 41.90 per cent, 34.76 per cent and 53.67 per cent respectively. This reveals that the disadvantaged social groups occupy a disadvantaged position in literacy.
4. 'Culture deficit' implies the culture of 'others', while the term 'others' represents those social groups, who strain under the weight of various forms of oppression and exploitation (Mclaren and Giroux, 1989).
5. 'Dead time' refers to schools that have no relevance for the lives of students, belonging to 'others' (ibid.).
6. 'Pedagogy' refers to the art of teaching. It is also concerned with the curricula and learning that take place in the classroom. It is also a process, through which knowledge is produced through curricula and teaching/learning processes in the classroom situation (Freire, 1972). Those who treat pedagogy critically refer to pedagogy as a deliberate attempt to influence how and what knowledge is produced within and among particular sets of social relations, through school practice. These writers basically refer to the practice and imposition of hegemonic culture on children from lower strata, through the practice of pedagogy in classroom interaction. Given this argument, the curriculum of a

school consists of a planned prepackaged academic programme and co-curricular activities that influence what a child imbibes from the overall practice and ethos of the school. This is also popularly termed as 'hidden curriculum' by many critics.

7. Gramsci refers to hegemony as the ideological ascendancy of one class over the rest of society, in an attempt to establish its own ethical, cultural and political values as the dominant social norms. Therefore, hegemony must be worked for, it is not preordained (Pink and Noblit, 1995: 180) and can be exercised mainly through religion, education, cultural systems, etc. In quite complex ways, this is visible in the ways that schools perform ideologically.
8. Redistribution was the primary aim behind the welfare philosophy of the Indian Constitution: the common provision of education, health, income, employment insurance, etc., to improve the lives of those who are temporarily or permanently without sufficient resources. It formed a part of a large, egalitarian reform for reaching greater social justice (Myrdal, 1967: 64). These hopes, however, are not being realised and are unlikely to be realised, because the idea of a welfare state is a comprehensive set of institutional arrangements that is incapable of generating non-partisan within its actors and this experience is typically encountered in India, as a soft state which is constantly under attack for its failure to fulfil its welfare policies.
9. The educational right of people is so vital that it is derived from the right to life and hence should not be treated as a mere pious wish of the state.
10. However, it appears that the Indian state has flouted the basic premise of Article 45, on the grounds that the Article merely calls upon it to 'endeavour to provide', with the result that India has fallen far behind schedule in making universal elementary education a reality, leaving millions as illiterates while they are capable of being educated citizens.
11. Jules and Apple, in their article, 'The State and Educational Reform' (in *Continuity and Contradiction: The Futures of the Sociology of Education*, edited by Pink and Noblit, 1995), argue that the state in the third world is a derivative of colonialism and hence not an indigenous social formation. They further argue that a significant dimension of the coercive function of the state is to eliminate indigenous systems of knowledge, while promoting rudimentary schooling, directed towards the inculcation of social control. Consequently, the education system is characterised by weak infrastructure differentiated by social stratification and pervasive elitism, directed to the recruitment of the local service class.
12. In his book *The Challenge of World Poverty* (1970), Gunnar Myrdal describes the political domination of the Indian parliamentary form of government by a privileged few, including big landowners, industrialists, bankers, merchants, higher military and civilian officials. Indian democracy, being trapped in a vicious cycle of exclusion and elitism,

forces millions to the margin of social policy, which essentially reflects an elitist orientation.

13. I wish to point out that civil society, in the broader sense of the term, can imply various levels of individuals and organisations that are formed by local communities, neighbourhoods, work places, NGOs, social movements, community-based organisations, e.g., local clubs and schools, churches and even a group of parents for a common purpose. The critical and uncritical subscription of a large number of actors such as academics, policy makers, international aid agencies, social activists and non-governmental organisations (NGOs), influenced by the historical shifts towards the idea of civil society, has made the concept more complex, ambiguous and, to a large extent, fluid. Worse, it has come to mean all sorts of things to its followers (Tandon and Mohanty, 2003: 11).
14. However, these possibilities may not take place unless state provides the space and opportunity for dialogue to take place.
15. In India, 63 per cent of education sector organisations see themselves as assisting government. While a similar percentage make direct education interventions, over half describe their work as innovatory and 50 per cent are working in geographical areas neglected by government (EFA, 2003/4, UNESCO).

CHAPTER 3

Understanding the Social Landscape of Manipur Valley

At the far eastern border of India, the lower Himalayan ranges, dotted with small green hillocks and blue rivers, cradle the beautiful green picturesque valley of Manipur. Nagaland bounds the state to the north, while it is bordered on the east by the Chin Hills of Myanmar, in the south by the state of Mizoram and in the west by Assam.

Manipur is located between 23.80 degree to 25.68 degree North latitude and 90.03 degree to 94.78 degree East longitude. The total geographical area of the state is 22,327 sq kms.[1] Of this, approximately 90 per cent is covered by hilly terrain that is sparsely populated by tribes. Thus, the valley occupies only about one-tenth of the total area of the state. It is at an average elevation of 2,500 feet above sea level. Manipur is a landlocked state, separated by several mountainous hills of Nagaland from the rest of India. The state is connected to the rest of the country both by air and road. One can reach the valley by road through National Highway 39, the Indo-Burma road, running from Assam through Dimapur and Kohima (the state capital of Nagaland) to Imphal, the state capital of Manipur. National Highway 39 thus links Imphal valley with the rest of India through railhead at Dimapur in Nagaland. In the pre-colonial days, for trading purposes, the Imphal valley was connected with Chasad in Burma, presently Myanmar, Silchar in Barak valley and Kohima in Naga hills. From her geographical proximity, Manipur could be India's favourable gateway to Southeast Asia.

Manipur is endowed with rich natural resources. The valley is a fertile plain, surrounded by mountain ranges. It is a land of hills, forests, rivers and dales with exotic flora and fauna. The valley slopes down gradually to the south and reaches Loktak lake, the largest fresh natural lake in northeast India. The lake, covering an area of 216 sq km, is fed partly by rainfall and partly by streams of river. It is the biggest natural source of fish, one of the important staple food items of the people of Manipur. Fishing is the main occupation and source of full-time employment for many. The terrain of hill ranges extends as part of the southern continuation of the Naga hills leading to Myanmar and encircles the plain valley. From Loktak lake, the land rises on all sides up to the foot of the surrounding hills. The hills are drained by numerous streams down the rivers and the lower valley. The climate of the valley is moderate due to its elevation. During cold season, the minimum temperature can be recorded as low as zero degree, while during the summer, the maximum temperature can be recorded as high as 40 degree centigrade. The spring months in Manipur are charming periods, during which nights are cool and days are moderately hot – a time when an abundance of flowering trees and flowers come into blossom.

A Brief Socio-Historical Account of the Origin of the Manipuris

The population of the state of Manipur is composed of various ethnic groups, each of which has unique socio-cultural characteristics. However, the main social division in the state consists of the Meiteis and the tribes. The Meiteis form the predominant Hindu community occupying the valley. Among the Hindu Meiteis, there are the Brahmins, locally known as Meitei Bamons, the Kshatriyas, the Rajkumars, and the *Lois* or the Scheduled Castes (SCs). In an attempt to link Meiteis with the Aryan race, British administrators such as Brown, Dun and Johnstone observed that the Meiteis share certain physical Aryan features. Johnstone, for example, described the Manipuris as a 'fine stalwart race descended from the Indo-Chinese stock', mixed with Aryan blood as a result of successive waves of Aryan invaders that passed through the valley of Manipur in pre-historic days. Since then, the race has been constantly changing through its interaction with the surrounding hill tribes, producing a homogenous people of great energy and activity, with much of the Japanese aptitude for acquiring new arts.[2] However, physically, the Meiteis have distinctive Mongoloid features apart from sharing a few similar socio-cultural traits with the people of Southeast Asia. This suggests that the origin of the Meiteis must be sought further in the east. Most of the theories of the origin of the Meiteis are predominantly based on surviving oral histories, legends, traditions, beliefs, myths, folk tales, individual memoirs and the writings of colonial administrators. Therefore, in the absence of authentic historical accounts, the origin of the Meiteis has been clouded by obscurities, more or so due to the influence of Hinduism (Brown, 1873; Hudson, 1908). Despite such uncertainties, their origin can be traced to the surrounding hill tribes (ibid.). They have been described as one of the few groups of Mongoloids who possess a written script and a fairly rich literature from the early period (Singh, 1982) and the royal chronicle traces the history of Manipur from 33 A.D. The Meitei *mayek* (script) (see Figure 1) is the original Meitei archive script that only a few can still write, since it is very ancient, although it has been recently introduced in school education.

Figure 1 *Meitei mayek*

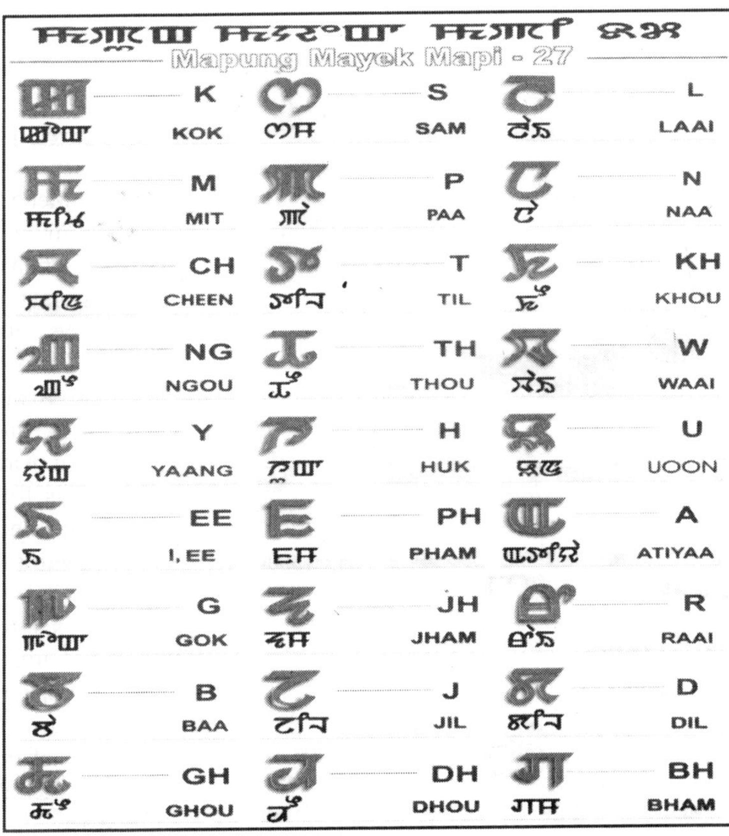

It is argued that a vast literature is treasured in Meitei *mayek*. These treasures include information on astrology, medicine, Meitei *puyas* (chronicles), and historic-legendry works including genealogies. Meitei *mayek* was introduced by King Khangemba during the period 1615–1616 A.D. Scholars argue that a mass of Manipuri literature is locked in the old script of Meitei *mayek*, since it gradually fell into disuse after the Manipuris adopted the Bengali script that was introduced, in the wake of Vaishnavism, by King Garib Nawaz in the first half of 18th century. Cheitharol Kumbamba, the Manipur chronicle notes that the Meitei script and all Manipuri books of the old faiths were destroyed at the instigation of King Garib Nawaj during the period 1732–1733, in order to eradicate the pre-Hindu sacred books, as Hinduism was introduced in the princely state of Manipur at this time.[3] One prophet, locally named as *maichou,* who is famously remembered among the natives of Manipur valley, is the Khongnangthaba. His followers attempted to prevent the onslaught on the Meitei culture but the attempt ended tragically as few Meiteis, including the *maichous,* could manage to preserve the remnants of the script. Hence, the script was not completely lost. However, the destruction of Meitei *mayek* on such a large scale caused irreparable damage to the old literary tradition and its people because the destruction of the archive script abruptly disconnected the people from their indigenous socio-cultural roots. Nevertheless, these accounts reveal that the Meiteis had a sense of history and most of their manuscripts are historical records (Dubey, 1978).

The tribes form the second largest population in the state and reside in the hills of Manipur, although some of them are also settled in various other locations in the valley. In the state, there are 29 tribal groups. Brown (1873) observed that the hill tribes, who inhabit the mountain tract, divided themselves into innumerable clans. This produced slight differences in language, customs and modes of dress but can be generally grouped under two main categories: the Nagas and the Kukis. The Naga tribes have different sub-tribes, including the Tangkhuls, the Maos, the Marams, the Anals, the Kabuis, the Marings, etc., while the Hmar, the Paite, the Zou, the Thadou, the Gangte and the Simte belong to the Kuki tribes. The Naga tribes occupy the hill areas in the north, northwest and the northeast of the central valley, covering about three-fifths of the state area. The Nagas are found to have close affinities with other Naga tribes living in the neighbouring state of Nagaland and have lived in contact with the plain people for many centuries (Singh, 1975). Apart from other factors, such as similarities in language and dress, the closeness of the two ethnic groups could be due to geographical proximity between the two states of Manipur and Nagaland, where a vague boundary was drawn only in 1842 by lieutenant Biggs and Captain Gordon (Johnstone, 1896: 53). Another source claims that the Nagas originally belong to the Ningthouja clan, one of the most powerful clans of the Meitei community (Constantine, 1981). The Kuki tribes live in the southern hill tracts of Manipur. They are described to have close cultural links with the Mizos of Mizoram and the Chins of the Chin Hills. However, James Johnstone observed that they migrated from the Malya peninsula and were first referred to as Kukis in the state of Manipur between 1830 and 1940. According to Jhaljit Singh (1975), the Kukis arrived in Manipur after being driven there by more powerful tribes; soon after their settlement they became good subjects of the Raja of Manipur and helped the king in maintaining peace in the hill areas. In a comparable observation, Johnstone described the Kukis as a wandering race consisting of several tribes, who had long been subjected to the Raja of Manipur, after being driven north by more powerful tribes. However, these theories regarding the origin of the tribes in the region have slender foundation due to the absence of recorded authentic historical accounts.

Although the historical evidence available on their origins remains obscure, there is a consensus that the Meiteis and the tribes originally belonged to seven distinct tribes, called *salais* (clans), with one common ancestor. The historical accounts on the clan chiefdoms of the state of Manipur reveals that the Meitei social organisation during the ancient period was based on a lineage system and *salais,* i.e., clan principalities. During the reign of King Pakhangba, the presence of seven *salais* was found. These *salais* were: Ningthouja, the royal clan, Angom; Luwang Kha-Nghanba, Sarang Leishangthem, Khuman, and Moirang.[4] Tracing the origin of the Manipuris from the surrounding tribes is the most credible tradition as observed by R. Brown (1873). The *salais* were vital to the Meitei social system. Hill tribal communities such as the Anals, the Tangkhuls and the Kabuis were also organised into the seven clans of the Meiteis. As argued by Gangumei Kamei, King Pakhangba is thought to be responsible for the creation of the Meitei *salai* system, which later became the corner stone of the Meitei society and the state. It was King Pakhangba who established the Ningthouja clan as the kingdom at the heartland of the Manipur valley, by subjugating other clans. The integration of non-Meitei groups into the Meitei lineage further strengthened the position of the Ningthouja chief in enlarging the Meitei society. King Pakhangba captured Kangla, the original seat of political power, religion and culture of the Meiteis. Thus, the name Meitei originally applied to the Ninghthouja clan. King Pakhangba is considered to be the first monarch to have performed the coronation ceremony and a line of 74 kings succeeded Pakhangba until the kingdom of Manipur was merged into the Indian union in 1949. The clan chiefdoms thus played an important role in the social and political organisation of the Meiteis. Singh (1988) aptly observed that the history of Manipur, from the beginning of the first century until the British occupation of the kingdom in 1891, is mainly the history of expansion of the Ningthouja dynasty at the expense of other *salais,* the Kukis, Nagas and neighbouring countries such as Burma (Myanmar) and Assam.

In the state of Manipur, there are also other communities that constitute a small percentage of the total population. These are the Muslims, locally known as Meitei *Pangals,* who belong to the Bengali emigrants, chiefly from the districts of Silhet and Kachar; they inhabit the south-central part of Manipur valley. There are also Jains, Sikhs and Buddhists who inhabit the Imphal region. There are as many as twenty-four languages spoken by the people inhabiting the state. All the languages spoken belong to Tibeto-Burman sub-family of the Tibeto-Chinese language family, except the Nepali language that belongs to the Indo-Aryan family. Manipuri or *Meiteilon* is spoken by the largest number of communities. Though the Nagas and Kukis have their own dialects, they use *Meiteilon* as the medium of communication among themselves and between each other (Singh, 1998: xiii). This may be due to the existence of numerous tribal dialects in the state. Hence, *Meiteilon* is the lingua franca of the state (Singh, 1982).

As previously stated, the social organisation of both the Meiteis and the tribes is largely based on kinship, clan and lineage system. Both the social groups practise animistic faith and such practice is a response to the functional needs of both the social systems (Singh, 1988). One of the accounts provided by Verrier Elwin notes the tribes of Manipur as animists up to the period of 1931 (Singh, 1991). Although it is correct that Manipuri tribes practised animism, it is more true to recognise that animism among the tribes is still prevalent today. In the present times, there are glaring instances of cultural affinity between the hill and the valley people that can be observed during worship or observation of festival of gods and goddesses. There are interesting occasions, where both tribes and Meiteis worship forest gods known as *Umanglais (Umang = forests, Lais = gods)*. One such instance is the worship of *Lainingthou Khoriphaba* installed at the famous Nambol Khoriphaba hillock, located at a distance of about 14 km south from Imphal capital. The *Khoriphaba* hillock is the abode of the King of God of Gods. *Lainingthou Khoriphaba* is worshipped by both the local Meiteis and the Kabui tribe (a sub-tribe of Naga tribe) who reside in the southern part of the *Khoriphaba* hillock. Unless there is a death in any of the *leikais* under the territorial jurisdiction of *Khoriphaba*, on every Sundays, the Kabui tribals and the local Meiteis make offerings to *Lainingthou Khoriphaba*. Though the Meiteis worship numerous gods and goddesses and all shades of philosophical reflections such as the unity of god (as found in abstract unity), the duality of concepts, e.g., spiritualism and naturalism reflect their world view and reality (Singh, 1988). Furthermore, the prevalence of practice of animism is also evident from the existing priest, *maibas* and priestess, *maibis* without whose service, religious festivals such as *Laiharaoba* (festival of gods) in particular and occasional worships cannot be either initiated or concluded. During the *Laiharaoba* festival, the *maibas* and the *maibis* play an indispensible part from the beginning till the end of the festival. The festival is celebrated in its most sacred form to ensure the prosperity of collective life of the community. Till today, the Manipuris seek the help of both *maibas* and *maibis* to cure many kinds of ailments, since they are adept in the art of healing ailments that cannot be cured by modern professional health care or doctors. Similar practice could be observed among tribes too. While describing the religious observations and practices among one of the Naga sub-tribes called Kabui, Brown observed that each tribal village has a priest who not only directs sacrifices but also acts as a physician, performing sacrifices and invocations for recovery of the sick. As such, animistic faith and rituals continue to play a significant role in the organisation of the lives of both the communities. This reveals strong cultural affinities of the inhabitants of the hill and the valley in the state. It can also be noted that, in the early period, both the valley people and the hill tribes observed grand puja of Lord *Pakhangba* during the month of *Mera* (September–October) in order to integrate the two social groups. During the puja, the tribes are fed with rice, bear and meat. Another cultural trait shared by both the Meiteis and the surrounding hill tribes until today's time is the appeasement of evil spirits – a practice that has been observed since the pre-Vaishnava period among the Meiteis.

Emergence of Hinduism

In Manipur, the emergence of Hinduism is recent. In fact, the process of conversion in Manipur began much later than in the neighbouring state, Assam whose population was vigorously converted to Hinduism by Brahmins from West Bengal. Beginning from the 14th century onwards, there has been a sequence of different stages, which marked the introduction of Hinduism in the state of Manipur. The penetration of Hinduism during the rule of Garib Nawaz (1709–1748 A.D.) has been described as the most important period, during which the king was initiated into Vaishnavism. This event marked the beginning of the Ramanadi cult in the state of Manipur. Thus, the type of Hinduism that got introduced in the state was that of Bengali Vaishnavism. Johnstone also observed that the process of conversion to Hinduism in the state of Manipur was along different lines and it did not produce the same deteriorating effect as it did in Assam, because the Rajas of Manipur assumed themselves to be of a greater position than that of High Pontiff.[5] Nonetheless, Hinduism became a state religion under the rule of king Garib Nawaz. The beginning of the 18th century thus saw the dawn of a new era in the history of Manipur (Roy, 1958). Many scholars observe that it is during this period that King Garib Nawaz, a revolutionary and zealous conqueror, assumed the political leadership of the state of Manipur for a long period of forty years. Apart from engaging in territorial expansion towards its neighbouring territories, he made rapid cultural integration of Manipur with the rest of India. Some scholars interpreted this cultural integration of Manipur with the Aryan Hindu culture as a ruthless, hegemonic attempt to subdue the Mongoloid culture of the Manipuris. Thus, as stated by Sanajaoba (1991), the entry of Aryan culture into Manipur gave a deathly blow to the Mongolian culture of Manipur because Meitei scriptures were burnt. Furthermore, the *Sanamahi* (Sun-God) religion of the Meiteis was destroyed by the king, who was influenced by Shantidas Godsai, a native of West Bengal.

After the penetration of Hinduism in the early 17th century, the majority of the valley population were forcibly converted into Hinduism while the tribes remained untouched by the process. During conversion, sometimes the inhabitants of a village were elevated en masse from the level of outcaste to that of Hindus of pure caste,[6] but more often it was simply single individuals who were often 'converted'. If the Raja chose, even a hill tribe could receive the sacred thread – a symbol of the twice-born caste[7] – on payment of a small sum of money (Johnstone, 1896: 88). The king punished those Meiteis, who refused to be converted to Hinduism, by sending them to the foothills. Brown (1873) argues that Loee (Loi) literally means the 'subdued', a name given to them after being subjugated to the Meitei were out-casted due to their refusal to convert to Hinduism. They later came to be known as the SCs or the Lois and the Yaithibis by local names (ibid.). Brown further reveals that Lois have been identified as one of the indigenous tribes belonging to Moirang, the southern part of the Manipur valley before the emergence of the Meitei community. Another historical account reveals that the Loi community, who are treated on par with SCs (constitutional status) elsewhere, formed an integral part of the Meitei community bearing surnames such as Singh and Devi among males and females respectively. In this way, the Lois community differs from SCs of the Hindu caste system, since the term is not ascriptive from birth. Hence members of the Lois were readmitted into the Meitei community by royal grace (Constantine, 1981: 38). Further, some of the Loi cultural practices are very similar with those of Meitei and, hence, the possibility of a common origin cannot be ruled out. Among the Meitei Hindus, there are the Meitei Kshatriyas, the Rajkumars and the Brahmins, who migrated to the valley. Thus, a characteristic of Manipuri Vashnavites is the absence of *varna*[8] categories. The Rajkumars are the descendants of various Rajas of Manipur. Another class of people is the Lairikyenbam, who retain Bengali titles such as Basu and Das. They are traditionally a class of writers who have been absorbed into the general mass of the Manipuri population.

Yet, there has been a great deal of Vaishnava influence in the lives of the Meiteis, particularly in their observation of festivals and religious worship. Singh (1988), in his study on the religious and cultural practices of the people of Manipur, highlights the different forms of Hindu religious festivals celebrated with great pomp by the Meiteis. These festivals include *Ratha Yatra* on the Puri model, *Durga Puja* on the Bengali model, *Deepavali, Dussera, Holi,* etc. Visiting the shrines of different Hindu gods and goddesses has also become a part of the cultural life of the Meiteis. Despite the existence of a majority population under the fold of Vaishnavism in the valley, the Hindu Meiteis are however ignorant of the Hindu religion they profess (Brown, 1873). This could be due to the reason that Hinduism did not successfully penetrate into the valley. Furthermore, many practices associated with mainstream Hinduism are not observed by the Meitei Hindus. For example, M. Sircar (1984) observed, 'There is no stratified caste system among the Meiteis. The Lois and Nagas live apart in their own villages without ritual obligations to Brahmins and Kshatriyas'. Caste system, *sati, purdah* and notions of pollution and purity, which were some of the evil practices of Hinduism, did not play any significant role in Manipuri society (Brown, 1873; Chandrashekhar, 1987; Singh, 1998). On the superficiality of practice of Hinduism among the Manipuris, James Johnstone (1896: 98) remarked, 'Though rigid Hindoos outwardly, they have a curious custom by which a man of low caste, marrying a high caste woman, can be adopted into her tribe, the exact reverse of what prevails in India, where a woman of high caste marrying a low-caste man is hopelessly degraded and her children outcasts'. When compared to the general Hindu caste[9] society of India, caste rules in Meitei society are much more relaxed, because the social structure of the Meitei society is essentially not based on ascriptive hierarchy. M.N. Srinivas (1962) observes, 'Every society has a social structure of its own that influences individuals' behaviour. It is this structure that largely governs inter-caste and inter-community relations among groups'. The absence of such a social structure based on caste hierarchy in Manipuri society has helped various social groups to develop a community life based on mutual cooperation. The social organisation of Manipuri society is seen as relatively unaffected by many aspects of mainstream Hindu social order.

Unlike the rest of caste society in India, in the state of Manipur, Brahmins do not hold high status. The Brahmins of Manipur traditionally lived off the cultivation of land provided by the king and trade. Further, the Meitei Kshatriyas, the Lois and the tribes were all employed in the *lallup* system.[10]

Traditionally, manufacturing silk and fishing are the occupations of the Loi class. However, in the present times, fishing is not only a pastime but also a full-time occupation among the Meiteis. In today's Manipuri society, it is also a common feature that Brahmin families run tea stalls, selling different kinds of local made snacks at market places, catering to all types of social categories such as tribes, non-tribes, Lois, etc. Although Brahmins perform rituals, their ritual position does not correspond to any form of secular social positioning such as owning assets in the form of land, political power, income or higher education. This is in contrast to the general pattern of mainstream India, where Brahmins hold high status in secular domains as they are considered to be the beneficiaries of primary westernisation. Like other social groups, they engage in agricultural activities and adapt to the Meitei lifestyle completely including the animistic faith (Brara, 1998), for example, the worship of *Sanamahi*, the traditional household deity of the Meiteis. *Sanamahi* occupies one of the three places of religious importance and worship in every Meitei household. T.C. Hudson states that the hold of Hinduism in Manipur was on a superficial level since the Manipuris are still animists. Thus, in his own words, Hudson stated that in Manipur where Hinduism is a mark of respectability, it is never safe to rely on what men tell of their religion; the only test is to ascertain what they do and by this test we are justified in holding them to still be animists (Hudson, 1908: 97). Further, the communal way of life and the cordial existence between the tribes and the Meiteis since the early times can also be noticed to date. Presently, despite tension and conflict between certain tribal groups and Meiteis, there are many instances where tribal villages have sprung up in Imphal valley (Roy, 1973). Further, the character and equality of local institutions, such as the *leikais* (villages) of Manipuri society, are far more superior to the caste-ridden feudal panchayats prevalent in much of rural India. A member in a Manipuri society lives in a *leikai* and hence one is always identified with a particular *leikai*. A *leikai* is organised on the basis of mutual help and cooperation. An individual family receives full cooperation and mutual help from the members of his/her *leikai* during familial activities/ ceremonies such as marriage, birth, death, feasting and agricultural activities like harvesting, etc. In Manipuri society, a *leikai* possesses many traits of what the French sociologist Emile Durkheim termed 'collective conscience', consisting of common values, beliefs and practices – a fundamental moral force for social solidarity among its members. Cooperation and reciprocity among the members of a *leikai* arise from such social solidarity. Considering this angle too, Hudson's argument is that the essence and the philosophy of Hinduism did not penetrate into Meitei society. Furthermore, the Meitei-isation of Manipuri society in recent times, through the re-emphasis of non-Hindu cultural traits, has diminished the hold of Vaishnava culture in their lives. In the present times, though the majority of Meiteis follow the ordinary rules of Vaishnavism, there has been a revivalist movement that is clearly reflected in their attempt to reinstate the original Meitei *mayek,* by introducing the script in school education and the practice of pre-Vaishnava rituals and festivals.

Social Position of Women

Manipur is a small state with a population of 2,388,634 lakhs.[11] Of the total population, the male population consists of 1,207,388 persons as against 1,181,296 females. It has a favourable sex ratio 978 – when compared with national average of 933. The women of Manipur are seen to hold high social status and enjoy freedom both in economic and social domains. Scholars such as Brown, Roy, Hudson and Sircar argue that the women of Manipur enjoy more freedom than in other parts of India. Allen in 1905 observed that the women of Manipur are capable of fulfilling all stages of their career and are allowed the fullest of liberty (Singh, 1998). They are not only the major economic contributors in the state, but also have considerable voice in social and political domains in the state. The famous *Nupilan (Nupi = Women, Lan = War)* or, women's wars (1904 and 1939) against the oppressive colonial administration still remains a memorable historic feature among the Meiteis. Interestingly, it can also be noted that until the colonial period, there existed a separate woman's court with formal authority solely based in the hands of women. These movements have strong social and political messages about the role of Meitei women in Manipuri society. Another account reveals how the political circumstances in the state forced the Manipuri women to leave their domestic domain and enter the public sphere by taking up multiple public roles. Manipur faced seven years' 'Reign of Terror', popularly known as 'Seven Years Desertion', from 1819–1826 in the hands of the Burmese (presently, Myanmar). During this period, the Burmese almost completely devastated the kingdom of Manipur and a great number of the population fled the place and sought safety in the adjoining places of Kachar and Silhet. Sudhir (2010: 180) states that the Burmese onslaught on the kingdom of Manipur caused a devastating male depopulation, considerably changing the sex role in the socio-economic and political relationships. Hence scholars attribute the sex role reversal of Manipuri women to political factors of the pre-colonial days.

In Manipuri society, today, the legacy of women's movements continues to exist in one form or the other. *Ima Meira Paibi,* literally meaning 'mother torch bearers', is one such legacy. *Ima Meira Paibis* consists of only married elderly women groups that exist in every *leikai.* The unique feature of *Ima Meira Paibis* is that it forms an important part of women's agency in their constant struggle to fight against social evils, such as male alcoholism and other factors that have been responsible for family break-ups, violence against women and the ruining of the domestic economy. Another potential strength of *Ima Meira Paibis* is their role in society as 'watchdogs'. They keep night long vigils to protect the males of the community, particularly the youths, for example, from being random and arbitrary arrests by the Indian Army, who are infamous for misusing the 1958 Armed Forces Special Power Act, termed as Black Law by *Ima Meira Paibis.* Thus, throughout the political history of the state, Manipuri women exercise their vocal assertions.

Concerning the economic contribution of women in Manipur, Brown (1873) observed that they were very industrious in comparison to their male counterparts who are lazy and indolent. Further, he observed that all the market activity, including buying and selling of goods sold in the public area, are handled by women only, who are also self-employed in weaving and spinning at home. In a similar description, T.C. Hudson (1908) notes the high and free position of Manipuri women and all the internal trade and exchange of the produce of the country being managed by them. In present times, the economic contribution of Meitei women not only through market operations but also *Marup* holds great significance. *Marup* or kitty – a kind of cooperative credit and savings organisation – is very popular among Meitei women and the operation of *Marup* spreads across several *leikais* and market places. Women's participation in *Marup* is an indication of both economic and social roles in the public sphere. It is through the help of *Marup* that most of the family expenses of marriage, funeral, child birth, feasting and education of children are met.

Less restriction on women's freedom of movement and women's various socio-economic activities outside the four walls have undoubtedly facilitated the social importance of women in the state. It is worth recollecting what Mrs Grimwood, wife of political agent, Mr Grimwood, praised the Manipuri women. On the women's freedom of movement, she stated, 'The Manipuris do not shut up their women, as is the custom in most parts of India, and they are much more enlightened and intelligent in consequence' (as quoted in Singh's book, *Introduction to Manipur,* 1987). Thus, a Meitei woman does not lead a secluded life, rather, she has ample opportunity to move beyond her own *leikai.* The fact that a woman can freely and safely move beyond her own *leikai* reveals the dramatic absence of crimes against women in the state.

Economic and Political Organisation

During the pre-British period, the economic organisation of the state was described to be closed, traditional, pre-capitalistic and self-sufficient. The economy of the state remained under the control of the king. Traditionally, agriculture has been the main occupation and the backbone of the economy for the people of Manipur. In the valley, wet rice cultivation was common due to the fertile land and favourable climate. Instruments such as axes and *daos* for felling trees, clearing jungles and small iron hoes for digging the soil were used. Hence, there was no extensive cultivation. Yet, the production of rice was more than either in Bengal or Assam[12] and Dun noted as many as 15 varieties of rice grown in the valley. It is said that the growth and development of the Meitei state formation from a small chiefdom into a fairly large kingdom was based on the wet rice cultivation. Hence, this form of cultivation was crucial to the economy of the Meitei state. Apart from this, fruit trees such as mango, pineapple, jackfruit, lemon, tamarind, banana, orange, berry, gulabjam and wood apple grown in large plantations provided another main source of cash crop.[13] High quality tea was also grown in profusion both for consumption and trading. In the hills *jhum* cultivation was practised.

During the pre-British times, comparative isolation from the wider economic system, geo-topographical difficulty and an absence of an organised trading system meant the state engaged in limited trade and commerce with neighbouring countries such as Burma, Silchar in the Barak valley of Assam and Kohima in the Naga hills. Barter system existed between the hill tribes and the valley population (Laiba, 1992). The cotton and silk industry also formed another important economic activity in the state. The superior quality of the silk industry is believed to have been introduced by Chinese invaders among the Manipuris. Weaving, a household-based industry, was confined mainly to the hands of women. Another famous industry was the salt industry of rich quality found in the state. It is noted that there were more than 80 *khongs,* also known as salt wells, in the valley and the hills. Along with these, traditional handicraft industries such as pottery, carpentry, jewellery and leather works formed other forms of economic activity in the state. During his stay in the colonial days, Johnstone observed the Manipuri men to be capable of learning anything and the women as famous weavers, who competed with and almost killed out manufacturing of clothes particular to certain tribes. Johnstone described the state as self-sufficient and the people of Manipur as the happiest of the happy, who had enough to live on.

Gradual changes in the economy and occupational structure occurred after the occupation of the Manipur kingdom by the British in 1891 A.D. (Dubey, 1978). British colonial policies attempted to integrate Manipur's economy with the global economy and compelled the Manipur economy peripheral to that of favourable British economic policies. The system of free trade introduced by the British damaged the main trades of the state. For instance, due to a decline in production levels of agricultural products, Manipur eventually became a net importer of rice from being an exporter of surplus rice. While there had been no developments of any form of modern industries, some of the traditional industries such as the silk industry, traditional handicrafts and artisan productions were also thoroughly crippled in heavy competition with the massive influx of cheap machine-made imported textile goods by the British (Singh, 1998). The state's pre-colonial self-sufficient economy thus experienced rapid erosion after 1891, as British colonialism rigorously propelled trade and commerce with heavy imports from British India into Manipur (Mackenzie, 1884). The kingdom of Manipur suffered the same fate of political and economic exploitation that other colonised countries experienced.

After the British occupation of Manipur, the state also became politically fragmented, particularly between the hill and the valley population. For example, before the British occupation of the state, the king appointed chiefdoms including hill men for local governance, but this was completely altered after the British introduced separate administration systems for the two population groups, e.g., the Meiteis and the tribes. This is a prime example of the divide and rule policy. Such divisive rule was completely ended after 56 years of British rule, by drafting its own constitution in 1947 through the Manipur Constitution Act of 1947 and the Manipur Hill People Regulation Act of 1947. Subsequently, the first assembly election was held in the state, with a seat allocation in the ratio of 30:18:3 between the valley population, the hills and the Meitei Pagans. Thus, Manipur became the first Indian state in which the members of the state assembly were elected through franchise, but the assembly was dissolved when Manipur was integrated into the Indian Union in 1949. Politically, Manipur was given the status of Part-C state with administration in the hands of central government, through the Chief Commissioner, appointed by the President of India. The legacy of a peripheral political economy continued in the face of increasing national security concerns at the border of India. The dissolution of the Manipur Assembly was vehemently opposed by some conscientious sections of the state. In 1956, Manipur was designated as a union territory. The local population, however, was not satisfied with this status and spearheaded for statehood status. Protest and *hartals* (demonstrations) were organised demanding statehood. Consequently, statehood was granted in 1972. This was seen as a 'red letter day' in the political history of Manipur.

During this turbulent period of political crisis, the central government in New Delhi attempted to silence the popular unrest by deploying heavy police forces which had repercussions for the people of Manipur. Further, after the merging of Manipur into the Indian Union, it was reported that many state government employees lost their jobs at the expense of introducing substantial numbers of Nepali ex-army personnel in the police force, an act so designed that New Delhi could command the loyalty of its police force. The handover of administration of the state to the hands of non-Manipuris resulted in a lack of proper judgement on the political economy, since the new government had little knowledge and respect for the local culture, with a heavy bias and prejudiced opinion of its peoples. The state was naturally ill-suited for this form of local governance, since it had managed its own internal affairs for centuries. Consequently, upon these developments, unrest both in the valley and the hills broke out. The first years of Indian rule had brought into Manipur a degree of unaccountability, financial corruption and nepotism that the state had not seen since the heyday of King Chura Chand's rule (Parratt, 2005: 125). Till today, the merging of Manipur to the Indian Union has been repeatedly debated. Some of the symbolic movements against the merging of Manipur within the Indian Union included resistance movements started by the charismatic leader Hijam Irabot in 1948 along Maoist line of armed struggle against the semi-feudalism and semi-colonialism, the formation of Meitei State Committee in 1960 and the organisation of the People's Liberation Army in 1978. It is also argued that the insurgency movements started armed struggles against the Indian army and the state security forces, termed as the 'occupation army'. Among the civilian population, there is a general feeling of repugnance, irritation and uneasiness, due to heavy deployment of armed commandos, armies and paramilitary forces in the state. However, Sanajaoba (1995) argues that the discontent of the

Manipuris was not deeply associated with either the secession of Manipur from the Union of India nor aimed at the revocation of the merging, but the issue was ignited when the aspirations of local people were gradually depleted. For example, to cite a case which Sanajaoba has rightly put forth, during the Second World War, Japanese and allied forces positioned themselves in the state of Manipur for a long time and so Manipur suffered devastation where no other Indian state had suffered. Later, there was legitimate Japanese assistance offered to the state for reconstruction programmes, but these were flatly refused by the Indian government. The Manipuris perceived the Indian government's apathetic attitude as systematic negligence towards the Manipuri people. Sanajaoba further claims that the merging of the Manipur state to the Indian Union sealed its fate and prevented various opportunities for the state to enter into the industrial age.

A Valley of Killing Field

The turbulent years that Manipur experienced continue to haunt its population even in the aftermath of attaining statehood. Subjection of the local population to the misrule of the Chief Commissioners, the presence of heavy military and paramilitary forces from outside the state, violent suppression of popular movements and the abrupt halting of the infant democratic government at the time of Manipur's merging, are cited as the major factors resulting in chronic political instability, corruption, lack of integrity and political will to put the state into the right tract (Parratt, 2005). All these factors have left their legacy on the present pathological political economy of the state. The present democratically elected state is viewed as anything other than the product of the overall socio-economic changes. It is an alien superstructure imposed initially under the British rule, which was consolidated in independent India (Karna, 1998). The failure of the democratically elected state has hardened the insurgency movement that ranges from the demand for autonomy of the state to complete independence from India. Even after attainment of statehood, Manipur still continues to grapple with chronic political violence and economic backwardness, with a tortured history of death and destruction, systematic violence and victimisation.

Thus, more than half a century of bloodshed has marked the life history of the people of Manipur. The epidemic and endless phenomenon of violence during the period of intense political chaos and its impact on the lives of people in the state can indeed be aptly drawn as an analogy with the Hobbesian spectre of the collapse of civil society, into conditions where 'every man's hand is against every other man's hand', life is harsh, brutish and short, as it was during the dark age of a conflict ridden England in the 17th century (Halsey, 1997: 69). Sporadic violent eruptions and brutal killings of innocent people, either in insurgency-related violence, intermittent clashes of militants with security and police commandos, or bloody factional fights within the underground insurgent groups and intra-tribal conflicts are frequent occurrences in the state. The setting alight of villages and slaughtering of human beings by factional rival groups of insurgents continue to haunt many innocent lives. Sometimes, the scene of such killings is so horrific that it continues to traumatise those who witnessed such a scene long after. Conflict and violence have also displaced many lives and communities who are forced to live in psychological trauma for generations. In fact, one often finds it difficult to express such traumatic experience in tangible terms.

Strangely, the interest of the state continues to strengthen the might of military power, by increasing expenditure on the defence forces in the state, drastically reducing expenditure on welfare projects for the people. Of the administrative expenses in the state, policing consumes up to 70 per cent of the total expenditure. The amount spent by the government in counter-insurgency operations in the past two decades was roughly equal to the plan allocation for the state in the year 1998–99, which stood at ₹ 4,250 million, while on the other hand, the state's annual expenditure incurred on social sector programmes fell by 21.1 per cent during the year 2000–2001 (Homen, 2005: 121). Another disturbing feature is that the budgetary expenditure on military and police forces crowds out social spending, by undermining various welfare projects solely meant for improving the lives of the people. The ruthless, calculated action of the state is a serious irreparable compromise to the lives of people in the state. The Indian army in the state operates like 'an army of occupation', while the failure of the state is evident in the extreme scarcity of good education, good infrastructure, job opportunities and poor living conditions of people. Much like the rest of India, the youths of Manipur are disillusioned. One also occasionally notices the deployment of heavy armed forces at strategic locations and the constant patrolling of towns and villages in search of insurgents. Paradoxically, despite such strategic calculations of fighting against the rise of insurgents, the insurgency movement in the state has been on the rise.

Another disturbing factor is the power sharing nexus between insurgents and politicians that in turn encourages the growth of insurgency, corruption, extortion and diversion of funds for development as the armed forces fight a redundant battle in search of the illusive insurgent enemy. Here, it is relevant to note that the neighbouring Myanmar government has often been blamed for providing shelter to a large number of insurgents of Manipur since it is an important transit route for easy smuggling of opium drugs and small arms and weapons. This is linked to the fact that Myanmar and its neighbouring countries have control over the infamous Golden Triangle, the world's second largest opium production zone. Despite the strategic heavy deployment of security forces, it is puzzling that the Indian state is still unable to take up any concrete step to stop large-scale drug and arms trafficking given its negative effect for Manipur in particular and India as a whole. Insurgency is not the only problem in the state. There are inter-ethnic clashes that include tensions between different tribal groups. The infamous ethnic conflict of the Kuki-Naga tribe has already threatened to intensify since much of the communities are forced to cope with homelessness and socio-economic instability as a result of displacement. Each problem is important and caught in a vicious cycle. The growth and endurance of these problems has meant that any authority of the state seems to have ceased to exist.

The regular chronic political instability means that innocent civilians are systematically caught in the crossfire, since they are sandwiched between army and paramilitary personnel and police commandos engaged in counter-insurgency operations on one side and the insurgents, on the other. The situation creates a war economy that feeds on conflict and violence. *Bandhs,* strikes, economic blockades and destruction of public properties are all common occurrences, ultimately resulting in the closure of *keithels* (markets). National Highway 39, as stated earlier, forms the lifeline for the economy of Manipur as it is the only viable road link between Manipur and the rest of India. On the route between Manipur and Dimapur in Nagaland, insurgents of both Nagaland and Manipur origin operate randomly. Therefore, the transportation of essential commodities, life-saving drugs and medicines from different parts of India to Manipur are often disrupted by both civil unrests and insurgents. Economic blockades often give rise to the inflation of prices for essential commodities and shortage of essential food supplies. With repeated state failure to contain such practices, it creates rampant corruption and makes it easier for informal and illicit networks to develop. This vicious circle means the toiling masses under grinding poverty continue to bear the brunt of negative effects. The overall structural transformation in the nature of the state, economy, livelihoods and social relations of Manipuri society emerges mainly due to this institutionalised violent conflict that reflects the larger failure of Indian democracy.

Situating Civil Society in the State

Situating civil society in the state of Manipur is complex. Its existence, structure and function in its varied forms need to be situated in the specific socio-political landscape of the state. First, I wish to point out that the genesis of civil society in the state can be traced during the colonial days. The anti-colonial movements (1904 and 1939) waged by the Manipuri women were one such popular movement, fighting against colonialism and the autocratic king. The first few years of British rule in Manipur saw protests and uprisings accompanied by incidents of arson, particularly in and around Imphal valley. On 15 March 1904 the state bungalow occupied by Captain Nuttal, a tutor to the Raja of Manipur, and Mr Dunlop, the Assistant Political Agent, was burnt down. Four months later, 285 market sheds for women at mother's market were destroyed by fire, which appeared to be pre-planned, since the fire started from all directions at the same time. A few months later, a new bungalow constructed for Mr Nuttal and Mr Dunlop was destroyed by a fire. The local administration took the incident seriously and tried to trace the culprits unsuccessfully. The Political Agent decided to punish the whole population of Imphal valley by issuing an order by reviving the *lallup* system in order to build the burnt bungalow. For this, all the inhabitants of the *leikais* were made to collectively responsible for providing all the necessary materials required in the construction of the building. The Rajkumars were not spared from the *lallup,* despite their relatively high social status. The Rajkumars felt offended and played the leading role in mobilising the *leikai* members against the order. However, the British administration remained firm in their order, due to which tensions and resentment increased. The women of Manipur viewed the order as an infringement on the right of the locals and they were disturbed mainly by the possible attack and arrest of their menfolk. To prevent this, thousands of women mobilised and demonstrated in the compound of the Political Agent, strongly demanding the cancellation of the order. The women's war, 1904, known as *Nupilan Ahanba* broke out, during which many women were physically assaulted and injured. The second women's war, 1939 later broke out, caused by the scarcity of rice available in the market. On 12 December 1939, women in huge numbers staged a demonstration against the rice export policy of the British in connivance with the Raja.

Thus, both the movements of 1904 and 1939 symbolised the anti-colonial and anti-feudal struggle of the people of Manipur. The idea of these movements was influenced by national movements against British rule that occurred in various other parts of India. The women's movements formed a turning point in the emergence of a political and national consciousness among the people. Till today, the Manipuri women's movement, most popularly in the form of *Meira Paibis,* continues to operate actively touching upon a wide range of socio-political issues on a large scale, as already addressed in this chapter. Local *Chanura* (young women) clubs are other civil society organisations, which are specific in generally addressing local issues such as health, hygiene, cleanliness, opening of local libraries, organising of local sports and festivals in their respective *leikais*.

In the state of Manipur, draconian laws such as AFSPA and POTA have only aggravated the dismal human rights situation and continue to be big threats to civil liberties (apart from producing a host of trickle-down effects). In response to gross human rights violations committed by state agencies, various forms of civil society organisations emerged and engaged in the protection and promotion of human rights. These organisations include Manipur Human Rights Alert (HRA), Coordination for Human Rights (COHR), Civil Society Coalition on Human Rights (CSCHR) and Naga People's Movement for Human Rights, etc. These organisations work mainly on issues related to human rights violations committed by the military, paramilitary and police personnel. All these organisations provide legal aids for victims, advocacy for human rights awareness, legal education on the protection of human rights, and campaign against AFSPA at the national and international levels. Furthermore, some of these organisations engage in sensitising the people against the apathetic state policy on public issues. For example, recently, COHR condemned the plan of the state government to construct mega-dams and demanded the state government to be transparent on the MoU between state and Government of India on construction of dams in the northeast region. Other organisations, such as the Manipur Democratic Women Front (MDWF) and the Manipur Chanura Leishem Marup (MCLM), are recently formed civil society organisations. While MCLM engages in organising and advocacy of issues related to RTI, MDWF was formed to check inflation and sensitise the state government to establish a price fixation mechanism for commodities.

Organisations such as the United Committee Manipur (UCM) and All Manipur United Clubs Organisation (AMUCO) are ethnic identity-based organisations that play a watchdog role against the possible alliance between the Central Government and NSCN(M) who want to create Greater Nagaland, which would threaten the territorial integrity of Manipur. Through the media, these organisations sensitise and create awareness among the general public on the issue regarding the activities of Greater Autonomous Council of Nagaland. Hence, their main aim is to protect the territorial integrity of Manipur. Kuki Inpi Manipur is another identity-based organisation, which was formed as a response to counter the offensive drives of the Naga secessionist insurgents, who had begun an ethnic war against the Kukis in the early 1990s.

Another religious-based identity organisation is the Imphal-based All Manipur Christian Organisation (AMCO) which is aimed to maintain harmonious relations among different denominations of all Christians in the state. Hence, these organisations have specific aims dependent upon representing the interests of its particular ethnic community. They are powerful organisations which are often successful in resorting to strikes, *bandhs*, economic blockades, destruction of public property to unrest both the state and the civilians irrespective of their logical/illogical demands. Federation of Regional Indigenous Societies is another identity-based organisation which is currently spearheading to introduce an Inner Line Permit System for the non-locals in the state of Manipur, since there has been concerns raised by the general population on the large-scale influx of non-locals in the state. There are also a host of voluntary organisations that work in support of government programmes and advocacy networks that exist for health sectors, such as Prevention of Drugs and Substance Abuse, HIV/AIDS, Rehabilitation Centres, Women's Welfare Organisations, Children Adoption Centres and Destitute Homes for Children, Old Age Homes, etc.

Besides Christian missionaries and individual private-run schools, other civil society organisations operating in the state include the International Society for Krishna Consciousness (ISKCON), the

Madrasas, Shree Digambar Jain Society, All Manipur Elementary School Teachers Association (AMESTA), Democratic Students' Alliance of Manipur (DESAM) and All Manipur Students' Union (AMSU) to name a few. All these are engaged in education-related issues in one form or the other. For example, AMESTA's main concern is youth-related education, organising seminars and workshops at school level, demanding the regularisation of teaching posts, timely payment of salary, issues concerning teachers' recruitment and making educational settings free from all kinds of disturbances, including violence and conflicts that disturb their regular operations. DESAM's main endeavour is to make education a 'free zone' by bringing reforms to the education system, mostly in the school education sector, in a radical way. Similarly, AMSU, besides intervening in education-related issues, is also engaged in the cultural integration of the northeast region, by organising and participating in cultural festivals and workshops. The work of the missionaries, missionary NGOs and private individuals mainly focuses on school expansion and literacy campaign in the state.

From the above brief discussion, it can be rightly maintained that the formation, existence and functioning of civil society organisations in the state is mostly a response to the particular socio-economic and political experience of various social groups, ethnic communities and the larger Manipuri society as a whole. Such civil society formations can range from the most microscopic order of *leikai* organisation to the macro-level order, responding to various diverse needs and aspirations of people including identity assertion, promotion of democratic values and human rights, social justice, struggle against draconian laws of the state and overall social well-being for collective life. In addressing these needs and aspirations, some of these organisations work independently of the state and act as a check and balance system against the state's excessive use of power. On the other hand, there are organisations that work in support of government policies and programmes. Notwithstanding, while these civil society organisations have diverse engagements, one can also notice the unity of these organisations. That, when state repression becomes oppressive and pervasive, it is often responded to by the masses and civil society organisations through creating counter-hegemony, which again forms another basis of civil society upsurge in the state.

Imphal: The Hub of Socio-economic and Political Intercourse

Before the British occupation of Manipur, Kangla[14] was the state capital. Historical accounts reveal that Imphal, popularly known as *Yumphal* (collection of houses), grew out of Kangla. Kangla was the ancient palace of the Ningthouja clan of the Meiteis who ultimately established their hegemony over six other clan principalities in the valley of Manipur. From the time of Pakhangba in the first century, the Ningthouja kingdom of Imphal gradually wielded enough political power to merge as the most dominant in Manipur valley. Hence, Kangla used to be the most important seat of political, military and economic power but also the centre of social, cultural and religious activities. Due to its legacy, Imphal valley continues to be a hub of social, economic, political and educational centres for the people of Manipur till the present times.

Imphal district is centrally located in the state of Manipur. Imphal east district occupies a total land area of 709 sq kms with a population of 394,876 people. It has a sex ratio of 991. There are 204 villages with a density of 557 persons per sq km (Economic Survey of Manipur, 2007–08). Agriculture remains the main occupation of people in the region. While the main food crops are paddy, potato and vegetables, sugarcane, maize, pulse and oil seeds are the main cash crops.

When compared with Imphal east, Imphal west is highly developed in terms of trade and commerce, with two large important bazaars(markets): Thangal Bazaar and Paona Bazaar. This is where locals and *Mayangs*[15] run large numbers of stores containing both imported goods and local products for export. Seen side by side are numerous small shops, run both by males and females. However, the largest and most famous market within Imphal is the mother's market, popularly known as Khwarimband Bazaar[16] or *Sana Keithel* (Royal Market). It is the largest trading centre owned solely by women. Every day, hundreds of women traders commute from far and near to the mother's market by public transport, for the transaction of mostly home-based products. The district is well connected to other parts of the state by a network of national and state highways, district roads and village roads. The mother's market, as observed by Brown, used to be exclusively in the domain of women, since men, except foreigners, were not allowed to enter. The mother's market provides a vibrant socio-economic world for these women traders and offers an exciting spectacle from early morning till late evening. The district is highly advanced in terms of small-scale industries such as handloom, handicrafts, cottage and the like. This constitutes the bulk of the industrial units and the growth of such remains highest in the district when compared with other districts. Around 61 per cent of the total workforce of the district is in non-agricultural sector.[17] The district also has a high female labour force of 40.51 per cent as against to 48.91 per cent of males.

In the district, the male population consists of 2,21,781 persons as against the female population of 2,22,601 persons, hence the sex ratio in the district is favourable to women at 1,007 per 1,000 men.[18] The district has a high density population of 856 persons per sq km as against that of state average, i.e., 107 persons per sq km, indicating that the demography of the region is highly developed. Among the social groups in the district, the Meiteis form the largest population groups, followed by the STs and SCs respectively. There are also other communities such as the Meitei Pangals (Muslims), Nepalis, Jains, Sikhs, Bengalis. The Imphal valley is thus a mosaic of various ethnic groups, comprising the Meiteis, the tribes and the SCs, who are the original inhabitants of the valley, while the Pangals, the Nepalis, the Bengalis, the Jains and the Sikhs are the immigrants. Being the state capital, the Imphal valley is the heart of the people of Manipur.

Education in Manipur: A Brief Historical Journey

The works of various scholars in those days before the British occupation of Manipur reveal the existence of an indigenous system of education. Books on the disciplines of history, religion, medicine, dance, drama and the philosophy of life and death written in Meitei *mayek* (Devi, 1989) were inscribed in copper plates and coins. It further points to the irrefutable fact that a mass of hugely rich literature of the Meitei community is locked in the old script of Meitei *mayek*, most of which was destroyed during King Garib Nawaj's reign, in his attempt to promote Hinduism. In recent times, there has been a serious attempt to reinstate Meitei *mayek*, by introducing the language as a compulsory paper in school education. The indigenous system of education at that time was, by and large, methodological and scientific by stressing all-round development of individuals (ibid.). Meiteilon (Manipuri language) and the Meitei *mayek* were important mediums in spreading such forms of education. However, importance of the script declined after the emergence of Hinduism in the state and the script got steadily replaced by the Bengali script.

The educational situation at that time was also influenced by the socio-political developments in the state. Manipuri society was in perpetual conflict with neighbouring countries, especially with Burma. For this purpose, all adult males were physically trained to remain fit. Hence, it was compulsory for every adult male member to learn how to use weapons of war such as swords and spears. On attaining maturity, the male members learnt the art of wrestling and other forms of physical training and, when grown up, they learnt the art of riding ponies. It was also customary for every male member to learn the art of hunting and capturing elephants and wild tigers from thick jungles. In this way, every male was compelled to acquire some sort of military education. It was also customary that every female and male member learn the art of dancing during their childhood days. Every *Umanglai,* or forest God, had jurisdiction over certain degrees of habitation. The inhabitants within the jurisdiction of *Umanglai* had to perform *laiharaoba* (festival of gods and goddesses) every year. Therefore, Manipur has a rich legacy of dance closely associated with its cosmology. Till today, it is still customary for an elderly person to play with a child of a few months old by gently saying *taadhing* (rhythm), which the child automatically picks up. Later, the child starts steadily picking up body co-ordination movements according to the rhythm, *taadhing dhin.* The deeper meaning of such forms of education could be grasped purely from the functional needs and importance arising out of the immediate socio-cultural milieu of those days.

In the absence of any established system of educational institution, the house of each *maichous* was regarded as an institution of learning, each with its own individual character. The Kangla, the sacred royal coronation hall was described as the University of Manipur. The kings of Manipur were great patrons of learning and culture. The king was responsible for funding education for all. The indigenous schools were the main agencies for the spread of mass education. However, such a form of education system started decaying by the beginning of the 19th century, when Manipur came under the control of British colonialism.

Going by these historical developments, it is clear that the Imphal valley had been the hub of learning and growth of educational institutions. Imphal was the central place where the growth and inception of the formal education system began during the British occupation of Manipur. Captain Gordon was the first British, who organised a primary educational centre at Imphal in early 19th century. Nuthal was another British official, who opened a school at Imphal with English as the medium of instruction in 1872, but the school remained dysfunctional due to a lack of local support, for they did not appreciate the English language. The locals feared that the new system of education would take away their freedom and therefore they viewed the new system with suspicion. Hence, for a long time, no English school flourished in the state. R. Brown (1873), discussing the sluggish growth and lack of appreciation of English education by the local population, remarked that this was due to the factor that the Manipuris wanted to remain ignorant and they are not a whit ashamed for their lack of knowledge.

However, in the course of time, when the English missionaries were permitted to enter Manipur with the consent of King Chandra Kirti, the Political Agent of Manipur, James Johnstone first opened a Middle English School in Imphal in 1885. This laid the foundation of the modern formal system of education in Manipur. During those days, primary education was taught in the Bengali script. Among the missionaries, it was William Pettigrew who opened a school at Imphal in 1894. His educational activities were extremely large and satisfied the British officials and the people at large. Gradually, primary schools were established in other districts of Manipur. The actual expansion of schools in the state, however, began after India's independence, especially during the period of 1949–50.

Female education in those days, however, was not encouraged. Parents were not willing to send their daughters to school. One possible rumour that discouraged the education of girls was the chance that these girls, soon after they were satisfactorily taught how to read, write and speak English, could be shipped off to England, where there was said to be a scarcity of marriageable women (Hudson, 1908). Despite such discouragement, girls were steadily absorbed into formal schools. Girls' enrolment in formal schools gradually increased by 1900. In succeeding years, the number of formal schools also increased gradually and reached 210 during the period 1931–42. During this period, the missionaries, especially the American Baptist and the North East India Missionary, did commendable work among the hill people by bringing tribal children to schools by opening more and more schools in the state. The period of 1941–45, however, had been considered to be the most unproductive period in the area of education due to the setbacks caused by Second World War.

In the aftermath of India's independence, during the period 1957–63, the territorial council took over the administration of schools and also the extension of grant-in-aid to private schools. Interestingly, as reported in the State Education Report (1992), it was during this period that the people of Manipur appreciated the council for opening, recognising and taking over a considerable number of schools, especially primary schools. By 1963, the period of territorial council came to an end and all the educational institutions were brought under the state education department. The report further noted the contribution made by the locals in terms of material, moral and human contributions. It was during this period that the council opened five private schools.

The attainment of statehood in 1972 seems to have provided an impetus to the spread of education in the state. In the year 1972–73, 336 private aided schools along with 42 junior high schools were recognised. Further, in the year 1978–79, 92 junior high schools and 685 aided and non-aided schools were taken over by the state. However, while examining the school expansion and management of schools for primary and elementary stages in the state, it is observed that a significant number of these schools, particularly the upper primary stage, are managed by private bodies. The trend further indicates that, despite the takeover of schools by the state government, the number of schools run by private bodies continues to be high. In the state, educational institutions run by private individuals and voluntary agencies thus continue to play an important role for the schooling of children. Significantly, Imphal district continues to be in a pivotal position in terms of school expansion established by various private bodies. The district has the largest number of mission schools, Madrasas, NGOs and private schools.

As stated in the forgoing chapter, Manipur has been throttled by gross political instability and economic backwardness. With massive underdevelopment, the state has witnessed a long history of superficial development policies and projects which have failed to transform conditions for the people in the state. People of Manipur still find their aspirations largely unheard and derided. The development paradigm of the state has invited criticisms that the state economy does not reflect the general development pattern of India, while scholars and local intelligentsia often raise concerns against the existence of democratic institutions in the state, without democratic governance and polity. Violence, bloodshed, extortion, *bandhs, hartals,* boycotts, destruction of public goods, powerful insurgent groups drawing legitimacy from inefficient, corrupt politicians and non-performing officials, who in turn get support from these groups, have become the order of the day. The crisis in human governance often poses one of the greatest challenges to education, for it greatly destabilises the normal functioning of schools, while constantly exposing children to a violent environment. It can be recalled that in the most infamous mass protest incident against ceasefire extension in 2001, a large number of school children participated. In the incident, school textbooks and reading materials were burnt and destroyed, which forced innocent children to be a part of the political unrest in the state. Such protest demonstrations are always manned by policemen, armed commandoes and army personnel, who, at any moment, can trigger violent action.

The pathological political and economic situation is deeply drawn into the present education system in the state. The current deepening crisis in education has caused tremendous anxiety, worry, restlessness and frustration among the general public, anticipating the future of Manipuri society to be at great stake. Further engagement of the local intelligentsia and pilot studies in school education reveal the increasing impoverishment of government schools in terms of quality schooling for children. These studies show that many government schools are crippled and operate without basic amenities such as toilets, latrines and drinking water facilities. To cite a case, according to the report of the Situational Analysis of Children in Government Schools conducted by the Institute of Social Work and Research (2009), it was found that students studying in government schools in Imphal east district have been facing a lot of inconveniences due to absence of toilets or unserviceable conditions, even if some schools have such facilities. Furthermore, the study found that only two out of 50 schools had toilet facilities.

The widespread general failure of government schools has caused restlessness, anxiety and tension among concerned local intelligentsia, students and parents. These tensions and anxieties are often released through workshops, seminars and the media, by expressing well-thought opinions and views with a clear vision, often prompting the state and society to provide quality education to all children. Further, as the local intelligentsia, academics and concerned individuals speak out, in the present education scenario, there is only an insignificant number of children who are from highly privileged backgrounds, able to be educated at elite private schools. This phenomenon runs parallel to the Darwinian law of natural selection of 'survival of the fittest', suggesting that it is only natural laws that recognise 'the fittest', unlike human laws that have compassion and magnanimity. Several concerns are also raised against the constant trapping of educational institutions by insurgents, sporadic violent movements and incidents such as murder, kidnapping and extortion made on school teachers. Concerns over these developments are commonly shared by all sections of society, including the most ordinary poor parents, who have reached a point of frustration over an education system which has largely failed in cradling and nurturing children and the youth of the society. The development is indeed a tragedy for a society, where humanistic and liberating education system have deep social roots among its people, since time immemorial.

Notes

1. Census of India, 2001. Provisional Population Totals, Manipur Series 14, Paper 3 of 2001, April.
2. James Johnstone. 1896. *My Experiences in Manipur and the Naga Hills*, London: Marston and Company Limited.
3. Lal Dena (1988) notes that in the aftermath of the introduction of Hinduism in the state, orthodoxy and conservatism arose particularly among the native aristocrats. With the advent of Hinduism, the Meitei script was eventually replaced by Bengali script. Along with this development, the native culture underwent a massive change. However, in recent times, the centrality of Meitei identity to Manipur can be observed by identity-based movements. The Meiteis have not only rediscovered and reconstructed their script; they have also started practicing pre-Vaishnava rituals and festivals.
4. J.B. Bhattacharjee (ed.). 2010 State and Economy in Pre-colonial Manipur, Nre Delhi: Akansha Publshing House, pp. 156–169.
5. Johnston, op. cit.
6. In the Hindu social system, varna is generally a reference category of the caste system. It is not only a functioning unit of social structure but also refers broadly to the ascribed status of different castes. The three upper levels – the Brahmans, the Kshatriyas the Vaishyas are assigned different occupations and are hierarchically superior to the Shudras, forming the fourth order. The occupation of the Shudras includes a multiplicity of artisan work. The untouchables, or the outcastes, constitute the fifth order that performs unclean and polluting occupations. G.S. Ghurye (1950) argues that the degree of their pollution was

reflected in various forms of disabilities imposed on them such as settlement outside the village boundary, denial of access to public resources, occupational segregation, practice of endogamy, etc.

7. In the order of caste hierarchy, Brahmins, Kshatriyas and Vaishyas are twice-born castes who can don the sacred thread around the waist and neck and whose culture and lifestyle is generally emulated by the members of low caste through a process of *sanskritisation*.
8. M.N. Srinivas (1962) defines varna in terms of the four orders, Brahmana, Rajanya (Kshatriya), Vaishya and Shudra as emanating from the mouth, the arms, the thighs and the feet of a primeval man, found during the later hymns of the Purushasukta. Srinivas further argues that the particular limbs are associated with these divisions and the order in which they are related indicate the status of each placed in the order.
9. The concept of hierarchy is deeply ingrained in the caste system. Caste is understood in terms of the principle of hierarchy. The principle is omnipresent and ubiquitous, not only in the nature of arrangement of social groups into different ranking but also in food (*kuccha/pucca*), occupation (pure/impure), space (sacred/profane), cloth (silk/cotton) and so forth.
10. According to *lallup*, or forced labour, every adult male in the age group of 16–60 years was bound to render ten days service out of every forty days to the Raja. Blacksmiths, goldsmiths, carpenters, etc., pursued their different crafts in the Raja's workshops, while the bulk of the population, the field workers, served as soldiers, made roads or dug canals. These men executed great public works for the benefit of the state under the *lallup* system (Brown, 1873; Johnstone, 1896).
11. Census of India, 2001. Provisional Population Totals, Manipur Series 14, Paper 3 of 2001, April.
12. Bhattarjee, op. cit.
13. Ibid., pp. 156–169.
14. The Royal Chronicle notes the existence of Kangla as the palace from the first kingdom of Manipur, i.e., Pakhangba, who became the king of Manipur in 33 A.D., just after the crucifixion of Jesus Christ in 29 or 30 A.D. The Chronicle further records that King Pakhangba used to assume the form of a snake by day and, by night, he used to be a man. This is the reason for the culture of snake worship among the Meiteis of Manipur.
15. *Mayangs* are any non-Manipuri people who come from mainstream India for the purpose of taking up business, or any other occupation. To the local people, the name also suggests outsiders, who belong to a different race and culture. Therefore, in most cases of reference, it has become rather derogatory to refer to outsiders as *mayangs*, due to various political reasons.

16. The market was established by King Khagemba in the 16th century. The market not only occupies a pivotal position of trade, but is also symbolic as the seat of women's power in the economic domain. *Ima* market continues to draw admiration and fascination for many outsiders who visit Manipur.
17. Census of India, 2001. Provisional Population Totals. Manipur Series 14, Paper 3 of 2001, April.
18. Census of India, 2001. Provisional Population Totals. Manipur Series 14, Paper 1 of 2001.

CHAPTER 4

Choosing Schools for Children: Seeing through Parents' Eyes

The explosive parental demand of schooling for children in the state of Manipur is evident in this chapter. The chapter examines how parental demand of schooling for children remains a deep-rooted realistic hope against all the odds, such as economic constraints, spiral downfall of government schools, corruption and constant violence in the public space – all of which pose a huge obstacle for achieving universal elementary schooling for children. In the state, even the poorest parents are clear about education goals, its vision, and hence are able to make judgements about the relevance of good schooling. The unresponsive, failed education system in the state however has pushed them into a hard dilemma with shock, frustration and a sense of helplessness that today's education system has failed to cradle and nurture a child. With a sense of deep frustration and helplessness, parents and children alike abandon government schools in hordes by shifting their allegiance to private schools. This emerging phenomenon has empowered private schools, while virtually leaving government schools completely impoverished to be internalised by only impoverished children whose parents are at risk of social exclusion as they are either survivors or intermittent income earners. The chapter examines some of these critical reflections, hopes and aspirations of parents on the present education scenario in the state, and how universal elementary education for their children is likely to remain a mirage despite their overwhelming support and constitutional promise.

Household Economic Activities: Agriculture

The Meiteis of Manipur practise many forms of industry, although most are involved in agriculture. Agriculture is a family enterprise and all family members including children are involved in guarding vegetables and crops from stray cattle and birds. The agricultural produce consists mainly of rice for immediate consumption and local trade. Rice is the staple food and it grows abundantly in the fertile soil. The economy of the state is predominantly agrarian and it is practised in a traditional way. It is greatly controlled by physical and cultural factors such as climate, topography and the socio-economic conditions of the landholders. In recent times, however, the only changes have been that tractors are used to soften the soil of the field with one crop a year. Agriculture remains the mainstay of livelihood for people and continues to be the main sector of employment absorbing the largest number of labourers, though it is a highly unorganised and unskilled one.

Agricultural land is symbolic to the people of Manipur. While examining the possession of land and ownership of land among households, it is revealed that 63 per cent of households own agricultural land ranging from less than 1 acre up to 3 acres, 45 per cent own less than 1 acre while 10 per cent of them own more than 1 acre and thus the largest land holding is up to 3 acres of land. Land ownership helps households save the expenditure on food as it meets the major household consumption spent on rice. Yet, as discussed above, the practice of agriculture is still rudimentary and hence not much surplus rice is produced. Compounded along with this are a host of problems such as lack of irrigation facility, low use of high yielding variety seeds and fertilizers and hence the productivity of agriculture is low. As such, not much income can be generated from the practice of agriculture. Yet, 65 per cent of households are in the agricultural sector, which is more or less subsistence type.

Another source of household income is derived from kitchen garden produce. Customarily, almost every household in Manipuri society possesses a homestead. In the homestead, households grow varieties of seasonal vegetables such as potatoes, sweet potatoes, tomatoes, beans, peas, chillies, mustard leaves, lady fingers, cucumber, ginger, turmeric, coriander, spring onions, cabbages, cauliflower, carrots, radishes, beetroots, turnips, gourds, pumpkins, aubergines, peas, cucumber, etc. Further, a village in Manipur is normally a long straggling series of houses each standing within its own enclosure with access to the river. Households grow vegetables on the fertile soil of river banks. In the absence of arbitrary boundaries of these banks, households falling within the area of river banks use the river bank for growing vegetables. It is usually the women who manage the kitchen garden, such as ploughing the soil, the spreading of cow dung that is used as fertilizer, fetching water for the plants, etc. These domestic products are used for household consumption as well as trading purposes which are carried out by women. In this way, households make substantial savings of income from their homestead kitchen garden as the people of Manipur valley thrive on green vegetables as part of their food consumption every day. Household income – big or small – is generated from both agricultural and vegetable products. There are also varieties of fruits grown such as apples, apricots, strawberries, oranges, limes, pomegranates, guavas, mangoes, pineapples, etc. The earnings made from these products range from ₹ 300 per month up to ₹ 600 per month. At least 75 per cent of households earn more than ₹ 300 per month from the kitchen garden while the remaining households earn more than ₹ 600 per month. The amount, although small, is indeed significant in a society where the majority of its members are left without any viable income from other sources of economic engagement.

Another source of major income among a few households is fishing which is a convenient practice as a large portion of the valley has access to ponds, rivers and lakes. Fish is an important article of consumption and sale. There are many varieties of fish and the supply is plentiful. The all time favourite pastime of fishing gives an employment opportunity to many of these households especially to women. During *Ekpal Lokpa* (the rainy season), almost all women engage in fishing in flooded fields, ponds, canals and rivers. At other times, fishing is done by women on a regular basis and the sale of fish even to the remotest area is done by women.

Weaving and Other Economic Activities

Next in importance to agriculture is weaving. Weaving is a year round pursuit among females. Almost all households possess a simple loom kept in the verandah of the house or *Shangoi*.[1] All women – educated, literate or illiterate – make an effort to provide self-employment through weaving. Almost every household owns a loom – be it a loin loom or a fly shuttle loom. The entire business of weaving is managed by women only. This includes *tareng masa* (spinning of wheels), *langchak* (bobbins), while better off families have large *tareng* used for arranging thread on a roller for the looms. Though mainly intended for household use, the cloth made from weaving is sent off to Imphal market for sale. The income generated directly supports their households. Only womenfolk sell these products, generating cash for household expenses including school fees for children.

Thus, in the absence of any viable industry – small, medium and large – households engage in different occupational activities[2] such as primary, secondary and tertiary. Going by these occupational groupings, 58 per cent of parents engage in tertiary sector working as agricultural wage labourers, construction workers, brick makers, incense makers, vegetable vendors, fishermen, weavers, small traders such as goldsmith, coal and cylinder business, running fast food shop, grocery shop, selling home-based products such as fish, vegetables, animal husbandry, piggery, poultry, carpentry, transport and construction workers, rickshaw pullers, etc. These households through these engagements earn intermittent income as daily wagers.

The income earned from such economic pursuits is used to meet daily basic necessities. On the contrary, 42 per cent of respondents belong to skilled workers.[3] These include clerical jobs in government

Table 4.1 *Occupational Categories of Parent Respondents*

Categories of Occupation	*Male*	*Female*
Carpentry	Yes	Helps in selling it
House construction	Yes	No
Brick making	Yes	Yes
Weaving	No	Yes, prepares threading, weaves and sells in the market
Vegetable seller	No	Yes, collects vegetables from home garden and sell it in the market
Fishing	No	Yes, collects fish from rivers, ponds and lakes, (sometimes roast it on fire) for sale in market
Grocery	No	Yes, collects all necessary items from bazaar for sale to meet local consumption
Fast food stall	No	Yes, collects all items from market and prepare them for sale
Piggery and poultry	Yes	Yes, helps in preparing food and feeding
Wood business	Yes	No
Incense making	No	Yes
Salaried	Yes	Yes

Source: Primary Survey, 2009.

sector such as police constables, electricians, artists, health workers in hospitals, government school teachers, auditors, etc. The high number of unskilled labour force among the parents indicates that many of these parents could not acquire skilful occupations due to a lack of necessary skills. In this case one's educational level is recognised as one of the most important factors governing the accessibility to social advantages including job opportunities. However, this may not hold a suitable argument in the state of Manipur where job opportunities in the service sector are fiercely scarce. For example, most parents, who have obtained a Bachelor's degree, engage in occupations such as poultry, piggery, construction work, sale of firewood, etc., whereas the same job can be performed by an individual who has not earned a formal degree.

Thus majority of parents who have completed graduation are employed as daily wagers or casual workers while some of them engage in self-employment ventures such as piggery, poultry, wood business, etc. Of these, most women respondents are found engaged in trading home-based products such as vegetables, fruits, fish and items of clothing woven at home. These products are brought to the local market and the main mothers' market. It is worth mentioning that the mothers' market is a fascinating site since it is operated and manned only by womenfolk. Busloads of women carrying all types of products such as fish, vegetables, bamboo shoots, fresh spices in big tin containers rushing to the mothers' market is a daily scene. The market is of considerable size, with covered sheds of tin and *pucca* (well-built) roofing as well, while a large open area is also fully occupied by women traders. The main marketing business begins in early afternoon. Another interesting scene is the common street site where one notices streams of women walking on foot, carrying loads of edible items such as fish, fruits, vegetables of all kinds, clothes, etc., heading for local markets. During this time, one notices that well groomed women enter the scene with *chandals*[4] on their forehead. The price of goods is fixed through bargain and haggling. It is also noticed that price determination is also affected by factors such as lineage, kinship ties[5] and the status of the consumer.

Data about the main income earner[6] indicates that 33 per cent of the women respondents are main income earners, while almost all the remaining women respondents contribute as supplementary income earners. The occupational structure of different households offers interesting developments. The occupational mobility pattern among different social groups indicates that they are free to exercise an unrestricted choice of occupation. As seen, though there have been avenues for mobility in various occupations, the economy of the state has not been able to provide facilities to absorb its population into various sectors of employment.

Unemployment problem for both the educated and uneducated remains acute in the state. The occupational activities of these households indicate that a significant portion of them are engaged in primary occupations. The majority of the population is engaged in agriculture as wage labourers, while some of them possess land. Therefore, 57.5 per cent of them belong to unskilled workers such as construction workers, farmers, brick makers, etc., against 42.5 per cent skilled workers. As much as 37.5 per cent of households have a monthly income as meagre as ₹ 2,000 to ₹ 4,000. Around 27 per cent of households have an income of ₹ 4,000 ₹ 6,000 per month, while 35 per cent of households earn an income of ₹ 9,000 and above per month. These households, though less in number, are skilled workers employed in the service sector in high positions including those of Commissioners, Deputy Directors, and auditors working in the government sector. Yet, as revealed in the present study, the majority of the households are employed as casual and unskilled workers, earning intermittent income.

Household Expenditure on Education of Children

It is understood that parent respondents enjoy different levels of socio-economic status. Yet, a large number of them are engaged as intermittent income earners and are always on the lookout for menial jobs to eke out a living. The pattern of household expenditure on various items, such as everyday consumption of food, medicine, festivals, various religious ceremonies observed during rites of passage,[7] feasting specially during *phairen-lamda* (spring months), shows that 20 per cent of households spend upto ₹ 2,000 per month, 48 per cent upto ₹ 6,000 per month, while 32 per cent spend more than ₹ 6,000 per month. However, it is found that all parent respondents, irrespective of their economic status send children to school, though there is sharp contrast of expenditures among households on the education of their children. For example, 25 per cent of households spend ₹ 500 per child per month, 22 per cent spend ₹ 330 per month for children's education, while a marginal number of households, i.e., 2.5 per cent, spend more than ₹ 1,660 per month. In contrast to these observations, 35 per cent of households spend as little as ₹ 160 per child per month. When one examines the financial status of these parents and expenditure pattern on children's schooling, it is revealed that educating a child is a huge financial liability. The most expensive school items start from school uniforms followed by stationery and textbooks. Yet, despite financial disadvantageous position of parents and a lack of possession of assets such as land ownership, income and wages, either working as white or blue collar workers, there is not a single household that neglects the schooling of their children irrespective of boys and girls.

Housing Conditions and Learning Facilities for Children

In Manipuri society, it is customarily considered to be auspicious that all the houses face eastward to feel the morning sunlight. Hence, the houses have a large open *mangol* facing towards the east. *Mangol* is the front porch where the space can be used for different purposes, including entertaining guests, informal meetings, or for study purpose of children, etc. In the *mangol,* the family members sit during the day as well as carry out all the household chores there. The southern side of the *mangol* is considered as the seat of honour and here a reed mat is always spread from morning till late evening. Children usually study on the reed mat before leaving home for school.

However, in today's times, most of the *pucca* (well-built) houses do not have sufficient space for *mangol*. These *pucca* houses on the contrary, have an adequate number of rooms of reasonable size, with the kitchen and hearth being separated from other rooms. In a *pucca* house, there are amenities such as potable water, electricity supply, sewage facilities, etc. These households have a good amount of ventilation, decorative furniture and other items such as tables, chairs and desks for children to study at, whereas children in *kuccha* (not well-built) houses are deprived of such amenities and hence proper study facilities too. In most cases, the walls of the *kuccha* houses are reeds plastered with a mixture of earth and cow dung, and the roofs of these houses are thatched with dry grass. These houses have narrow windows for ventilation, and may not provide sufficient light to enable one to read or write. Of the total households interacted, 65 per cent of parents live in the *kuccha* houses, while the remaining households live in semi-*pucca* or *pucca* houses. *Pucca* houses are relatively larger and constructed of better materials such as wood and bricks, while *kuccha* houses are made of posts, beams, bamboo and mud. A semi-*pucca* or *pucca* house can have more than two rooms, while the *kuccha* house can have just one room with the hearth, the kitchen and the bedroom together. Therefore, children in *kuccha* houses, in the absence of basic study facilities, squat on the mat or floor and write on slates or paper balanced between their knees, creating physical discomfort and distracting their concentration level. In most *kuccha* houses, there is a combined room where beds, hearth and kitchen are located. It takes about one and a half hours, or sometimes longer, to cook a complete meal by means of firewood and paddy husk. Traditionally, among the Meitei households, the hearth is considered sacred and should be kept burning with low intensity all the time. Thus, the chimney coming out of the hearth and the kitchen is a natural cause of great discomfort and distraction for a child studying in such an environment. Apart from such inconvenience, family discussion and gossip mongers from nearby neighbourhoods usually sit around the hearth, particularly in winter, sometimes creating a nuisance and thus a great disturbance to a child's study.

Housing facilities can create an environment that operates to either hinder learning or promote learning of children. The housing condition and house type are therefore indicators of the general condition of the household and various facilities available within. Therefore, the presence or the absence of these facilities has a bearing impact on the motivation for learning that a child has. Therefore, children living in *kuccha* houses have generally demotivating and poor learning environment. Though, of course, the quality of the schooling that the child receives remains a crucial factor in the learning capability of the child, which is particularly true for poor households, since quality of schooling can compensate a child for his/her deficiency of home environment.

School Choice: Mapping the Future of Children

Existential situations of households in choosing a school indicate that space, travel and familial organisations are basic reasons for the choice of a particular school. This argument stands true mostly in case of poor households. Among poor households, financial constraints, lack of private and public transport play a key role in the whole range of decision-making of school choice for children. Added to these, constraints are also developed as a result of parents daily work responsibilities and the location of their households to the availability of public transport facilities. On his school choice, a parent who is a farmer thus reasoned:

> I always engage in seasonal jobs, sometimes in agricultural work, sometimes non-agricultural work; while my wife is busy in weaving and household chores. In this situation, I am not able to arrange even private school for my children. I send them to aided school which is less costly and is quite closeby. My children can walk down to school and return home on foot. There is no need, either for a cycle or a transport to reach the school.

School choice is also closely tied to a sense of local community, of which the household forms an extension of the locality in which the school exists. An Imphal-based affluent respondent, whose children are studying at Maria Montessori School, shared:

> My elder son and daughter attend Maria Montessori School. So my youngest child can join her siblings. It is local as well, since the school is just few kilometres away from our home. Three of them travel by school van while leaving for school and return home together. I don't have to make separate trips for each one of them; so it's easier for us.

Another father who makes his livelihood from poultry, referring to one of the famous sought after private schools (Bethel), located in his locality, observed:

> I didn't feel that it is a very good school at least academically. But the distance between the school and my home is favourable for my children, though the roadways are not safe at all. My child is very good in Sanskrit studies but could not continue in the previous school since there is no good teacher to teach Sanskrit for higher classes. So, I shifted him to the present school considering other options. Well, there are nearby dysfunctional government schools.

Access to public transport, the local timetable, the pattern of busy roads, open spaces, the physical location of the school and of course, time, as well as particular occupational engagements of the parents are important factors in deciding the type of school parents choose. However, parental choice for the private school system over other forms of schooling remains overwhelming. As in other parts of the country, parents in Manipur have also completely lost faith in the system of government schools. Sending a child to a private school among almost all households has now become a social norm. As shown in Figure 4.1, it is startling to note that an overwhelming 82 per cent of parents choose private schools as against to 15.5 per cent of households who send their children to government schools, while a marginal number of 2.5 per cent households send their children to aided school.

Figure 4.1 *Percentage of Households Sending Children to Different Schools*

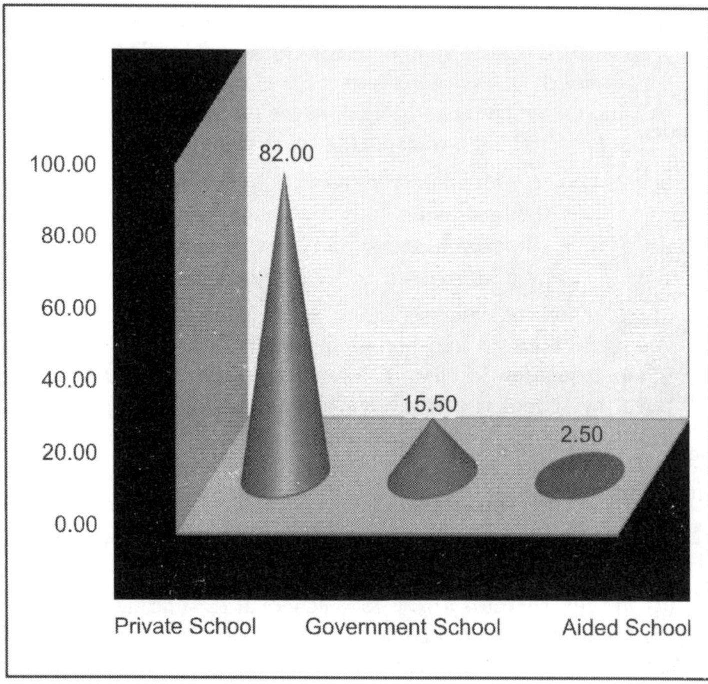

Source: Primary Survey, 2009.

In search of elusive quality education, a phenomenon of structural shift of school age population to private school has emerged, even though the concept of quality education continues to evade private schools as shared by conscientious parents.

Writing about the development of parental choice of schools in USA in early 1980s, David Hogan argues, as a matter of legitimate rights, parents exercise ample opportunity in school choice as they are the better judges of their children, and that the principle of equal opportunity requires that all parents, irrespective of their social background, should have the effective ability to send their children to the school of their choice. But, the developments in late 80s and 90s in state-run schools pushed parents much harder to go for a harder choice of school. While the performance of state-run schools was failing rapidly, the phenomenon provided a successful road map for private schools to flourish in no time. The same trend could be experienced vigorously in various parts of developing countries including India. In similar lines of articulation, while writing about postcolonial educational developments in the Third World countries, Jules and Apple (1995) argue that developing country, being a transition state,[8] is under tremendous pressure since the educational role is purely administrative with a limited capacity for regulation as the actual provision of education is done by private entities. This includes missionary schools that have a strong western influence. In the state of Manipur, these developments could be seen from the early times with the establishment of many Catholic schools, which later acted as ideal models with a strong impact on producing more private schools, charging high fees where majority children from urban affluent families traditionally attend. These are some of the similar emerging trends that prompted scholars, such as Apple (2001) and Torres (1995), to extensively engage in neo-liberal policies in education, with its initial roots in the West.

These policies, they argue, are guided by a vision of weak state and strong market, promoting what is private is necessarily good and what is public is necessarily bad. The idea is that consumer choice is different from the welfare tradition as the guarantor of democracy for people in choice making, and hence education will be largely self-regulated. Efficiency and cost benefit are its thriving force. Neo-liberal policies strive to pass the cost of educational services to clients through user fees, increasing the participation of the private sector in education causing a drastic reduction in social expenditure by the state. Torres further argues that the new political agenda is associated with a drastic shift away from the welfare state policies that began in the 1980s in developed countries, including the period of Margaret Thatcher in Britain and Ronald Reagan in USA. However, one needs to be cautious against such policies in the political agenda of developing countries, where its social formation is entirely different from the West, most of whom were early colonisers themselves and industrially advanced countries. Most importantly, issues of equality have been systematically neglected among advocates of allowing parents to choose schools for their children.

Reflecting on the debate of the development of private schools in the state of Manipur, one could notice that in a short span of time, these private schools became very successful in terms of what they offer, such as the whole package that is considered essential for the future of children in this era of fierce competition. The package may include the general feel good factor atmosphere of the school, discipline and morality, habits of cleanliness, school uniforms, emphasis on English language learning, commitment of teachers, weekly tests, examination systems, homework assignments, performances, competitions, grading, class attendance, accountability, class consciousness and so forth. These factors are found visibly missing in government schools but play a fundamental role in giving parents an edge of selecting private schools over government schools. Thus, in the words of a conscientious parent, who vehemently argued against the way the government school functions:

> In true sense, I prefer government schools because it is cheaper and less expensive. But it is extremely sad that in government school, there is hardly any student in the class. Children play mischief, without anybody's care. From home front, we send children in early hour in the morning without proper feeding so that they reach school on time and can attend class on time. But, in school, what the teachers do is extremely unwanted. What is the whole point when teachers don't care for these kids on reaching school after so much of hassles?

Another upright parent added her unhappiness over government school:

> There is strictness in private schools; government school teachers are lazy, bask in the sunlight, gossip, waste time in gambling, but never fail to collect a salary every month. So, there is no need to bother much for the welfare of teaching children. They don't want to cultivate any sense of sacrifice for children; they just give homework to children without teaching them in the class. But in private school, if teachers don't work sincerely, they'll be penalised either through non-payment or termination. In government school, there is no performance and hence there is no competition. One compares such performance with drama shows in a theatre. During a drama show in a theatre, when there is no audience (students are missing in classroom), there is no performance, so there can be no drama and no competition.

Similar opinion was voiced by a 40-year old parent, who is a cook, taking relief from busily serving her customers:

> Government school teachers want to relax. They engage in bad habits like smoking cigarettes, gambling, etc. Female teachers

> engage in knitting, form peer groups to bitch and gossip around. Teachers open register only to register children's name; that is the only job they perform. Government teachers don't teach. Most of them are trained but fail to respect the values and principles of training. There are seven to eight teachers for four students only. Since, there are no students; there is no teaching at all.

Almost all parents opine that government schools are dying and that there is chronic shortage of students in government schools due to the steady absorption of these students in private schools. The glaring example is Phoijing Upper Junior High School. A worried government school teacher, showing her concerns over the decaying of the school, reflected on the situation in the following words:

> There is no child in the school; situation was discussed in a meeting. The meeting was called by the head teacher. We realized that all children have joined private schools. The discussion was mainly focused on how to increase the enrolment of children and how to retain them in the school. The suggestion that came forward from all teachers is that retention of children depends on the performance of the school and therefore performance must be compulsorily improved. Facilities such as furniture, tables, chairs, desks – all are available in the school. But there are no students. The number of teachers is thirteen while the number of students is fourteen. So whom do these teachers teach when there are no students?

The experience of the teacher further suggests that teaching involves exchanging and sharing experiences between teachers and the taught, with a determinate end, that of promoting learning on the part of the students, with a fair amount of dialogue in a classroom situation that is found to be missing in the school cited above. Teachers have a social role that consists of a set of rights and obligations that goes with the position he or she occupies by virtue of being a teacher. Thus, role performance of a teacher is in conformity with societal expectations. As argued by many, a teacher's role is seen as an extension of what is valued in a society. Drawing inspiration from the phenomelogist, Erving Goffman, 'The presentation of Self in Everyday Life', it may be argued that the role of a teacher can be compared to a theatrical performance, just as the role of a teacher is a dramatic metaphor as expressed by many parents above. The role of a teacher in a school is readily interpreted as a form of role playing in a classroom, something of a theatre in a miniature. Teachers, equipped with all the necessary requirements for theatrical effect perform before their students in a lecture. Parsons (1968) in a discussion of the teacher's role argue that the role of a teacher in a classroom does the function of selecting children for their social future and occupational roles. The functionalists believe that teachers have taken over from parents, something of their prior task of nurturing and developing the child. It is further argued that with an increased importance on the role of the teacher in socialising children, this may lead to a requirement that teachers should be made more accountable to the community at large, particularly the immediate community such as the parents. As many parent respondents tend to compare, here the notion of a school teacher as an actor putting on a performance, is seen that the teacher must set a particularly high standard of moral probity and scholarly zeal. In the light of the foregoing argument, antagonism between teachers and parents arises when the former fails to perform its roles in terms of interest of children, which more or less represents the interest of the parents. A parent complained:

> From our experience about whatever is happening in government schools, we can count on private schools. Methods of teaching in both government and private schools are different in terms of norms, guidelines. Rules in private schools are better prescribed and managed in private schools. But, in government school, the teachers are there solely for salary, not for teaching. It is heartrending because we are unfortunate losers when government school teachers are non-performers.

On the contrary, the fact that private schools are perceived as better than state-run schools by parents brings out more accountability in the schooling system. In a private school, the teachers are accountable to the structure of management and regulation. They are generally seen to have a stake in the integrity of their profession. Fingers running through her wet hair, basking in the morning sunlight, sitting in a relaxed mood on the mat spread in the *mangol* of her home, a mother, who is a vegetable seller and also the head of a local Self-Help Group organisation voiced out:

> Government school is like a free zone. Strictness is no doubt a factor of sending my children to private school. Teaching in private school especially in lower classes is really impressive. Children can be disciplined at least upto class X. So, there is a lot difference between the two. Government school teachers just don't care about school improvement, and they've no control over

school matter. But private schools are not like this. Teaching methods, behavioural patterns of these teachers are somewhat different from those in private school. Of course, both produce differential influence on children.

A father of two school children, who works in a piggery and wood business, taking some time off from his daily routine engagement, shared his observation:

> Private school is better disciplined. We have faith in their accountability for our children. In private school, the management can become accountable, because, when we demand, we get parental support of other children. But, the situation is just the opposite in government school. The free salary government teachers collect per month fails them to be accountable with damaging effect on children. We want quality but we don't trust in government system.

Similar views were expressed by other parents too. For example, take the case of a father, a carpenter who is proud of sending his children to one of the best considered private schools, Saint Joseph School, Imphal:

> In a private school, teachers are accountable for disciplining and instilling moral values in children. The teaching method is also very strict. We send our children to private school simply because we've faith in them. Teachers are so compulsorily responsible to mould the child into a human being. So, I believe investment in a child is compensated if I send them to a private school. Till now I've found private school really good. Private school is my preferred choice. Children in government school become increasingly lazy. But private schools are so strict that children after being educated there are likely to improve themselves and naturally become good.

Such views are commonly shared by parents of all strata of society as another retired service personal from Defence Service said:

> I personally prefer sending my children to government school, but government schools are failed. How can I as a guardian send children to such a school to learn something?

The pathologies of government school have indeed infected not only the hearts and minds of parents but those of young school-going children too. For most of these parents, the wish of a child of choosing a particular school is given considerable thought. Take the case of a mother who thoughtfully shared her children's sarcastic and mocking opinion on the status of government schools in Manipur:

> My children look down upon government schools as cowshed, shabby and bleak place, with no future. Imagine even a tiny child from the start of his school is capable of forming such a negative attitude about a government school image. It shows the child's contempt of poor condition of government schools.

Another respondent, a mother of four school-going children, expressed how her children simply refuse to attend government school despite their grinding poverty:

> Children don't want to attend government school. Government school environment numbs children rather than improving them. Children in government school are asked to dust around. These kids are in pathetic and unhygienic condition with running nose, saliva on their chin; wear torn clothes they are filthy to the extreme.

Thereafter, she added:

> They start for school without bathe or stationery. Let children go to private and come back neat and clean. My children can't be forced to opt for government school. It is this helpless situation that is actually compelling me to send them to private school only.

Citing what was aired in the daily morning news, the mother continued in anguish:

> In today's morning radio news at 7.30, it was declared that government schools don't teach children. Choosing a private school has become almost universal and unconscious choice among households. Children are refusing to go to government schools. All their friends are going to private school. As a guardian, I can't force them against their wish. My neighbour sends one child to private school, two children to government school since both were failed while studying in private school.

Going by the weight of parental opinion, it is children who have no roots, who cannot purchase books and stationery, and orphans and hungry children without proper clothing are the ones who attend government schools. A government school is indeed depressing and it is never a happy experience for both the children and the parents alike. Therefore, children attending government schools have a bleak future and hence the future prospect of a child in a government school disappears into the void. This observation, in a deeply profound sense, is truly a constant traumatic engagement for the poor, hardworking parents, whose daily engagement is mainly on making both ends meet. A rickshaw puller, who is a father of three school-going children, blaming his existential situation of poverty, shared:

> Presently, my children go to government school, the choice is not in my hand. Government school teachers don't care at all. I am so disappointed, I am so poor; it is my fault. If I was employed, I could have satisfied my children's educational needs.

In a similar vein, another rickshaw puller, a parent of three school-going children, expressed his anguish over his inability to send children to private school:

> I can't afford private school. I send my children to government school. My children understand because I am so poor. Deep down in my heart, I am not at all satisfied with government school and also the idea that my children attend such failed school. I am worried for the future of my children. I want my children on equal footing with kids of rich parents, but there is no hope. Government school is meant only for poor families.

Some parents strongly assert that government schools exist by default. Yet, poor parents due to their destitute circumstances endure endless capacity to tolerate government schools that are almost perished. A parent respondent of two school-going children with a sense of guilt referring to her daughter's plight bluntly put:

> Due to our family poverty, I send her to Government Tangtek Junior School. I am aware that my daughter's school environment is not good at all. Teachers come to the school to pass off their time and collect salary. But, I simply can't do anything about it. Every day, I am engaged in making meagre earning of few rupees to support family's daily need.

As observed from these parental narrations, the majority of these parents end up blaming their own destiny that they are unable to exercise their school choice for sending their children to a particular school since the cost difference between a government school and a private school is quite substantial. Therefore, these parents, despite their strong dissatisfaction and protest against government schools, continue sending their children to government schools without expecting any future prospect.

Morality, Discipline, Grading, English, Speech Forms, etc.

It is alarming that among the parent community, there is a whole-hearted acceptance about the deliberate failure in government schools, the moral order and discipline in particular. Next to family, schools are seen as the most effective agencies in socialisation of children including discipline in myriad forms. Next to family, school-going children most of their time in a school. In this context, school is seen as the only means of socialising children that probably no other organisation outside the family has so prolonged a hold over the lives of so many young school-going children. Therefore, schools as custodial institutions are the caretakers of the young and can exert great influence in inculcating values in their students. In this context, Paul Rabinow in *Foucault Reader* (1984) describes 'school' as a disciplinary and a grading mechanism. He further explains how discipline presupposes a mechanism that coerces by means of observation and what is most important is functional surveillance that is extended not only to the overall behavioural and dressing patterns of children but also school layout, its fencing, punctuality, regularity, absence, lateness, personal hygiene, cleanliness, performance, etc. These strictures though required in all formal schools are strictly followed in private schools.

The above disciplinary observations practised in private schools were delightfully shared by most parent respondents. For example, while citing her views on school environment, a parent stated:

> I am happy with the school environment. I as a parent feel safe, because my children's school has bamboo fencing across the boundary. So children don't move here and there, it restricts them from venturing into unwanted loitering.

The concept of discipline and moral order indicates not only the physical environment such as location of the school, school boundary and its fencing but its totality such as speech forms, dressing, cleanliness, health and hygiene, strictness, periodical test performance, examination results and scholastic achievements that are scrutinised through the prism of children's performance and overall behavioural pattern.

Like other parent respondents, a widow, mother of two school-going children and who runs a small grocery shop in front of her home, shared her critique and seriousness about the whole issue of schooling culture in the state. While narrating her appreciation about discipline and morality maintained in private schools, she augments her views by exhibiting personal habits of health and hygiene among private school-going children. She considers the maintenance of discipline and morality as essential for personality growth in children:

> In private schools, during assembly hours, teachers observe children very carefully whether they have long nails, or keep their hair tidy or not. Private school children can't grow long hair; they've to trim their nails regularly, maintain dress neat and clean, and can't apply perfume; they can't even slouch in the school verandah. Actually overall good habit formation is taught in private school but these are not taken care of in government schools.

Another young lady engaged in coal and gas cylinder business appreciated private schools by despising indiscipline of government schools as follows:

> In private schools, teachers come on time, right from the start of teaching sessions. They teach students regularly. It is not that I am overwhelmingly appreciating private schools. But in private schools it is guaranteed that out of five teachers, at least two of them will be very sincere, strict and serious. There is discipline in them. Private school is my preferred choice. While sending children to government school for study purpose, I don't see improvement in them at all, but in private school, children improve their behaviour because every time, the teachers keep an eye on children's behaviour and encourage them cultivate good habit formation.

Apparently, another observation regarding private schools is that competition in the form of examination has become a norm and the standard and quality of the school is determined by the number of students enrolled and the rankings students attain in Board examinations. Precisely, because examination production is a crucial factor of parental choice for a particular school for the reason that top-ranking students determines the reputation of the school that parents choose. A father, who provides pick and drop facility to school children, shared:

> My child is studying in Joshep School which is quite famous and reputed. It is the best school for boys. The school produces at least four to five rank holders every year in matriculation. There is also monthly test conducted. This lessens the burden on children at the end of the year during final examinations.

A widow, who is in weaving business, while simultaneously tending her kitchen garden, opined:

> Teachers in Bethel school try their best to teach children well and produce many rank holders. It simply can't happen if the school environment is bad. In government school, the rate of passing of students in Board examination is very low. All rank holders are from private schools.

However, despite an overwhelming parental support for private schools, conscientious parents simply do not want them to be an examination factory, or performance, ranking and results alone; rather, the whole package of cultural indicators and class advantage embedded in these schools, including the feel-good factor of the general atmosphere of the school, quality, English medium and overall ethos of the school, are taken into account. Parents are concerned much more with what Bernstein calls the 'expressive order of the school', i.e., the complex behaviour and activities in the school which are to do with conduct, behaviour, character and manners of children.

Thus, appreciating the culture of private schools, parents whose children are sent to different private schools, shared:

> Children from private school know how to behave and talk appropriately, say, with seniors, juniors. I didn't notice these changes in my children before sending them to Bethel school. They've started forming good habits after sending to Bethel school. I notice these marked changes and improvements in their overall behaviour.
>
> I myself did schooling in government school. In government school, pattern of speech, teaching methods, behaviour of the teachers are somewhat different from those in private schools. These have differential influence on the development of behavioural patterns on our children, don't you think so?
>
> My perception about my children's school environment till now is good; the school is also strict in maintaining moral behaviour and discipline among children. I've noticed about my children's changed behaviour. My children know about appropriate behaviour; how to speak to others politely.
>
> I prefer sending my child to private school because there is discipline in study pattern and children become dutiful. However in government schools, the way teachers teach and behave to students is improper. Corporal punishment and unwanted treatment is meted out to a child. But disciplining of

> children should be done in a playway method. Without understanding the attitude of the child, they start beating. In every school, there are plenty of activities through which the bond between teachers and students are easily established. Such a bonding is absent in government school. The trust factor is missing.
>
> In private school, there is moral and character formation among children. They are stricter than government schools. Anyway children are better trained in their behaviour and learning abilities in a private school.
>
> I am a rickshaw puller, my earning is meagre and sometimes I go back home empty handed. Despite all these heavy odds and struggles, I still prefer sending my children to private school. In a private school, children who have completed at least IV and V standards, can read and write, but this is not possible in a government school. Government school is a waste for children.

Parents are therefore convinced that apart from improvement in overall behavioural pattern, there is some amount of teaching/learning taking place in private schools while government schools are completely failed in enabling children to become functionally literate. Parents unanimously agree that sending children to private schools enables them at least to become literate. These parental observations cut across all economic strata, such as salaried and non-salaried, rich and poor including farmers, daily wagers and rickshaw pullers alike across regions such as rural and urban.

At a stone's throw distance, away towards the south from the heart of the mother's market, there is Keisampat town with some small shops existing. These shops are manned by both men and women. In one of these corners, there is a fast food stall manned by a female in her late 40s. She is quite active and looks after her business from dusk to down. Several elderly women, including her 80 years old mother-in-law and *leishabis*[9] from the nearby households, lounged around her stall to enjoy evening tea, *sengju*[10] and snacks. This woman delightfully shared some of her impressive observations about teaching/learning imparted in private schools:

> There is depth of teaching/learning in private schools. For example, when private school teachers teach about the fruit-apple, they teach very thoroughly. They not only explain that there is an

apple, which is a fruit but also by demonstrating the process of planting and growing it.

A conscientious mother who supplies coal and gas cylinder, shared her views in the following words:

> Government school teachers send their own children to private schools. Teachers in government schools don't teach if they don't want. In government system, there is nothing called responsibility. But in private schools, teachers join on time, right from 10 a.m. in the morning and stay on till the end. Teachers teach students on time and regularly. In government schools, teacher absenteeism is plenty. If this is what private teachers do, then there'll be reduction in their salary and if they don't teach, they will be thrown out of the school. Children get upset with government teachers. Government school might give facilities or not, I've never seen it, but in private school, there are plenty of facilities and good infrastructure facilities. So, naturally overall environment is far better in private school than that of government school. In private schools, all students seem to be uniformly good in dressing, maintaining discipline, cleanliness, habits, homework performance, etc.

Moving away to the south from Keisampat for a distance of almost 17 km, clusters of households are located at Phoijing Chingning village, in rural Imphal west district. Among the villagers, there are householders who generally work in the kitchen garden in the morning hours till forenoon until the time lunch is served. While walking through several houses, a father of four school-going children, who is a trained pharmacist by profession, was found working in his kitchen garden, taming the soil with a spade. After a hectic engagement in tending his kitchen garden, keeping his spade aside, he set down in one corner of his *mangol* and said,

> The standard of teaching in private school is high. Children of class V in private school are better equipped than those learning in class VIII of government school.

Interestingly, a government school teacher residing in the next house, hurriedly shared her experience as a serving teacher in a government school:

> Look! In government schools, there is monthly salary that compensates any misdealing and non-performance of teachers. So ultimately there is a marked difference in the performance of the

> teachers in private and government schools. Government teachers take teaching profession for granted. They start everything late. A child in a private school starts learning methods of conjugation at an early stage. This helps him in learning faster than those in government schools. When we are to teach *Mapi Mairik* (Mapi = Mother, Lairik = book) in proper order, government teachers teach the book in reverse order. Instead of making children learn alphabets first as A, B, C, D, children in government schools are taught to learn words first. So, parents don't want to send children to government schools where the order is missing in every sense of the term.

The above observations are uniformly shared including government school teacher themselves though a lot of blame is laid on the parental negligence of children sent in government school as schooling of children is also intrinsically a joint task of parents and teachers, in as much as a child requires education not only at school but also at home. As the same teacher showed her concerns:

> When government school children don't have the parental support in getting homework done, it can sap the morale of the child. They don't have the right kind of study habit at home. Their parents don't bring them up in right manner and never bother to see what is happening to the welfare of their children. Home background is not encouraging and so one can't blame the teachers alone.

Yet, the teacher complimented on children of government school saying, 'But these children will shine, I assure, if taken care of in the manner parents of private school-going children invest in their children'.

Nevertheless, the candid and open acceptance by the government school teacher on the issue of non-accountability of state-run schools is the reflection of her other fellow colleagues' views whose children also go to private schools. Even government school teachers are in favour of private schools that they do not even want their children to be in their own schools. Many parents observed such a candid attitude of government school teachers as a form of acceptance of their own failure in performance to the extent that these teachers have lost faith in their own capabilities of delivery. Many perceive of this observation as an important reason as to why they, as guardians, do not prefer their own children to be in the custody of government school teachers who have lost credentials as responsible teachers and guardians. In the words of a parent respondent:

> It is certainly a serious issue when government school teachers send their own children to private schools rather than to their own schools. It is quite not possible for us to send our own children to government schools when government school teachers have lost faith in themselves and there is no question of entrusting my children in them.

Apparently the present study has also found that English medium instruction (which was once a language of distaste during the British period) in private schools is a big selling point for school choice making of parents. A parent respondent reflected on what is fashionable in today's Manipuri society, 'In today's Manipuri society (Houjik Matamgi Manipuri Samaj), it has become a trend and prestigious to speak English'. Further, private education is considered synonymous with English learning as the parent further expressed,

> Nowadays, education means private school and one has to be educated in private school to pick up English language or else it is meaningless. Speaking English is considered so desirable because when children are sent to market places to purchase a medicine for example, they have to know English since everything is written in English. Private school is what English learning is.

Hence private schools have now become synonymous with English medium which is most sought after by parents. A parent respondent, who is a weaver shared, 'For the present day, it has become a trend to send children to English school medium which is private'.

Thereafter, in retrospection, she reflected:

> We also question ourselves as to why it has become a trend. Moreover, children in private school start conversing in English as soon as they join school and it automatically becomes a natural habit for them to pick up English.

The feeling that English medium private school is the most preferred school strongly prevails among low economic strata too that even a rickshaw puller goes crazy after private school that is synonymous with English learning. 'I send my daughter to English education where there is moral and character formation and they are far stricter than government school'.

A parent respondent, whose children study in classes II, III and VIII, shared her satisfaction over her decision of school choice:

> I am satisfied with our children's school. It is private and English. Students from other villages come to get education from the same school since it is an English medium school.

As observed in the present study, parents selecting private schools exercise more potential choices. And, while exercising their school choice option, they are more likely to select schools that more closely match their expectations. It is this matching phenomenon that helps private schools to establish a clear set of goals formulated and shared by the schools and the parent community as well. Private school teachers, for example, turn up to school on time, keep the students busy, and maintain discipline. In all these respects private schools convincingly strike the parents. Benches, desks, electricity connection, doors, windows, ventilation, uniforms, neck ties, shoes children wear make an impression of private schools though without much critical scrutiny. Students are also more likely to achieve scholastically in schools that establish high academic standards, enforce disciplinary rules which are far better managed in private schools. This is perhaps the most compelling reason why private schools provide successful learning environment for children as perceived by most parents. Further, as argued by Chubb and Moe (1985), private schools do not encounter the myriad of bureaucratic problems that beset with government schools and as such private schools can accomplish their goals with minimum interference and this is most visibly measured by performance and results in examinations. Another major organisational advantage of private schools over government schools is that the principal in most cases is also the manager, instructor and decision-maker. It is this accountability and relative autonomy that raise the expectation and likelihood among the parents that goals will be accomplished. If this is seemingly what parents want for their children, the image a particular school conveys through its students is a powerful influence on school choice making of parents. Many parents explained, for instance, examination results could dramatically provoke their school choice making. Therefore, while exercising their choice, parents are likely to select schools that closely match their expectations as argued before. For instance, to note a parent's statement whose opinion is also uniformly shared by other parents, 'In today's times, we all prefer sending our children to private school because private system is so attractive since what they do is our choice'.

Despite these observations, acceptance of private schools among parents is but without critique. For example, the hollow claim of English instruction made by many private schools is another illustration of this problem as observed in the present study. There is a great deal of variation in the credibility of private schools of English instruction too. For instance, there are low quality private schools charging low fees where English is imparted as medium of instruction with teachers themselves knowing a few sentences with most of them as unemployed youths who have completed certain qualifications as expressed by one of the conscientious parent respondents:

> The Meiteis falsely speaking English – good or bad English – believe that wearing neat and clean clothes, neck tie, uniform, speaking English – good or bad English etc., are superior. Private schools are very particular about fencing walls, concrete buildings, playgrounds, instruction in English, but the fact is, parents who don't have food to eat can spare the money for purchasing food items at least if they stop spending that much money in private school.

The parental observations further indicate that even the poorest parents readily compromise their means of basic living such as food items and other essentials for the sake of their children's education by sending them to relatively high fee charging private schools. For some parents, therefore, what exists in private schools could make a good impression without necessary meaning attached much in terms of quality education. Secondly, as expressed above, these private schools seem to be physically and culturally cut off from the cultural environment of those children attending private schools because within the school enclosure another world exist, with a life of its own such as dresses, particular norms, etiquettes, class culture and so forth that appear to have little relationship with the day-to-day life of the children's own society outside. Let us take the case of English language as the most preferred medium of instruction and interaction in a private school environment. When lured by these schools due to

Anglicization of children, even parents of low economic strata struggle to meet the educational expenses by choosing relatively inferior private schools where English is the medium of instruction. But, English language has no support in the home environment of these children unlike children of higher socio-economic status whose home background has strong similar cultural support. Therefore, children of lower economic status are the biggest losers since their home background has little scope of relevance with their school environment and hence their marginal success. In another sense, the economics of parental choice of different forms of English medium private schools and the politics of language in school education have sharpened the basis of social stratification among people.

Anxiety-Ridden Parents

Therefore, the present study has found that there is a blend of both pessimism and optimism which so marked the feature of the advocacy of parental choice of private schools over government schools. Despite the weight of advantages of private schools as discussed by parents, there are also dissenting voices which is a matter of serious concern. As seen above, relatively better private schools serve the interest of only those children whose parents can afford, thereby leaving out a major chunk of children of poor parents, especially those below the poverty line. The cost difference between government and private schooling is substantial. Private schools are the very institutions that provide a benchmark against which government schools can be compared that private schools have been permitted to exist on the ground that parents cannot be coerced to accept the functioning of government schools that traditionally perform for the welfare and future prospect of poor children with minimum cost. However, the phenomenon of spiral downfall of government schools in the state has empowered private schools to exploit the vulnerable parents who, in the absence of any alternatives available, rely heavily on private schools. This has caused a situation of chronic shortage of students in government schools while producing a phenomenon of chronic burden of overcrowding in private schools with serious impairment on teaching/learning processes in classroom. The situation has become a cause of worry and anxiety among parents. Referring to her children's private school, a parent complained:

> My children don't learn much in school since the teacher-pupil ratio is really bad. Overcrowding of children in classrooms has become a huge problem in private school.

Another parent respondent, who is a part-time contractor and whose children are in Maria Montessori, expressed his dissatisfaction:

> I've seen the system. Standard in private school is high but the teaching staffs are not able to teach as per the requirement of children. What they don't know is left to the students as home assignments. Teachers don't know what they ought to know and even skip some chapters. Teacher-pupil ratio is high. Number of students is so huge, in class IV itself, i.e., 46; it's 62 in class VI and 96 in class I. Since children don't understand in the classroom teaching, there is the need to hire private tutor.

On the role of private tutor in learning improvement among children, another parent respondent stated:

> Without private tutor's assistance, it has become impossible. There are around 50–70 students in a class, much ahead of the required number of students. This makes the teachers difficult to give due attention to all the students in the class. Hiring a private tutor then becomes essential. Children learn stage by stage or else what learning they can acquire in the classroom when there are so many children in one class. A teacher can't inspect all students and hence only few are benefited but the average students are ignored. Even while choosing a private tutor, I ensure that my children go to a tutor having less than four children.

Thus, one of the major complaints parents have against private schools is the overcrowding of children and children's inability to comprehend what is taught in the classroom. This has necessitated the parents to hire private tutors that have become a norm which is particularly true mostly for children attending private schools. According to the present study, there are as many as 72.5 per cent of parents whose children are dependent on private tutors not just as tutors but also as a guide, a mentor or a counsellor. This is specifically true of householders who can hardly find time for their children due to prooccupation with family business or earnings and for affluent families who are deeply concerned about their children's rankings in examinations. The present study reveals that for majority of struggling parents whose survival issues have virtually rendered them into helpless situation, the feeling is that private tutors can enhance a child's ability to understand what could not be learnt in classroom process. It is also believed that private tutors can help a child in learning in advance, get a better deal in examination and keep children engaged in the care of a tutor to avoid trapping in the bad company of local boys as one parent respondent shared his reflections:

> I'm so busy. I don't get time to even meet my children, let alone studies. I don't help them academically. Sometimes my wife comes out of the kitchen, just to see about their studies. By the time we return home in late evening, children are at the place of tuition and it is time for them to sleep when we retire to bed. This is what we also realise that if our children go for tuition, they don't have the chance to go to drugs, because, at least tutors take care of them. The influence of peer group on bad habit is less likely to be there on them since they remain busy with the tutor. Teenage period is also the most important period and I feel parental role is big. And, once children in this period are not directed in the right direction, they may go wrong in the future.

A van driver, whose occupation is to drop and pick up school children, with a fair knowledge about the trend of tuition system and its demand in the state as a matter of trend, citing the case of affluent parents, sorrowfully shared the negative developments related to tuition system in today's Manipuri society:

> All parents believe that through private tuition, there is possibility that children do better in examinations. The entire private business becomes so merciless. There is so much of exploitation of children demanded by parents and society, putting them to unrealistic and difficult situations. Affluent parents are exceptionally running after tutors all the time and making their children's life hell. Class differences are also noticed. We don't have money like affluent parents have. These families drop and pick children by car while sending children to coaching classes. Tuition business is flourishing in the state. Even advance booking system exists. As soon as the examination is over, booking starts in a fast manner. At the time of booking, one has to make full payment; for mathematics, the fee is the highest. There also exists secret tuition system where parents separately hire a tutor who charges exorbitant amount. Hiring of separate tutor is deliberately done by desperate parents who want their children to be rank holders in Board examination. Before sessions begin, tuition starts and continues till final year examination and in this manner,

> the full course is completed. This is a general and normal practice. Almost every child is sent to private tutor these days.

Thereafter, considering the poverty situation faced by the people in the state, he further added:

> This trend is unexpected in a place like Manipur where almost all households seem struggling all the time. But many poor families painfully disconnect from such trends, because they are poor.

Here, again in the prevailing system of hiring private tutors, it is only those children attending private schools are also the ones who require private tutors, while children studying in government schools cannot afford to hire even a tutor who charges nominal fees. Take the case of parents who are daily wagers and whose children are studying in government schools. With a sense of guilt on her face by gazing on the ground sadly, a parent respondent, who sells vegetables and whose husband is a carpenter, shared her agony:

> I don't feel good about my children's school environment at all. There's teacher absenteeism problem in which the situation is acute. Even when teachers are present, they don't take interest in studies. The principal doesn't maintain rules and regulations. There's no discipline at all. I am aware about all this. Teachers know that nobody is going to complain against them. Despite these grievances, I can't afford sending my children either to private school or hire a tutor since it is hugely expensive.

Considering the above parental voices on the demand for private tutors, private schools too fall short of parental expectations in terms of scholastic achievements and learning abilities of children. And, as such, it is indeed important to know the fact that in private schools too, children do not learn as expected. A government school teacher, while contemplating the much hype appreciation and false claims about private schools, reflected on private schools existing in Manipur as follows:

> In private schools, few children say, from one to twenty can be counted. The rest are thrown out when they reach the stage of class VII, VIII and IX; the structure of private school is just like a pyramid.

She further narrated how children who are disqualified in private schools are easily drawn into bad company such as substance abuse and alcohol for they go astray with no proper place to be absorbed in simply because they are so embarrassed to join government school after being thrown out of private school. She substantiated her observation by citing an incident of few tribal students who were thrown out of private school but did not want to be in government school and later were drawn to drugs. Her main argument is that in private schools, there is a large number of enrolments at lower class which decreases at higher stages. Further, those children who are not neglected by parents and whose studies are taken care of by private tutors are capable to sustain themselves in private school up to a certain level such as the Board examination while those who are thrown out of private school find it embarrassing to join a government school and hence go astray without being absorbed in any alternative. Another common observation is that private schools and hiring of private tutors are concerned with examinations and performance of students only at the neglect of other value systems to be instilled in children. The fact that a large percentage of parents send their children to private tutors because the tuition system is oriented towards examinations as also admitted by a parent respondent, who is a salaried employee:

> Tuition system is oriented towards examinations and getting ranks. Through tuition system, one gains familiarity with the examination pattern, and is, therefore, likely to perform better in examination.

The politics behind the private tuition system is therefore oriented towards competition and examinations so that the reputation of the school can be elevated, which again serves a selling tactic employed to gain fame for the concerned school. This could, however, on the other hand, prove to be extremely terrifying and horrendous experience for children and parents alike in which the experience could be drawn parallel as the 'haunting' in the ghostly sense to use Meighan's analogy while trying to understand the way society's values invade the classroom that is mostly observed in private schools. For example, Meighan argues, teachers in a classroom feel that everything therein is within their control and direction though it is not true in reality. He further observes, the classroom is haunted by the ghost of the creators of language and most importantly the ghost of executors of disciplinary rules and regulations at the neglect of other human considerations. These rules simply haunt and do not spare the tender child as lamented by a conscientious mother who critically looks into the whole system of private schooling where punitive and regimental rules prevail.[11] Thus, in her words:

> Syllabus is tough for children. It is vast, difficult and unsuitable. I am noticing these problems every time when my children struggle. The school is also ruthlessly very strict and the actions the school take for disciplining kids are horrendous. Their motive could be correct but the extreme disciplinary rules are not suitable for my children's age.

In a vehement complaining tone, the mother continued:

> Children become deranged. It is torturous. Every sort of rating is done through marking. In case my child feels sick and can't attend school, then the class teacher will reduce his marks.

Children when sent to carefully chosen private schools are burdened with heavy homework assignments, examinations, weekly tests and are constantly nursed under strict school regime to the extent that these children start losing faith in parents. The mother continued:

> Our children don't trust us; they are under the constant control of their teachers who are always strict. So, children trust the knowledge of their teachers only, not ours.

Thereafter, she shared her experience:

> Once there was homework assigned to my child. The homework was related to few animals which are not available in the state of Manipur.

By exclaiming softly, she continued:

> Imagine! We could not name the animal even though we knew; instead, they simply trust what their teachers say.

Despite various drawbacks, children continue to flock to private schools in the absence of alternative choices. The mushrooming growth of private schools has endangered the government schools. A parent respondent, also a daily wager, who was equally worried about the mushrooming growth of private schools compared the phenomenon by drawing a metaphor of the fertile seed of the famous eatable plant, *shougree* (bimlipatam jute or ambary). The seed grows on any type of soil when even slipped from anybody's finger in much the same way private schools mushroom at any place. On the mushrooming growth of private schools in the state on the one hand and the helplessness of poor parents on the other, she shared her observations and concern as under:

> Everywhere, there are schools. Even cinema halls, instead of providing entertainment facility are converted to schools. Establishing schools have become a lucrative business. No doubt, these schools try their best to improve their reputation. But, the growth of these schools is due to complete failure of local government schools. In government schools, teachers are extremely indisciplined because they don't expect challenges from the parents of these children to correct them. We, parents, are virtually dragged in survival issues. We don't have time to fight to correct the system.

Therefore, as against the proposition of neo-liberalists' school choice, though quite appealing at a glance, remains a formidable difficulty for parents who are either survivors or intermittent income earners such as poor farmers, daily wage earners, rickshaw pullers, to name a few. It is also noticed that economically and socially deprived parents are worst hit due to their meagre income. On the whole, while some parents' exercise of school choice can boost their children's moral and educational attainment, its accumulated effect is certainly to increase in educational inequality and social polarisation to be born only by children of poor families. Secondly, as observed above, the feasibility of strengthening local government schools is not in sight in the absence of trust and faith among parents, teachers and the local community whose collective social resources could generate social capital. Thirdly, parental involvement, though necessary, is not efficient enough to improve the state-run schools without serious state and community commitment to serving children of poor parents by improving schools in low income neighbourhoods and their surroundings. Because putting the fallen schools right on track is not only a herculean task for poor parents since it involves continued dialogue and also fighting of attitudes and perceptions of all those authorities who run the system. The problem therefore lies squarely in the unresponsive system itself. Because, what has surfaced from the parental concerns in the present chapter are chaotic implementation of schemes, decline of inspection system, lack of transparency, corruption among officials and politicians in recruitment of teachers, teacher inertia, feminisation of teaching profession as some of the silent features that continue to plague the functioning of government schools. Some of these parental reflections are addressed in the following section.

Whither Accountability: Why It Matters

Parents agree that government school teachers are qualified in terms of training skills they acquire and qualifications in particular fields when compared with private school teachers most of whom are unemployed youths with certain qualifications and can utter few words of English. A parent respondent, wife of a construction worker, grieved about government school environment:

> Government school is like a free zone for children since both the parents and teachers are not accountable to children. But, government teachers are qualified. They unlike private school teachers acquire training in B.Ed.; PGT and are also trained in DIET. In private school, if a person knows few words of English and has the basic knowledge of mathematics, then, he is considered qualified to teach without any specialisation.

However, despite being qualified, much to the disappointment of parents, government school teachers are seen to be most inactive and found engaged in a variety of pastimes rather than discharging their responsibilities and hence reducing teaching activity to the minimum. This appears to be a consistent pattern and also to be a way of life among government school teachers. The fixed well-paid salary structure is another factor that makes them unaccountable to their teaching job. These are the factors that have forced parents to lose faith in government school teachers, leading to ultimate desertion of government school by children in hordes. The issue has been sufficiently highlighted in the foregoing chapter.

Yet, there are instances where only few government teachers, despite all odds, are committed with shining accomplishments. 'What happens to the government school according to your experience as a government teacher' was asked to one of the parents who is a mathematics teacher in a government primary school. The teacher, by chiding away authorities responsible for the failure of the system without any hesitation, shared his lived experience. By pointing to departmental failure, he argues, teacher accountability can be derived from a variety of factors. For example, inspection system, an important instrument to keep the accountability of teaching profession in check is no longer operative in the state. Referring to the inspection system prevalent in 1970s and 1980s,[12] he took the case of Nambol Higher Secondary School where he was serving as a mathematics teacher. In a delightful and thoughtful mood, recalling his past days, he narrated:

> In those days, in my school, there was inspection system for three times a year. Inspectors, without notifying, used to visit schools and enter classrooms after taking permission from the class teacher. By requesting the class teacher, the inspector could enter any class. The inspector then started asking questions to students to test the efficiency of teaching skills of teachers on particular subject, for example, one particular inspector asked the spelling of Mohandas Karamchand Gandhi to the students and they also checked on other subjects like mathematics. Even the Education Minister once used to accompany the inspectors.

Thus, failure of the inspection system has been largely contributed to general failure of teacher accountability. Inspection system is seen as a vital link between the education department and individual schools but is no longer operative in government schools in the state. Failure of the inspection system has delinked the highest educational machinery from various schools by completely washing its hands off, cutting dialogue between teachers and educational administration where school decisions are taken and mediated.

The Government is Blind

Chaotic and patchy implementation of schemes poses another great challenge for government schools. Going back to his personal long-lived experience, the mathematics teacher further recollected:

> There is no scheme implemented in my school and the government is running blindly. The school gets teaching/learning material aids. But it is the school that purchases charts and other materials for sports. Teachers discuss the matter and report it to zonal education officer. The officer openly responded us to manage on our own or to let it be the way it doesn't cause great inconvenience.

Thereafter, he continued:

> But recently the new development is that, textbooks are distributed to students from class I to class VIII. Distribution of textbooks itself is good enough for them. For every year, teachers

> are given grant. Out of this total grant, certain amount is deposited in the account of the underground outfit, PREPARK. The transaction is done at a higher level. Now, of the remaining grants, we've started purchasing books for children. Feedback from the students is that, unlike before, students started having separate exercise copies after this distribution of items was started. This is good in many ways because children feel happy and excited about it. Out of the teachers' grant, we also purchase games and sports items.

On teacher absenteeism, in an exciting but mocking tone with a chuckle on his face, he narrated how the irregularity of a sports female teacher and long absence from the school was caught by members of DESAM:

> She was caught by DESAM. DESAM issued a complaint letter against her absence and irregularity. Then, she was forced to pay fine to DESAM. She was then transferred.

But, as he wanted to clarify further, 'She was not entirely responsible for the problem; she was irregular because there was no sports student'.

The above enriching lived experience of his own school by a parent respondent is a widespread phenomenon of the situation of government schools in the state of Manipur. The instance of tracking down absentee teachers by DESAM, a student organisation supported by KYKL (an insurgent group), also points to the failure of the state to the extent that these groups freely operate like parallel government system in a win-win situation.

Among parents, there is unanimous deep concern about the prevailing corruption in the recruitment of teachers that has emerged as one of the most important issues responsible for the collapse of government schools. The issue is, the curbing of mushrooming growth of private schools is possible only if there is improvement in appointment and recruitment rules of teachers who would contribute to improving government schools. Recalling what few parent respondents shared, he too complained:

> For this to happen, there should be a sudden brake on rampant corruption within the system of school governance including recruitment of teachers, implementation of schemes, arbitrary transfer of teachers, etc. But we can't think of such drastic possibilities in the system. Government is repeatedly responsible for

> the entire failure and the failure is just like a curse for ordinary poor people like us.

Yet the profession of teaching is respondents extremely important as expressed by one of the parent, who is the principal of Saint Anthony School at Chingmeirong, Imphal. Being in the profession for many years, she shared:

> The job of a teacher is extremely respondents and important. To be in a profession of teaching, one has to be vigilant enough. Group counselling for teachers is required and constant watch on teachers is also important. I am quite particular about selection procedures and recruitment of teachers. It is certainly a blunder to play with a child's future.

Therefore, it is not to blame teachers alone. At the time of recruitment, government selects not only disqualified candidates but also those who lack subject specialisation. To cite an example as stated by a government school teacher, who is also a parent of two school-going children:

> It's not possible to teach social science subjects while having background of specialisation in Hindi. There is no sufficient number of teachers recruited either in our school. It is quite appalling.

The teacher continued:

> If a teacher is vocal and wants justice, he is transferred to far places such as Ukhrul/Senapati (hill districts) for his duty in the form of punishment. The corrupt and unfair system have its own consequences on school children too. The teacher, after having transferred, is disconnected from the students and a new teacher who is altogether different in teaching styles, experience and skills in the particular subject will be introduced to the students. It certainly affects the students in more than one way. Worse is the case, when there is no substitute teacher because children suffer the worst in such a situation. The fallout is students' unrest in the form of *bandhs*, strikes, boycotts, etc. The glaring example is the case of Government Nambol Higher Secondary School. In this school, there is often boycotts and strikes observed by students against the transfer of teachers. In every *leikai* such similar crisis exists in government schools. The system operates blindly.

Feminisation of Teaching Profession: A Risk

Interestingly, while there is a concern about the significance of increase in the number of female teachers in other parts of India, feminisation of teaching profession in the state of Manipur is not doing good favours to its children; rather, it disturbs the routine teacher performance of government schools. Based on his own experience, the mathematics teacher referred to earlier cautioned against the risks of feminisation of teaching profession in the state. Women teachers in the state constitute of almost 75 per cent outnumbering male teachers. Generally, the presence of large number of female teachers could encourage greater gender equality, and as role models, they could expand the aspirations of young girls. However, recounting his lived experience of his own school, the teacher observed:

> If one takes his school as an example, out of 15 teachers, only two of them are males. Female teachers reach school late, at 11 a.m. in the morning, whereas the teaching timetable starts at 10 in the morning. His female colleagues are burdened with household chores and hence are not punctual at all. This has adverse effect on children. In the morning, children come fresh, with full of enthusiasm to learn, but there is no teacher around and hence they feel extremely discouraged. Syllabus is not completed in time but normally exams are held without even completing the course; students start protesting but ultimately they are the sufferers.

The educational crisis in the state as revealed in the foregoing discourse indicates that parents and children alike have reached the vantage point of frustration that there is an outpouring of calls for urgent reforms and reconstruction in the system failure that is responsible for the collapse of government schools. The parental narrations reveal that it is not only government school children who are at risk but also the teacher themselves who equally feel a sense of worry at the prospect of closing down government schools due to chronic shortage of students since children leave government schools in hordes.

Good Schooling Compensates a Fallen Society

Despite the deepening crisis in the present education system, there is little consensus among all parents that a good responsible education system can actually compensate even a fallen society. Asked, 'Why do you like to send your children to school'? Parents, one and all, have huge expectations from education and its role for individual and society. Today, as in the past, parents and the community alike look at school to help create or sustain the values they feel are highest for their own society. Some of the most candid and profound observations parents of poor and rich strata have made on the role of education in society are as follows:

> Why shouldn't we be sending our children to school? We expect education to take care of our future generations and protect them from unwanted elements. The future of children is the future of *leibak* (society). But the present-day education system has crushed this vision.
>
> Through education, we expect children to acquire and develop knowledge to become wiser, moral character formation, socialisation in the right direction, development of personality and achieve lifetime skill and so forth. If today our children are educated, we would be able to produce a good society.
>
> During schooling, children get socialisation with teachers and peer groups for 10–14 hours in a day in a school environment. Education trains one to be a good citizen. Knowledge through education is a lifelong benefit. Good education can do well for future generations. Sending children to a good school enables them to realise their goals. So sending children to school is not only good but this is only our hope for our children.
>
> As a parent, my utmost concern is to make my children perfect human beings in the future. If guidelines are given to children, they'll automatically be able to direct themselves without being dependent on others. My son is very keen on the study of space. His interest in space study directs his mind and imaginations towards his future goal. These aspirations serve as a litmus test to guide future aims and objectives in his life. All children have a target of their choice and interest. We must encourage them and it is our responsibility to raise them by sending to a good school.
>
> In order that he becomes an educated person and participates in modern-day society, I am putting my best responsibility to educate him well. My child, if sent to school, will not take drugs, steal things from others, also will not be carried away in wrong direction by peer groups, etc. To become more alert, more knowledgeable and able to face life situations are reasons for sending children to school.

> Education is a matter of prestige; earning knowledge is as important as leading a dignified life and understands the world around us. If one is educated, one can utilise one's resources and potential, for example, I, being an illiterate earn ₹ 50 in a day. This'll certainly be different for an educated person. So life can be more fulfilling if one is educated.

> Through education, children become knowledgeable, aware of self, can find a dignified place to live in society. When there is no education, there is no knowledge. An uneducated person is bound to suffer. Education is essential. An educated person is held so prestigious and respected by the *leikai* and the society. After getting the light of education, children bear its fruit. They'll get decent job and their future life will be in peace. They'll be reaping the benefits of education.

Thus, the parental concerns depict that there is huge expectation from education which is indeed in crisis. According to parental perception, education has intrinsic values in itself. It is a means for individuals to improve personal endowments, build capacity, overcome constraints, make critical choices and fair judgements, face struggles of life nobly and gracefully, acquire practical knowledge for a living, give direction to life, necessity for participation in modern life and a solution of all problems and so forth. Education can direct a child to a desired future goal that will help him to become a perfect and a fulfilling human being in future. In addition, through education a child will be empowered to direct his own life independently and also be able to face all struggles in life.

Therefore the role education plays in the life of a child is overwhelming as perceived by parents. The ordinary parents' vision of education is much closer to those of timeless visionaries such as Emile Durkheim, Max Weber, etc. Durkheim, while writing, in late 19th century, propagated education as a *social fact* which is indeed a *sui generis* both from the individual and social ends, emphasising both on the individual and social significance of education. This argument stands similar to many of parental observations reflecting on their own situations.

Parents unanimously perceive that education trains the mind of a child to be critical and judgmental, can discriminate between what is right and wrong. Born as a human being, if the person is still uneducated, he or she is just like blind and deaf. Moreover education is a basic tool of social transaction and meaningful participation in modern society besides inculcating moral values in a child. As revealed in this chapter, parents send their children to school with the hope that they will achieve, most importantly, status and dignity with the ability to utilise resources judiciously and choices of profession.

Thus parents have a clear vision of personal, social and economic benefits to be reaped through education. This vision of education the ordinary parents hold runs parallel to the views of sociologists, such as Max Weber, whose writings in early 20th century argued how impressive educational qualifications could be equivalent to noble blood or distinguished ancestry as the litmus test that persuades others that the individual in question is entitled to high prestige and a desirable occupation. The significance of such argument is, parents undoubtedly use education as the main indicator of not only occupational achievement but also status and other forms of socially desirable attributes that can counter any form of handicaps their children are likely to face in their future life. What is truly striking and remarkable is the level of consciousness among poor parents whose educational vision treats education as an end in itself. The parental concerns, attitudes and ideas regarding the education of their children largely reflect the deeper aesthetic values generally treasured within the culture of Manipuri society that has deep roots in its own historicity since time immemorial.

Economic Returns of Education: Only Half Truth

Contrary to the popular assertion, the present chapter has revealed that employment and jobs hardly hold as pivotal among parents in the motivation of sending children to school. On the relationship between education and employment benefits, it is interesting to share some of the observations these parents made:

> Never think for job since we can't link the two actually. Because, education is for life or symbolises life itself, not necessarily a job.
>
> Education is the best bet in one's lifetime. Even if there is no formal employment, an educated individual can establish his own private enterprise. Self-employment for his life's sustenance and life skill itself are earned through education.
>
> There is no linkage between job and education as I visualise the worth of education. As a human being, my child must be a man of

> merit and knowledge. Never had I thought of linking education of my children with a job, since education is a lifetime necessity.
>
> Educated people are abreast of what is of national importance and issues affecting them. It helps one in fuller participation in societal affairs. Educated people are much stronger and empowered and can fight injustice. So, sending children to formal school is not just for job security, but for developing the full growth in them.
>
> Education helps one to face not only the challenges of life in the right spirit fearlessly but also in expansion of one's choice making.
>
> Education is essential in almost all walks of life; modern-day demand is education; education is the solution of all problems; why should anybody be deprived of education so long as he or she has an opportunity to be educated.
>
> As a guardian, we feel good when our children are educated. In future, when they grow up, they will be perfect individuals, they will be able to be responsible for themselves, and they will stand on their own feet.

These are some of common sentiments echoed by parents. The parental responses and concerns add up to a fairly understanding of the most valuable empowering attributes of individual and societal benefits of education as also addressed by parents in the foregoing section. The approach that parents hold about the educational agenda thus goes beyond any doubt of myopic aims of education, and is one such that of timeless wisdom that promotes values of scientific temperament and teachings of humanity, to mention a few, which are in fact rooted in ancestral wisdom that was in vogue during the ancient educational practise of Manipuri society. For example, Devi's (1989) discourse on the history of education in Manipur, before the advent of Hinduism in early 17th century, reveals how teaching in various disciplines such as History, Religion, Medicine, Dance, Drama and Philosophy of life was by and large methodical and scientific by stressing on all-round development of the individuals as briefly addressed in Chapter 3. The famous scholar, Jyotirmoy Roy (1958) adds, the valley had the fortune to cradle saintly lives like Magang Guru Punsiba, Luwang Guru Punshiba and Khuman Guru Punhsiba who have illuminated man in the domain of knowledge. So, the valley had the opportunity to nurse its own children through education system of all-round development that continue to remain a cherished dream in the hearts and the minds of today's parents even with the spoils of time.

Zone of Terror

As discussed in previous chapter, every violent incident in the region forces civilians at the crossfire and life ultimately becomes standstill. Parental narrations depict a close relationship between the quantum of violence and the educational loss of children in the state. Further, parents, like any other community living there, are also equally affected. Describing how the present-day Manipur has become a zone of terror for all, quite unlike before in the past days, when there was much of peace, a parent who is a retired defence personnel, reflected his poignant experience of the changing times of Manipuri society today:

> Times have changed for the worst. In the past, during evening hours, we used to study on a mat, spread in the courtyard. But, in today's time, as soon as sunset begins, we ask children to go to bed. In today's time, it is never safe even within the boundary of your own home. In today's time there are many incidents of killings, kidnappings, there is no value for life; Manipur has become a valley of killing fields and coffins.

On the issue of trafficking of school children in crossfire, he continued:

> General strike is taken seriously and hence during strike, teachers and students can't participate in school. On the way to school, armies and commandos often beat up students and harass them. So, naturally schools are closed for the sake of students' safety.

A parent, who is an electrician, shared his concern:

> With increase violence in public places, children's life at such places has become really unsafe. Certainly, their attendance is also on the decline. Syllabus to be completed remains incomplete and this encourages private tuition system. There is insecurity all over the state. Every time, we are disturbed thinking of unprecedented violence such as bomb blasts, killings, etc. The feeling that whether one will be killed or alive is the same for all. Deaths and killings are so frequent in the state that normal schooling of children is always disturbed creating mounting frustration in both children and parents as guardians.

On children's stress and difficulty to cope up with schooling in continuous violent situation, a parent, who is a trained pharmacist, sadly reflected:

> Whirling violence has caused tremendous loss; exams are postponed due to sudden violence. Destruction caused by violence is beyond my words and expressions. Violence has become a trend of the present Manipuri society. In the past, people used to be panic and remained inside their homes on hearing sounds of gunshot. But, now, everybody takes such incidents as normal as these occur frequently. When there is repeated violence, it starts looking like normal incident without thinking the damage it has caused to our lives. There is sudden stoppage of vehicles, roads and market places. Insurgent groups also often call for *bandhs*. When there is blockade of public vehicles, children can't attend school. Sadly, despite all these, teachers compulsorily complete the syllabus and naturally children find it difficult to cope up in such situation.

Recalling the most infamous widespread incident of ceasefire in the state of Manipur on 18 June 2001, a mother of three school-going children recounted her sad tales:

> The ceasefire incident has caused great education emergency to children. During the incident, there was emergency called for law and order situation, followed by mass protest and bloody deaths of youths. *Bandhs* were immediately called for, creating tremors, anxieties and distress in us. In such a volatile situation, school children are critically affected because they were forced to be a part of mass protest. The cyclic process of violent incidence handicaps the teachers to complete the school syllabus. Each of us feels insecure when there is immediate closure of roadways while our children are still at school.

Occasional feeling under the reel of violence, a school principal by taking a deep breath nodded:

> Yeah, very often, we've violence. We are asked to observe sit in protest holding up placards in times of violent emergencies caused by disappearances, killings, arbitrary arrests, etc. Insurgents impose on us that we should be a part of protest and they use children as means of protest. So, I send children of classes IX and X for protest. Insurgents also demand money from us as tax once in a year. There are many insurgent factional organisations asking for money. So, I maintain a register when they collect money from the school. I pay to local insurgents ranging from ₹ 5,000–10,000.

> We want educational institution to operate freely from these distractions.

Having witnessed a series of emergent conflicts, a mother who runs a fast food stall recounted those unforgettable, bewildering incidents of widespread violence in Imphal during the ceasefire:

> I wish all sorts of violence get over before the school session begins. Every parent has the same wishes. The cases of death of Chitarajan and Manorama keep social life under seize, heated and burning. Such violent incidents flare up emergencies, anxiety and tension. We are always in civil war. During day time, we are sometimes in normal condition, but in the night, we are just experiencing terror. But since we are in Zero Mile,[13] Indian army can't torture us. In an environment like this, our life is always uncertain with anxieties and restless. Violence is affecting all of us on a regular basis and not just schools and children. Restlessness and tensions, anxieties, emergencies are very often in life. That's not life. Sometimes, violent incident erupts like volcano.

Parents in utter frustration and shock, voice out that outburst of violence, anywhere, anytime in the state has affected one and all. Worst is when protest against killings, kidnappings and arbitrary arrest gets intensified and goes on for end number of days during which daily wage earners, in particular, start suffering the pangs of hunger. A rickshaw puller said, 'Violence attacks the poorest of the poor, affecting our livelihoods. We are daily wagers and hence violence can deprive us of day's meal altogether'.

Similar view was endorsed by another parent, who is a rikshaw puller:

> We are worst affected, because we are daily wage earners. If work is stopped, where we will get money to eat and survive, leave the rest of other issues.

Violence of any kind at any time has become a customary experience for the people in the state that some parents went to the extent of calling such incidents as too normal, as in the words of a father:

> Look! if you think you are going to be caught up in such incidents and are afraid to go out of your house, it is like saying, don't sleep, you'll have nightmare.

Apart from the occasional educational emergencies faced by children, parents were equally alarmed about the impinging psychological trauma in children brought up in a violent and conflict-ridden society as volatile as that of Manipur. The volatile situation of the present Manipuri society has distorted the image of the kind of society which was otherwise once a peaceful society where violence and gun culture were completely alien. In a society gripped by violence, one can notice how youths go astray, children being demonised and deprived of childhood. Often the people of Manipur are forced to put up with a glut of commodified violence in everyday media as well. Parents did not spare even media whose main role is to do social engineering but continue to ignore such coverage since the society is constantly gripped by violence of macro-level concerns. Thus, in the words of a conscientious parent, who is an artist:

> Media highlights of violence have become an instant gratification for us as an audience. Media is no more interesting without a piece of information about violence in society. Media coverage is full of kidnappings, arbitrary arrests, disappearance of individuals, individual and insurgent outfit confessions and clarifications, strikes, *bandhs*, blockades and so forth. Newspapers thus no longer send right messages; obviously children do not get the right message about the image of their own society.

The point the parents want to reflect is that a violent state sending such an image naturally destroys the faith that children can nurture for their very own society by living up in perpetual restlessness and anxiety with a heightened sense of insecure feeling. What none could imagine has become real; that today violence and living with violence has become a social fact; and that the present generation is so accustomed to turmoil and living in amidst of constant outburst of violence that they are forced to falsely reconcile with the idea that violence is a normal incident in society. These are the gruesome experiences and how ordinary people including children cope up and negotiate with violence in the conflict-ridden state of Manipur. The above concerns of parents stress the fact that schooling of children is hugely damaged by occasional violence and that educational right for children cannot be treated in isolation from the societal crisis. Education as a matter of right is related to other rights, most importantly right to life and feeling safe and secured which continue to be still elusive in the state of Manipur.

Right to Education: The Formidable Challenges Ahead

Strong evidence supporting the social dimension of children's education as a matter of social norm is evident from parental responses. On compulsory education, I asked, 'Would you support elementary education being made compulsory and fundamental entitlement for all children?' Parents are concerned of the fact that childhood is a precious period in one's life. If children attend school, they do not waste time, idling away at home; they can socialise among peer groups, can encourage and motivate themselves in studies with a future goal. These are some of the basic reasons why children have to be compulsorily sent to school. There is an overwhelming response in supporting the crucial aspect of this right, mostly, because of the fact that childhood period is the most precious period in one's life and hence formal education, if made compulsory will benefit all children, especially the poor. However unfortunately, the chronic political violence in the form of rampant corruption and poor governance of the state has virtually smothered parental hopes and aspirations for the educational right of children. Crudely exposing the level of corruption in the state, some of the sentiments parents vent out are worth highlighting:

> Elementary education and making it fundamental is indispensable because, a child in a growing stage is in his most fresh stage of mind. Therefore, educating children at the right stage is a matter of necessity. The spirit of the Act is too good but in Manipur, it is like a tragedy bound to happen to its children. The state is too corrupt to implement any Act in a fruitful way. In the name of implementing the Act, needy children will not be benefited. Corruption at every stage is the worst nightmare. At the last end of implementing the project, nothing will be left for children's share.
>
> These days I've not heard of SSA. Nobody knows where SSA is heading for.
>
> I certainly support the concept of making elementary education fundamental right. But as the present situation of government school suggests, the Act will remain useless since there are no children in government schools.
>
> Right to education and making it fundamental is good, but it is not possible to implement because Manipur state is too corrupt and money sanctioned for its implementation will be slipped in between the fingers of the officials.

Recruitment of teaching jobs is based only on connection, many people have sold off their property just to bribe the politicians and top officials for return of a job. Some of these individuals have become mentally deranged due to shock because they've lost huge amount of money after selling off immovable property such as land. When there is so much of corruption at every level, government is not ready for such a revolutionary transformation for children's education. The sorry state of affairs of the state is deliberately reflected in Shumang Leela[14] (dramas and plays) by artists to sensitise people about corruption.

Aah! Right to education and making it fundamental right for all is the best. But, I don't think, the state is in a position to implement it, because nobody knows who executes all these tasks. It is so painful that 90 per cent of education officers do not even look after the education affairs.

If right to education is implemented, we don't have to pay fees and spend so much for educating our children as we do right now; but I certainly doubt whether it can be really achieved, because, I simply don't trust the system. All officials in the hierarchy, teachers and officers will be hand in globe to siphon off the resources for themselves, will smoother all resources that come in the name of children.

It will simply empower people and will have major effect on poor children. But the right to get due share by children will be unfailingly trapped by the system itself.

If a new scheme is implemented, it's just like dropping a lump of sugar among beaming ants. Ants are also living beings; each struggles to taste the droplets of sugar by grabbing it at any cost. This is the same with the right to education project.

It is a good idea and correct too, but how revolutionary it will be when all children from poor background can attend school of equitable quality.

The parental reflections reveal that school education for children cannot be treated in isolation from the larger realm of operation of political culture of the state and hence right to education can be achieved if the culture of political violence is strongly fought out. In addition, in the midst of sporadic violence, the right to learn for children on a progressive scale is denied due to education emergencies. On the whole, parental hopes and aspirations to the concept of making elementary education fundamental entitlement are overwhelming. With this massive support, it is not just the constitutional argument alone that clinches the case of universal elementary education as a much desired social goal. However, as emerged from the foregoing discussion, a common variant of this hope is that, as things stand today, the parental aspirations would likely to remain a hope against hope. Therefore at a time when public schools are failing beyond reparation and when private and public schools are sharply and deliberately stratified, the idea of provisioning of equitable quality education is simply a mirage for children of poor households and hence the idea of universal elementary education would remain elusive for these children.

Notes

1. It is customary that moderate and well-to-do families among the Meiteis of Manipur possess *Shangoi*, a detached shed made of wood or bamboo and mud with either tin roofing or dry straw with three sides closed, usually located in front of the house. The shed is used for multipurpose activities such as weaving, recreation, ritual ceremonies, feasting, etc.
2. Primary occupations include age-old activities such as hunting, gathering of wild fruits, nuts, fishing, harvesting of trees and other commodities from nature such as agriculture, forestry, fishing, mining, etc. Primary producers might also be termed as 'red-collar workers' due to the outdoor nature of their work. Secondary sector includes activities such as purposeful tending of crops and commercial livestock and agriculture. Secondary production increases the value (usefulness) of a previously existing item by changing its form. The farmer, for instance, applies hybrid seeds, fertilizers and modern technology in the form of cultivating and harvesting equipment to increase the yield of crops. Those who engage in secondary sector are often termed as 'the blue collar labour force'. Tertiary production involves the service sector. Service occupation such as barbers, cobblers, rikshaw pullers, retail clerks and a range of personal and business service sector fall in the tertiary sector. It refers to a range of personal and business services involving a rapidly growing share of the labour force (Alexander and Hartshorn, 1988: 1–2).
3. A skilled worker/earner is the one who is capable of working effectively, exercising considerable independent judgment and of discharging his duties responsibly. He must possess a thorough and comprehensive knowledge of the trade, craft or industry employed, whereas unskilled worker engages in activities that involve the undertaking of simple activities that does not require the exercise of little or independent judgment or previous work experience. However, a familiarity with the occupational environment is necessary. Hence, the work performed by an unskilled labourer may require in addition to physical exertion and familiarity with a variety of activities (Tyagi, O.S. et al., 2002).
4. *Chandal* is a sacred mark on the forehead. It symbolises a sign of purity.

5. Each of the salais among the valley dwellers consists of number of subgroups called Yumnaks (Hudson, 1908). It is through Yumnaks that one can immediately link oneself to the other. Members belonging to the same Yumnaks closely identify themselves with each other. The relationship through such kinship ties influence bargaining and fixing of prices at market places.
6. A main income earner is defined as the one who had worked for the major part of the year, i.e., the one who was engaged in any economically productive activity for 183 days or six months or more during the year and a marginal worker is the one who worked any time at all in the year(Census of India, 2001: xxxxvii).
7. Arnold Van Gennep in his book, *The Rites of Passage* (1960), describes the life of an individual as a series of passages from one stage to another, where each of these stages in a person's life is deemed to be completed only after ritual ceremonies are performed. These rights are occasioned by celestial changes such as day, month, year and so forth. The Meiteis of Manipur observe different passages of rites in a person's life in particular periods of time without which the person cannot be fully integrated into the society. Most of these rites are observed during the Meitei lunar months of *Phairen-Lamda*. *Phairen* also known as the *Asit-tha* is a period during which the Creator is believed to give the souls of all creations and *lamda* is a period during which ploughing of fields begins.
8. In a transition state, the structure and policies inside and outside of education are in formation and are filled with conflict as they seek a coherent way of restructuring the relations between education and transformed economy, a radically different political power structure and a social and ideological agenda that seeks to overthrow the vestiges of entrenched elites of the old hegemonic relations of domination and subordination.
9. Among the Meities, *leishabi*(s) are unmarried girls who enjoy relatively free movement among *leikai*(s).
10. An all-time favourable snack, taken mostly during evening hours. It is shredded mixed green vegetables garnished with sesame, dry crush pea and dry fermented fish called *ngari*.
11. The parental concern has been one of most contentious issues at the centre of Sociology of Education. In early 1970s in USA, there was, as there is today a mood of great public urgency about the problems of schooling. That among many crisis, it was increasingly noticeable that schools, instead of meeting the student's needs for growth and development, regimental and controlled rules, in an essentially authoritarian manner stifled intellectual and emotional growth of children. This necessitated the parents with support of progressive educators to question schools on their regimental rules, lecturing and recitation that

could greatly undermine the intellectual independence and natural curiosity of the child (Cosin, 1972).

12. Discussion with local experienced teachers has revealed that in the state there was much improvement, not only in the expansion of schools but also school administration when Territorial Council took over the educational administration during 1957–63. During the period, performance of government schools was under constant vigilance and school inspection was carried out in accordance to the norms of inspection including regular visits of inspecting officers to inspect the work of teachers and progress of school programmes as laid down by the Manipur Education Code. The Territorial Council ended by July 1963 by bringing the education administration under the State Education Department.
13. Zero Mile is a zone where army personnel cannot fire or misuse their power under AFSPA, 1958. The rule is applicable only in select locations of Imphal area.
14. The Meiteis have a special natural talent for histrionic art. *Shumang Leela* also known as Yatras is an old age form of entertainment performed at the centre of an open round or a courtyard of any house owner who sponsors the cost of the performance. Hence, the performance of *Shumang Leela* does not require any stage. The audiences, consisting of usually the entire village or the *leikai* sit around on mat or *moorah* brought by them. During *Shumang Leela*, the actors perform acts reflecting a variety of current social themes on any issue such as political, religion, crime and sometimes with satirical and grotesque performance condemning the ills of the established social institutions including corruption in the state.

CHAPTER 5

Has the State Failed? Inside a Government School

The present chapter brings out the extremely challenging learning conditions of children by examining the nature of school provisioning, in terms of physical dimensions of school resources of the Government Junior High School.[1] Critical issues of equity and quality of schooling of children are fairly determined by the availability of these resources. The chapter also makes an attempt to examine the role of teachers as an important dimension of human resources, by examining their contributions in upholding the moral ethos of the school children, who otherwise would have not survived and, hence, the survival of the school would be under threat. This further illustrates how important it is to maintain the dialogical relationship between physical and human dimensions of school resources to make schooling effective, vibrant and more attractive for children. Apart from this, the chapter also examines the constraints of educational opportunities of children, caused by sporadic violence and conflict in the region. And how, in this process, children in government schools, in the absence of any alternative learning opportunity, are the hardest hit.

Research studies on school quality reveal that there is interlocking relationship between various dimensions that constitute school resources – physical as well as human. Physical aspects of school resources include infrastructural facilities, such as building, space, parks, playground, classrooms, furniture, equipment, etc. These determine the very organisation of teaching/learning activities that play a pivotal role in motivating children to learn. Operation Blackboard,[2] Mid-Day Meal schemes[3] and SSA[4] are the most recent schemes and projects that are designed to address issues of quality school education and to achieve equal excess for all children. Other forms of academic inputs in the form of instructional facilities and materials such as usable blackboard, textbooks, globes, chats, library facilities, science kits, newspapers, radio, television sets, games equipment, etc., when utilised in school, can be effective in facilitating learning capacity and cognitive achievement of children. On the other hand, the absence of attractive and stimulating learning environment can have the effect of discouraging the schooling of children. For example, when children are made to squat on the floor and write on slates or exercise copies balanced between their knees, it creates obstacles in the physical setting of the child, thereby, contributing to the child's physical discomfort. Dilapidated school buildings, the absence of adequate teaching/learning material aids, and an overall demotivating school environment can sap the morale of both teachers and students on a daily basis. Apart from this, the study of essential facilities and whether they are found missing in schools or not, is indeed significant since the availability of these facilities in public schools is a reflection of public initiatives and allocation of resources by the state.

The School Building

To a student, the school building is a temple of learning, where a large part of his/her life is spent. It is the most visible form of school education and is the first criterion in examining the aspect of physical facility available for a school. Availability of a school building, however, does not guarantee the minimum infrastructural facilities required for smooth classroom transaction, for example, if the building is in dilapidated condition. A small portion of the sample school building is made of bricks while the major portion is made of wood and mud. The roof is made of tin, surely constructed years ago, and there are holes leaking which results in the destruction of walls, furniture and the scarcely available limited teaching/learning material aids in the classroom. A male teacher who has been teaching Hindi complained:

> There're holes in the tin roofing because of which, there's leaking of water during rainy season; teaching/learning process in the classroom is seriously impaired especially during rainy season, particularly when there is wind and storm. Leaking of the roofing further dampens parts of the wall and ultimately damages the wall.

A female teacher, who is also teaching Hindi in class VII, joined the conversation and expressed with dismay, 'During rainy season, it becomes unmanageable; the classroom becomes muddy; so slippery that students and staffs sometimes slipped off'.

In a dampened school environment, where the roof is dripping, the walls are damaged and the rooms are dingy, teaching/learning can hardly take place. Flooring is not made of *pucca*, but of mud, and not of the same level.

At the backyard of the school, parts of the building are uniformly broken up to the height of knee level. The physical condition of the school building indicates years of neglect which nobody is concerned about, though it is a cheerful feeling to witness the efforts of the cook, who cleans the school building, sweeps and mops the floor. Although a non-staff member, she plays a vital role in keeping the school environment presentable.

It is natural that a functioning school has a sufficient playground facility and space for the students to engage in physical exercise, games, sports and extra-curricular activities for their mental and physical growth. In the sample school, there is but little space as the school does not have such a playground facility. The lack of available space, in the form a playground, has virtually shut the potential growth of other non-scholastic development in children. The school is no doubt easily accessible from all crossroads, since it is situated on the main road. However, the school is dislocated among the local houses and is therefore not an ideal place for a school to operate smoothly.

Thus, in the words of a teacher who has been teaching Hindi:

> Foul smell of human excreta from latrines of nearby houses disturbs us so badly; it is not in the best of health, disturbs the teaching/learning process in the class; it's all the more during monsoon.

Teachers, who were standing nearby, showed similar concerns about the awful and constantly disturbing condition with disgust. Another reason why the location of the school is not suitable is that the little space available for children has become a grazing ground for the cattle of the houses located nearby the school. Any sign of effort to relocate the school near empty fields or similar areas was not in sight, since the school, as one of the functioning schools, is considered to be 'good', as claimed by the locals, and is the pride of the local people. Despite such symbolic attachment, the locals do not seem to express a desire to improve the school, except leaving it to the hands of the teachers, who have a limited role in its functioning, though most of them belong to the local area and neighbouring towns.

While looking around the overall surrounding environment of the sample school, it was noticed that mosquitoes were swarming around the backyard of the building and in the dark corners of the classrooms. This can be attributed to the dirty surroundings of the school, especially the backyards that are surrounded by shrubs, bamboos, trees and wild grasses. In front of the school building also, there are patchy, wild, grasses growing which remain without being tended upon. The school verandah is not properly maintained and has cracks. In the absence of a cycle shed, part of the verandah is used for this purpose. This may further facilitate the damaging of the verandah.

In order to reach the school, 30 per cent students travel a reasonable distance of 3 km, while 3 per cent travel for more than 3 km. This is against the prescribed official norm that a child studying at elementary stage must be served by schools within a reasonable distance of 3 km. The distance a student travels is even more than 7 km, as is the case of the tribal students residing at Waroiching hill. The Waroiching hill is separated from the main road by a long, isolated, narrow, land that is surrounded by paddy fields on both sides. Moreover, the officially prescribed distance norms may not be suitable for a hilly region such as the case of Manipur state.

When one considers the mode that these children commute, it is found that 50 per cent children commute to school by walking, while 50 per cent by cycling only. This further suggests the urgency of building a cycle shed. The school head complained about not having one:

> A cycle shed at least for 50–60 cycles is urgently required; the non-availability of cycle shed facility is causing disturbance so much since part of the verandah space is used as cycle shed and particularly in rainy season, it becomes unmanageable since the flooring is partly of mud and using the verandah for cycle shed constraints free movement in the verandah.

The fact that children from various *leikas* travel long distance to attend the school strongly suggests the non-availability of a functional government school in various *leikais* of Manipur. Secondly, even if there are government schools available, they seem to remain dysfunctional and exist by default, while not much is known about the provisioning of schools and schooling situation among remote hill tribal villages.

Classrooms, Furniture, Windows and Doors

No doubt, the school has doors and windows, but not all are in usable condition, especially the windows. The windows are half-broken and unstable. It is horribly depressing that classrooms are dark, dingy, with papers littered around, and one is constantly nagged by the dusty smell. Ventilation is extremely poor with insufficient windows that are partly broken. Leaking of tin roofing and an unhygienic surrounding physical environment are contributory factors in dampening the classrooms. Classroom walls are not attractive and there is not a single picture hung on the wall, rather, one sees cobwebs and cracks. In the absence of school chowkidar, it becomes difficult to keep the classroom environment neat and clean. This can be most discouraging and can dampen the learning ability of the children.

There are six classrooms for instructional purpose, which is more than sufficient, considering the number of students, though the head teacher complained about their inadequacy. The most serious problem is that the rooms are partially separated by torn mats, with passage of easy entry to the next room, so that one can move from one room to the other. Hence, these rooms are hardly separated from each other except one which is used for cooking mid-day meals for children. The rooms are *kuccha* (not properly built rooms), dim and dingy and their condition is completely devoid of decoration. Of the furniture, provided in the classrooms, the desks and benches of the school hall, where classes are held, are found to be in proper condition. However, the tables and chairs for the teachers were shaky, while desks and benches in other classrooms were not only in very poor condition, but also insufficient.

Teaching/Learning Material Aids

Teaching aids play a crucial role in imparting quality education in any school. Usable blackboards and chalks are necessary items of teaching/learning aids. The blackboard as argued by Jossy Bass, in the absence of the modern equipment such as white board, or flashy slides, film strips or projector, provides the best and the simplest means of on-the-spot organisation of school classes. It also offers the teacher a tool to focus and shift the attention of the class. It forces the teacher into physical movement and remains the best audio-visual aid, not as flashy as slides or film scripts, which are provided in few private schools. And except, for want of chalks and erasers, the blackboard never breaks down, causing disturbance in classrooms. Unfortunately, to a great dismay, blackboards in the sample school are no longer in proper usable condition. The blackboard is no longer found to be black, as there are white patches here and there, and even if one tries to write hard on it, it cannot be distinctly seen. The sample school lacks even the most basic, modest facilities of teaching/learning aids.

Table 5.1 *Teaching/Learning Facilities in the Classroom of the Sample School*

Items of Equipment	*Adequate*	*Not in Proper Condition*	*Completely Lacking*
Usable blackboards	✓	✓	
Chalks, dusters and bell	✓	✓	
Globes, maps and charts		✓	
Mathematics kits		✓	
Science kits		✓	
School textbooks and stationery		✓	
Library			✓
Children's book bank			✓
Game materials			✓
Audio-visual aids			✓

Source: Primary Survey, 2009.

In the head teacher's room, there is one long table and two strong, long, wooden desks provided. There is one wooden chair meant for the head teacher. There is no separate room for administration work. Equipment such as bells, globes, maps, charts of flowers, vegetables, trees, mathematics and science kits are kept in the head teacher's room, though some of these items, such as globes and maps, appear somewhat new. The availability of these teaching/learning material aids does not seem to have had any relevance on children in classroom interaction since they are hardly utilised.

Items of stationery and books are kept in two small wooden almirahs placed in the head teacher's room. She complained in disappointment:

> There is no library facility in the school; the concept can't even be imagined, even if there are teaching/learning aids, these are regularly beaten up by rats.

A partially torn country map and two maps of important national leaders are seen hanging on the wall of the head teacher's room. Textbooks, globes, charts and a dictionary were seen kept on the top of the wooden almirah. A literature teacher stated in a complaining tone:

> These items are purchased out of the teacher's grant of ₹ 500 given every year by the state government. Teachers' handbook, plan book and dictionary are additional items that we purchased out of these grants.

However, teachers complained about the underpayment of only ₹ 300 instead of ₹ 500 since ₹ 200 are deducted from the total grant released. The books and stationery items, purchased out of these grants, are distributed to students studying from class III to class VIII students. The distribution process began during the year 2004–05 as a follow up programme of SSA. Though inadequate, the above facilities bring certain relief for school children who cannot afford even a pen and other necessary stationery items. Majority of students (i.e., 80%) received books and stationaries from the school as shown below in Table 5.2, though, quite inadequate as they are:

Table 5.2 *Incentives Schemes at the Sample School*

Facilities at school	*Yes*	*No*
Uniform facilities		✓
Attendance scholarship for girls		✓
Stationery items*	80 per cent	20 per cent
Textbooks	80 per cent	20 per cent

* Only 80 per cent students receive stationery items and textbooks.

Source: Primary Survey, 2009

Teachers are however quite disheartened to be chronically disturbed by the entrenched corruption among education officials, as complained by one of them:

> All of us were paid ₹ 200 less than the due such as ₹ 500 as registered on paper as record signed by each teacher. This is very much against our conscience. The practice is quite terribly discouraging for us. Such malpractices can be noticed whether in the sanctioning of mid-day meal programmes, building of kitchen room for mid-day meal or distribution of salary for teachers and release of school development funds.

There is an electricity connection in the sample school. However, it is available only from 8 a.m. to 10.30 a.m. and that too, for alternate days. The electricity connection in the sample school is, therefore, not that useful, as it should have been for classroom teaching/learning purpose, as classes begin at 9.30 a.m. and end by 2.30 PM. Once again, it is the teachers, not the state education department, who make regular payments for electricity bills of ₹ 120 per month. Teachers, wherever possible, seize the opportunity to discuss about the poor condition of the school with zonal education officers, but have turned a deaf ear, despite these repeated complaints by the teachers.

When inquired about the poor school infrastructure, school fund and its improvement, one female teacher commented:

> There are funds for improving the school infrastructure, but the state machinery is fully corrupt; we're extremely powerless. When there's funding of 100 per cent, only 10 per cent reaches us; education is the dirtiest zone, you know.

Similarly, the head teacher chided the inspection system as a complete failure. Recollecting her personal experience, she said:

> I often call up from my personal mobile to come over to our school at least once to discuss on the deficiencies of the school but they never listen to us, they are hell bent on leaving everything to us.

It is an unusual phenomenon that school teachers are obliged to invite inspectors to inspect the school, rather than conducting surprise inspections at schools in order to keep track of the duties and performance of teachers and to test the students' progress by interacting in classrooms. Failure of the inspection system, as evident in the present sample school, is an attributing factor for the fast failing government schools in the state. One reason provided for non-cooperation of the zonal education officers, who are also the inspectors, was explained by the head teacher as, 'In spite of their entitlement, inspectors aren't provided with travel allowance; hence there's no inspection of schools'.

Basic Conveniences and Ancillary Facilities

The quality of a school is supplemented by a number of essential, basic facilities, such as safe drinking water, electricity connection, toilet facilities, first aid kits, immunisation facility, availability of trained and experienced teachers, desirable teacher-pupil ratio, etc. For example, in the academic session of 2007, there were 35 students in class V and 32 in class VIII. This is an ideal norm as long as the teacher-pupil ratio is concerned.

While examining basic conveniences of the sample school, it was noticed that on the back of the school, there are two toilet facilities – one for the students and the other for the staff. The toilet is made of brick wall and tin roofing with mud holes dug as pits, which is used both by boy and girl students. This prompted a concerned female teacher who expressed discomfort regarding the sharing of toilet both by girl and boy students. As she further expressed, 'Children of class VIII are grown up, a separate toilet facility is a must, this is not a matter to discuss'. The toilet is simultaneously used for latrine purpose. However, the toilet remains non-functional, as the head teacher disgracefully puts it, 'In a situation where water is not available, the toilet that is simultaneously used for toiletries purpose is in a pathetically horrible condition'.

The teacher, sitting next to the head teacher, voiced out about the sorry state of affairs of the school:

> Student themselves fetch water by drawing from the pond which is a few yards away from the school, but there are lots of complaints from the local people; drawing water from the pond is discouraged since students use latrine bucket while drawing water from the pond, the owner of the pond is also a Brahmin.

The emphasis here is not so much on who owns the pond water, but the bucket used simultaneously for latrine purpose is unhygienic to be used for drawing water from a public pond, used by the local population for various purposes like bathing, cooking and feasting, etc. The teacher continued:

> We vehemently complain about the problem of water shortage, latrine and toilets to the zonal education officer. But there is no use of such complaints. We ourselves contribute money about ₹ 400 to ₹ 500 each, to repair latrine work. Since it is related to the work of cleaning latrine, there is no way we can bargain, we just pay what's demanded.

On the issue of basic convenience such as drinking water facility, the school cook shared her grievance:

> Drinking water is fetched by using the water pump installed in the neighbouring village, Khajiri Mamang Leikai. It's at a distance of almost 1 km from here. In order to fetch forty litres of water per day, four or five children walk a distance of almost 1 km two times a week during normal season but almost every day, in summer season. When the students find it difficult to fetch water repeatedly, I assist them.

When the school fails to provide basic conveniences like either drinking water or toilet water, students are punished and bear the brunt of such deficiencies. It is an unusual form of treating students, offending the sense of justice for the children and is an indignity imposed on them, assaulting their self-esteem. This is morally an outrageous incidence, where children from impoverished homes are forced to encounter an impoverished school that barely meets the basic requirements of quality schooling.

First of all, a school is considered a temple of learning as one traditionally believes in. Children come to school for learning purpose. Making children engage in any form of drudgery, such as fetching water, reveals that there is hardly any difference between home and school environment for these children, as an overwhelming 90 per cent of them are engaged in all types of odd household chores, ranging from cooking, attending to cattle rearing, kitchen garden, sibling care, fetching water to firewood collection for kitchen, etc. Unwanted school experience of this kind, by any school-going child, cannot be anybody's desire, at least the parents' whose ethical sensibilities are offended. In the absence of such basic essential facilities, such as toilet facility and drinking water facility, there is also every possibility that children are found missing from the class, since they can easily move out either for toilet, or in search of water, or both. Hence, classroom learning for these children may not take place at all, while they are the ones who are most in need of regular class attendance and learning.

Table 5.3 *Basic Facilities at the Sample School*

Basic Facilities Available at the Sample School	*Yes*	*No*
Drinking water facility		✓
Electricity connection and supply facility	✓	
Toilet facilities	✓	
Separate toilet facility for girls		✓
Chairs and tables for teachers in classroom	✓	
Desks, benches for students	✓	
Immunisation facility at school		✓
First-aid kits at school		✓
Provision of regular medical check up		✓
Almirahs available in classroom		✓
Shelves		✓

Source: Primary Survey, 2009.

The school does not have a first-aid facility nor the children are provided with an immunisation facility that must be made available once a year. There is no regular medical check-up facility in the school. Availability of medical help and an immunisation facility at school can drastically reduce health risk for school children, but the cost is continued to be borne by poor parents. Interestingly, in the absence of first-aid facilities provided in the sample school, it is the teacher themselves who arrange for the basic first-aid kits.

In the sample school, there are no incentive schemes, such as free uniform facilities and attendance scholarships for girl students. The provision is basically designed to facilitate the schooling of girls, in order to bridge the male–female gap in schooling. Yet, despite the absence of such facilities, the number of girl students in class V was 22 outnumbering boy students, whose number was as low as 13, while in class VIII, there were 16 girl students, in which the number was the same as that of boys.

Mid-day Meal Scheme

The mid-day meal is one of the most important incentives to attract children to school enrolment, attendance and their ultimate retention in school. The sample school shows the potential usefulness of the incentive scheme of the mid-day meal[5] that began distributing on 14 November 2004. Cooked rice is distributed, it is either the *yensang* (cooked vegetable) or *hawai* (lentil) distributed to children on an everyday basis. As per the official norm, cooked food is to be distributed among children of class I to class V, but the school provides the facility for all students studying in classes VI and class VIII too.

There is no sufficient utensil such as plates and glasses for cooking, eating and drinking purposes. Three cooking utensils and one frying pan have been donated by the school head. Another problem, as explained by the cook, is the non-availability of a separate kitchen room to prepare the meal. Therefore, the meal is compulsorily cooked in one of the classrooms, adjacent to the classroom where classes are held. This naturally causes a constant disruption for children. The cook complained about the uncomfortable situation as:

> This creates major disturbance, children simply can't concentrate on teaching/learning in the class as they become all the more hungry. It is funny, their mouths start watering when they feel the smell of *yensang*, but then, the smell of *yenshang* prepared and the fuel smoke in the kitchen causes great inconvenience for students and teacher both.

Despite such organisational difficulties of providing the mid-day meal facility, one of the oldest serving teachers of the school explained its significance in the following words:

> Distribution of cooked mid-day meal is the best form; all children of the school come from families below poverty line; distribution of cooked food is a great relieve for poor households living in hand-to-mouth existence. Most children come to school hungry. The mid-day meal facility has become a supporting mechanism for sustaining the school since majority of the parents send children to this school for the sake of food.

This suggests that the mid-day meal scheme in the sample school is an important factor for not only bringing children into the school, but also for retaining them because it relieves the parents from the burden on them of feeding their children at home. When children are provided with meals at school, it is obvious that their families feed them less at home, as teachers shared the plight of the parents:

> Some parents ask for distribution of mid-day meal before sending children; if we say yes, they are ever willing to send their children to our school.

In reality, a child should be given 100 grams of protein consisting of milk and lentil per day. The reason for thus is that such nutrients would support the nutritional intake of children and retain capacity and stamina so that the child's concentration level is not diminished quickly, while relatively difficult disciplines, such as mathematics and science, are taught in the afternoon session. A conscientious teacher, who was keen to share her ten days' training experience in the area of mid-day meal, organised by All India Teachers Federation in the year 1995–96 at Imphal, expressed her disliking and the quality of the food items distributed for mid-day meal by the school. She observed:

> It is unwise to treat all states equally so far as food items of distribution is concerned, for example, milk is a much desirable part of the dietary items to be distributed to children here, since there is larger concentration of calcium in milk, so that a child when served milk can retain concentration till the last class. In case milk is not available, *nunghawai* (soyabean) can be distributed instead of distributing poor quality rice, collected on ration supply. We are ready to prepare soyabean in our own pressure cooker from our own homes but the government is not interested in changing food items that is more nutritiously useful to children. The idea of mid-day meal provision also means supplementing the child's nutrition that was deprived when the child was in the mother's womb.

Despite many tangible benefits of the mid-day meal programme on children, the scheme is implemented in a chaotic, haphazard manner and such lip service to children of the sample school in the name of school provision reveals nothing much beyond the extent of corruption at every level. In another sense, this is clear evidence, as to how schools address poverty as an important test of the schooling system, when other parameters are failed. It also illustrates how government schools, in the name of the provision of welfare policies, have become like charitable organisations, where children of poor households take refuge in the name of schooling.

The argument is, if expansion of social opportunities and choices of children through education can counterforce weights of constraints, and all those difficult circumstances, by virtue of being born into a poor family, the more crucial issue is the accountability of the state in the just and fair provisioning of school education. Interestingly, this idea was the essence of the origin of the Compulsory Education Act, 1870, that first originated in Britain, and later in British India which, over a period of time, resulted in the making of elementary education a fundamental right. The original aim of the Act was to bring educational reforms based on compensatory programmes. Reform, through education, was considered to be the most efficient mechanism of breaking the vicious cycle of poverty among the poor. The concept of eliminating mass poverty requires uplifting children of poor families to escape from their situation, by making them acquire competencies to succeed. However, despite such reformative objectives, public schools today are still designed through the culture of poverty to maintain the distinctiveness of school poverty to be internalised by the majority poor children.

From interacting with the head teacher and a couple of teachers, it was understood that the state government neither sanctions money in time, nor a sufficient amount and hence, there are widespread complaints against the delayed payment of cash for the mid-day meal programme. The head teacher expressed her woes:

> Government sanctions money sufficient for ten or fifteen days only, instead of twenty days, which is the official norm. In addition, as an official norm, mid-day meal is served for children studying from class I to class V. But children of all classes including those studying in class VIII are served food since the teachers are not comfortable to let these students just watch in hunger, while serving food to other students.

It is the teachers who collectively bear the cost for the excess expenditure incurred for mid-day meal. Secondly, when a smaller amount of dry rations is distributed every month, it is natural that children are fed less than is due to them.

For overall maintenance, such as buying up for firewood, vegetables and cooking materials, the school ties up with local shopkeepers, as elaborated by the head teacher, 'Since we don't receive money during the stipulated time, payment is made after money is sanctioned on a much later date'. The head teacher expressed the displeasure of bureaucratic hurdles and corruption, and complained about the non-receipt of a single paisa spent on mid-day meals, even for more than a year. In her complaint, she stated:

> The government has appointed only one cook, instead of two, as per the norm. The cook is also responsible for the work assigned to a chowkidar; she is not just a cook but also performs as a chowkidar.

In affirming the complaints of the head teacher, the cook too shared her grievances:

> With added responsibilities, I am at the same time underpaid. The actual pay is ₹ 2,350 per month, but ₹ 200–300 are deducted per month. There is huge burden on me. I am the only one, who is actually managing the overall maintenance of the school, without the help of a chowkidar or any other helper; one helper; should have been provided to me by now, but they haven't yet. Problems of water shortage and poor hygiene are other common issues. I've to often take care of these inconveniences.

Theft and Corruption

A clean, separate kitchen, away from classrooms is not only ideal but is also recommended to prepare mid-day meal, so as not to distract classroom teaching/learning environment. The sample school does not have the facility for a kitchen room nor does it have a kitchen box. In the light of the urgent need of such a separate room and also due to repeated complaints by the teachers demanding for a separate kitchen, heaps of bricks and sandstones were parked within the school boundary. This was supposedly the material required for building the kitchen room. However, the material was no longer seen within a few weeks, as the head teacher explained in a surprise tone:

> Nobody is aware about who kept the materials, when and for what purpose. These materials remained in one corner of the school boundary for few days; but suddenly, on one fine morning, the building materials disappeared in the absence of the teachers' knowledge. The materials were never brought back.

The above incidence indicates the lack of accountability, transparency and coordination between the school and the state education department. Even after the school community and the education department were well aware of the fact that building a separate kitchen room is the crying need of the school, the plan was nipped in the bud due to the corruption of the education department and the lack of vigilance on the part of the teacher community. The opportunity for building the separate kitchen room was lost, for which the school community continue to lament.

This is a case of stark illustration where, on the one hand, the dynamics of corruption and unaccountability on the part of the state as an overwhelming powerful dominant is deeply entrenched, while on the other hand, the teacher community as a residual category remains dormant. The state, which is the promoter of public school systems, has become hostile to its own policies that are self-contradictory.[6] On the contrary, the availability of the facilities discussed through the provisioning of school education, constitutes the crucial aspect of quality education that can also powerfully influence learning improvement, enrolment, retention, completion of elementary stage and most importantly, learner's achievement, such as the cognitive achievement, though it requires a separate treatment, since the present focus does not deal with learner's achievement.

Quality education is thus visualised in terms of its product or output that is the learner's achievement, both in terms of scholastic and co-scholastic areas, viz., the performance of various subjects of study, habits, attitudes, values, life skills necessary for becoming a good citizen. However, this present focus does not address the issue of learner's achievement. This is closely associated with the condition of learning and teaching environment. It is a complex issue to understand since it looks at attitudes, values, etc., although the quality of education, though difficult to capture, is of interest because of what it can do for people.

The difference between poor and quality education matters in terms of what, how, and how much children learn. This remains not only a burning issue but has also caught the attention of many scholars who have interest in how equality of educational opportunity[7] works, and how it can be achieved in public schools where the majority of children come from poor households. In its essence, quality education and access to equal opportunity is an important potential instrument to help achieve greater equality between those who start life with different sets of economic and social advantages.

The above argument is close to the structural-functionalist proposition such as that of Parsons and Durkheim who view education as an agent of social change, promoting greater social equality and social integration. Echoing Durkheim, education, as a social fact, is a means of maintaining social solidarity, a necessary condition for the society to perpetuate itself, which is a *sui generis*. Making sense of Durkheim's proposition is rooted in developing equally the potentials of every children of the society (if solidarity is expected to prevail in society, justice for all is required) through state-run school systems and such equal access is one of the most important features that can be provided in any democratic society in which the main task lies with the state. As the argument suggests, every individual has the right to develop themselves equally by creating equal opportunities for all by the state as a duty bearer.

The central debate is that ensuring an effective educational system is seen as a powerful means through which societal reform can take place, by equalising school facilities for all children. Secondly, expansion of such facilities is an essential requirement of more rapid elimination of gross inequalities, or else differential access to school accentuates inequities in economic and social opportunities. In more or less a similar concern, quoting, P.C. Mahalanobis, Mrydal in *The Challenge of World Poverty*, argues, 'By and large, it is the rich people who have the opportunity of giving their children the type of education required for posts of influence and responsibility in the country ... the power and privileges of a small group of people at the top tend to be not only preserved but strengthened .... This has created an influential group of influential people whose natural desire is to maintain their privileged position and power' (1970: 201).

This observation apparently presupposes the views of classical thinker such as Max Weber, who treats education as the source of a new principle of control as instrumental rationality or bureaucratic domination, while the Marxian tradition treats education as a site of ideological reproduction of interest of the dominant class (Alberto and Allen, 1995: 10). Both views, though differ in fundamental ways anticipate debates that concerns education as a site of expression of cultural domination of the powerful few. Further, quoting J.P. Naik, Myrdal points, 'educational development ... is benefiting the "haves" more than the "have nots". This is a negation of social justice and planning proper' (1970: 201). Therefore, when schools are sharply and deliberately stratified, quality aspects of school education and how it reaches the children of poor households, as a matter of social justice, holds an important key issue in the discourse of education as a matter of right for the poor.

The Teachers

When the new sociology of education began to affect research paradigms in the sociology of education in Britain towards the end of the 1960s,[8] it opened up a wide range of issues for investigation which were previously considered to be trivial. The new paradigm examines a number of interlocking relationships and interactions between school environment, teachers and students. Thus, role theory, symbolic interactionism, phenomenology were the new emergent areas that got prominence in school education. One of these approaches is the sociology of inter-actionism, which gained much more prominence in the later period.

The new paradigm, sociology of interactionism, underlines the significant role a teacher plays in classroom interaction with students as an important process of improving teaching/learning processes in classroom setting. The approach emphasises students' perspectives to teachers, school environment, pedagogy, curriculum and overall school processes as the major areas of sociology of education, assessing quality schooling of children. Thus, the new sociology of education began to examine non-physical dimensions, such as teachers, as one of the most important human resources and utilisation of their knowledge, skills, talents, time and wisdom, that greatly influence the overall school environment, specially the students as H. Gracey discusses in detail in her paper, 'The Craftsman Teachers' (in Woods and Hamersley's book, *Process of Schooling: A Sociological Reader*. 1976), that the teacher's primary task is to present the curriculum in such a way that not only knowledge shall be acquired, but it will also become part of the children's general power to cope with intellectual problems and personal difficulties to enable them become aware of a wider world, and make them feel deeply and vitally connected with it. This will enable the child to move from the world of childhood to the world of adulthood with a positive self-feeling.

In the sample school, despite many physical handicaps as discussed above, it is observed that a few teachers have taken the greatest challenge to keep the ball moving. One of these challenges comes from teachers' contribution to the overall functioning and sustaining of the school, while other government schools are failing at a fast track.

Teachers' Qualification and Training

Unlike the popular trend in India, in the sample school, the number of female teachers far outnumber male teachers which is unique in the state of Manipur. Of the total teaching staff, two are males while thirteen are females. Therefore, the gender bias in the teaching profession is no doubt skewed in favour of females. It is in one sense, positive, since it reflects the official efforts of recruiting more female teachers. More than half of the teachers, i.e., nine of them are trained while the remaining six are untrained. Nine teachers from the school were randomly selected and were asked a range of questions about his/her social background, training exposure and its usefulness in teaching, qualifications, experience in teaching, aspirations, their role and contributions to teaching and other additional roles they perform besides teaching.

The study observed that the teachers in the sample school are relatively privileged in terms of social status and economic security, such as their salary status and other privileges, when compared with their counterparts serving in private schools. On the issue of salary status, all teachers are satisfied with the amount that they receive, which ranges from ₹ 8,000 to ₹ 15,240 per month, except the male teacher who is paid an amount of ₹ 4,500 per month since his appointment is on ad hoc basis. All teachers who are enjoying permanent status are comfortable with their salary amount but are extremely frustrated at receiving their salary three or four months late.

While studying the teachers' social background, the teaching force is drawn from all sections of society. The parental education status of these staffs reveals that all parents, except that of one teacher, are literates. They have completed functional literacy and elementary education. However, occupationally, the parents are either farmers or engage in some form of family business. Only one father of a respondent was found to be a Sanskrit scholar, whose teaching profession has some amount of influence on her while taking up the job of a teacher. As long as their economic status is concerned, all belong to economically well-off families.

Teaching experience of these teachers ranges from 2 to 25 years of time span. Of the total nine teachers interacted, five of them are trained in the conventional sense of the term. The most common type of training, they received is Junior Basic Training, B.T. and B.Ed., which usually last for two years. All teachers are quite sensitised about SSA programme in the state, though many have reservations and grieve about the way it is implemented. For example, as per the provisions of teachers' training under SSA, a teacher must be trained 20 days each year in his/her service course, 60 days refresher course for untrained teachers who are already employed as teachers and 30 days orientation course for freshly trained recruits. These norms are, however, by and large, violated, for example, not a single teacher was given a refresher course under SSA. The course content of training was not only patchy, but also irrelevant. One English teacher, teaching students of classes III and IV, narrated her experience while attending the training programme under SSA:

> The course content was irrational and irrelevant. The content of the training was designed basically for the lower class such as nursery and K.G. classes; it's not suitable for teachers teaching higher classes.

Others expressed the usefulness of training programme designed for value education incorporating subjects like AIDS, STDs, problems of drug abuse and its prevention at school level, etc. The response indicates a mixed reflection on the suitability of the course. But, on the whole, the training failed to achieve the targeted goal since individual teachers were randomly picked up for the training. Most teachers, however, consider the training course indeed useful and helpful in teaching. On the usefulness of other training programmes, a female teacher who received the Junior Basic Training, expressed a sense of satisfaction about the training she received:

> The training is helpful in classroom interaction with children in certain, specific ways, such as maintaining silence and discipline in the class and I use those training methods of teaching I received during training. It is really useful.

How to maintain discipline in a classroom is the common training that most teachers had undergone. The idea conveyed is: discipline trains students and it also moulds them. The exercise of discipline in classroom transaction presupposes a mechanism of controlling students in a classroom so that a meaningful classroom orientation can take place between the teacher and the taught. Moral education and discipline are seen essential in teachers' training as commonly shared by almost all teachers. This sounds very familiar with Durkheim's concept of disciplining the youngsters by the adults with humanitarian feelings. It is a kind of educational rehabilitation and this also implies a reform of pedagogy. Durkheim's argument need not be lost in unsympathetic critic, because, for him, discipline over the youngsters could mean damage control from societal chaos and breakdown of institutions. Therefore, imparting training skills on how to discipline and control students is a necessary part of any training course conducted for school teachers.

Inside the Classroom: Maintaining Order and Discipline

A teacher in a classroom can be overwhelmingly powerful, to the extent that the classroom situation is completely under his/her control. A teacher can show his/her tantrums, temperaments and gestures of all kinds. The school, through its agencies such as the teachers, becomes a sort of permanent observatory where the pupil is subjected to habits, rules, orders, through a technique called discipline. Interestingly, as the teacher commented on the importance of training and controlling of students, it points to the important observation of how classroom interaction between the teachers and the taught in many ways reflect ways teachers exert control over students and discipline them.

In classroom interaction, many teachers find it difficult to use extreme forms of coercion while dealing with students, such as canning or pulling up ear. Hence, a teacher may use other subtle forms of coercion. In an interaction process of a teacher with students of class VIII in the sample school, it could be noticed how teachers were concerned with classroom control in instructional phases of lessons. On the one hand, the teacher sets out to engage and maintain the attention and effort of students to motivate their participation in classroom process, while simultaneously trying to control and discipline students. This was visibly noticed when a social science teacher, while setting the stage off in classroom, tried to ensure that all students completed home assignments, while simultaneously checking that all students have access to the necessary materials so that no student will come up with excuses for not performing their assignments.

The teacher-students conversations in the classroom are as follows:

Teacher: 'Right, children, look in front'. (Students look up, try to be attentive). 'Before we proceed, can I ask you all if you have completed yesterday's homework or not?'

Students: 'Yes Ma'm (some of them look distracted since they have not done their assignment, that too from boys side; boy and girl students sit separately)'.

Teacher: 'Bring all your exercise copies, submit them immediately, then we go to the next lesson, all right'.

All students rush to the teacher's table with exercise copies at their hands (while some sit back, mostly from boys' side only, all copies are kept on the table for checking during her free time).

Teacher: 'Ok. Those who did not do homework, get up. (Students did not bother yet to get up). Boys! Are you hearing me? I said get up, come here'. (It seems that those who usually don't perform homework without genuine reason get beaten up two times of canning).

Teacher: 'Come! I said, hurry up, we're wasting time unnecessarily'. (As it appears these students are habitually neglectful of home assignment and get canning regularly).

All eyes of the students look towards the boys' side. Five of them get up. Shyly, they slowly move towards the teacher who is waiting with a cane in her hand.

Teacher: 'Stand in row. Why did you forget what I said? Tell me why; stretch your hand, hum! Ehh,! Ehh'! (Two times canning were given to the palm of each of the students in row) but leaving the last one who is a girl student.

This, in one way, is demonstrative of the teacher's claiming of being superior position vis-à-vis the students. A fellow student loses face before other fellow students because she/he was penalised as wrong doer before their own peer students.

Student: 'Ma'am I had chicken pox; I couldn't do'. (In meek tone, keeping head down).

Teacher: 'Oh! How many months? Are you all right now?'

Student: 'Yes, Ma'm, feeling better'.

Teacher: 'Have you vaccinated? I have to ask your parents, were you given full round of vaccination? If you hadn't, don't come. It's dangerous for other children'.

All are quiet, except one or two boys try to snatch books from fellow students. Yet, they are under control. Except for the girl students, reasons for the students' failure to perform home assignments were due to the lack of a necessary item, such as the textbook of social studies. The school promised to distribute textbooks but failed to do so in time. The result is, students have to bear the pang of physical and moral pain while being beaten up in front of their own classmates. Also, the dearth of stationery items and school textbooks can sack the morale of the students and the teachers as well.

The interaction of the classroom was often disturbed by the heavy noise of shouts by children of class VI in the next classroom. At interval, the disturbance caught the attention of both the teacher and the students. The teacher was repeatedly feeling signs of disturbance, rushed to the next class, gave one shouting, 'Who is your teacher, what subject are you having, go and ask for a substitute teacher. We aren't able to hold class'. The teacher comes back, looks at the students straight and asks them to maintain silence to begin lesson. It also shows that she is simultaneously keeping a check on the behaviour of students in the classroom, so that she can begin her lesson. Thus, making the classroom environment as an official environment, serious not funny, important not trivial, gospel not moonshine, powerful not puny, interest consuming, not as a casual background and thus, as grounds for enthusiastic participation, not yawns and arguments, etc. (Woods and Hammersley, 1976: 109) all add up as responsible etiquette on the part of teachers in classroom interaction with students. Yet, not all teachers are powerful enough to create an aura of this kind in classroom interaction. Another element of exercising teacher's control in classroom interaction is through putting students to the task of making them answer to questions in the classroom after being taught, such as reading out in classroom, as the most common method adopted by teachers. There is cyclical interaction of negotiation in classroom situation. The teacher provides frequent slots for the participation of students asking questions, integral to the topic she is expounding, thus using student's motivation to generate attention and learning sort of. This was commonly seen practised in the classroom process of the sample school. This is most probably due to the fact, that teachers cannot control students through pure coercion, which is often difficult to achieve.

The classroom encounter is seen constituted by the teacher via the enforcement of certain rules, defining student activity that could be identified as knowledge and meritorious, intelligent, unintelligent and lazy students, who either confirm or defy classroom norms. All these myriad of classroom cultures can be grasped from a classroom setting and that too, during teacher's interaction with students, while teaching topicwise lessons. In a situation of such a setting, the teacher works to organise the gathering of students, in a way that she is the hub for knowledge and a focal point of attention. The teacher spends a bulk of her time, facing the students, talking to all of them simultaneously (it is the teacher who talks most), while maintaining a balance of attention to all. For this, the teacher starts official classroom proceedings by setting the stage for the lesson, rather than starting it off straight.

Thus, in a conversation of a female teacher, teaching social studies of class V, the teacher begins the chapter related to Hunger Marcher's Day and Women's War in Manipur. Here is an observation of the actual conversation between the teacher and the students:

Teacher: (Standing right in the middle of the classroom) 'What's today's new lesson? Children'.

Students: 'Ma'am, Ma'am, ahh, ahh'.

Teacher: 'Com' on, it's nothing new. You all know it. What we're going to discuss is very popular indeed'.

Teacher: (Pointing to the student, sitting in the last row, 'extreme right) Tell me what you remember about today's lesson, I briefed you all, yesterday'.

Student: (He stands up, keep mum, no utterance of any word).

Teacher: (In sympathetic tone, looks at the student) 'Sit down, be quiet, all of you'.

Teacher: 'Look at Chapter 6 – An Educational Journey. (Students open page hurriedly, search for the chapter).

Teacher: 'Got it right! All of you, ok, children. Be attentive, after the lesson, we discus questions at the back, ok, be attentive'. (Two–three students sharing the same book, snatch the book from each other, immediately place it in middle after small scuffle and remain quiet).

The teacher starts reading the text as follows:

'In the history of Manipur, 27 August is observed as Hunger Marcher's Day in memory of those who died in the struggle for food. The policy of rice export was pursued as a part of colonial

> administration for a long time. The catastrophe occurred during Moirang Koireng, the first Chief Minister of Manipur, in 1965. Before the outbreak of war against hunger on 12 December 1939, people of Manipur suffered tremendously due to the shortage of food. Yet, the colonial government allowed Marwari businessmen to sell rice outside Manipur. Rice was continuously exported and, hence, the people faced shortage of food for their own consumption. In protest against the unjust treatment, women of Manipur began to hit the rice mills with sticks. At that time, women used to pound and grind rice grains with their own hands. Women marched to the state durbar as a sign of protest against the state but these women were charged with bayonets. This led to the famous women's war of 1939 in the history of Manipur. The women's agitation of 1939 was one of the most important events in the colonial history of Manipur. The deep rooted cause of the movement was directly related to the irregularities and malpractices in the administration of the state. Just after the establishment of the colonial rule, the outside traders gradually began to capture the monopoly of trade which at one time was under the management of womenfolk. Under the free trade policy introduced by the colonial government, the British authority began to export a large quantity of rice from Manipur. The rice export policy that introduced from the beginning of 1897 began assuming a peculiar character in the year 1925 and after this the Marwari traders began to take over the monopoly of the export industry from the local traders. As a result of this, the price of rice rose rapidly and it touched a dangerous situation. The immediate cause of the outbreak of the women's movement was directly related with the prevailing export policy of the authority and milling activities of the Marwari traders. The serious economic problem created by the colonial authority was further intensified by the shortage of food grains due to which, many went on hunger without food.'

Soon after the text is read out, the teacher immediately ordered the students to look at the questions printed at the back of the textbook. Few questions read by the teacher were as:

> Teacher: 'What is Hunger Marcher's day?' (She looks at students, all around, suggesting them to participate).

All students remain quiet, no sign of participation, few students look on, and the room is in complete silence.

The teacher goes on reading questions and answering the questions too in a running manner. Students keep turning the pages of the book, trying to catch up and figuring out. The classroom remains silent.

The above method employed in classroom interaction by the social science teacher is one way in which teachers generally try to maintain classroom discipline, by engaging the students in light conversation to attract students' attention. An interaction of this sort may not demand to test the students' knowledge or intelligence. In talking to the whole class and engaging them, the teacher is constantly checking the behaviour of signs of intention and attention of the students.

However, sometimes, even when a teacher tries to maintain classroom discipline through slots of questions, this may not be enough for teachers to command students' attention and take classroom under her control. In such situations, a teacher may employ certain parameters such as introducing an interesting issue to the students, apart from discussing lesson topics. Such a topic can be well beyond the knowledge of the students but something the teacher is really familiar with.

Very interestingly indeed, a situation of this kind was observed. That, beyond the lesson topic, a teacher of English literature, in the sample school, was found interacting with students about a conspicuous flower found in Manipur, its process of planting and rearing up in a unique way. In a classroom of 14 to 15 dyads (students) of class VIII, the teacher was standing at the right corner, holding the textbook at her hand. She was the hub, the focal point of student attention, at that very moment, all eyes of the students glued to the direction where she was standing.

The teacher began as follows:

> 'It's very interesting, if you really would like to know the process of planting, *leihao* in your own homes. *Leihao* is a Joy Perfume Tree, also known as Champa in Hindi. It is golden yellow flower; grown on a large evergreen tree, with a close tapering crown composed of ascending branches with extremely sweet heady fragrance. This fragrance has made *leihao* a delicate and very popular flower among households in Manipur. *Leihao* is not planted in every household. They are used in religious offering. First of all, it's an expensive flower, a rare flower. By planting *leihao* at your own homes, you can continuously make earning. That way, you can

generate income continuously. I tell you, the very productive method of planting the flower and how to grow it fast. You all can practice it at home; it's a very simple process'.

Thereafter, she began the narration of the process of planting *leihao* as follows:

> 'You mix soil with cow dung and hair. Hair is not to be wasted as we generally do after cutting it. We often cut our hair and throw them away waste. But you don't know how hair is such an important ingredient in enhancing the fast growth of *leihao*. If you put some quantity of hair in the soil, mixed it with cow dung, for few days, when the hair starts decaying, it is an excellent fertilizer for the growth of *leihao*. Once growth takes place, it branches out at a fast speed; the branches can be cut into sections, and again grow them in the same process. One can go on with the process in a cyclical manner. Selling the flower on regular basis can generate good amount of income for you without much effort. This way, you can easily meet your day to day expenses'.

The students found the English teacher's experience as uniquely interesting. During the above narration, firstly, students found the process of growing *leihao* in their own homes quite an amazing story to listen to. This could be guessed from the absolute silence maintained in the classroom. It also indicates that the skill or the knowledge of a teacher can be a powerful weapon to exercise his/her authority in the classroom. And, the authority is recognised by her students. Presenting the authoritative appearance and possession of superior knowledge is considered, not only normal, but also essential with an expectation of students, conforming to the claimed status of the teacher. The argument bolters Basil Bernstein's observation that every aspect of schooling is part of the controlling process that operates at two levels. Firstly, the teacher has control over students and knowledge in classroom. And, the failure to maintain control is seen as weakness and hence lack of authority and of being exploited by students.

Another aspect of teachers' control over their students is that teachers, due to their prolonged proximity with their students on day-to-day basis, naturally feel that they have legal right to comment on, and hence control over the clothing, hairstyles, footwear, language, behaviour and cultural interest of their pupils. In addition, society gives teachers the right to access to what is called, 'guilty knowledge' about pupils (Chapman, 1986). The main message conveyed here is, teachers become too knowledgeable about the pupils and their backgrounds that a particular trait or characteristic can be made for particular students. This leads teachers to unfairly invade the personal lives of the students and their backgrounds, and chances are that students are treated differently. This is one of the important observations found in the present study. For example, when the question, 'if children opt for private tutor or not when they fail to understand much of what is taught in the classroom' was put, the same teacher responded:

> All children have come from families below the poverty line; their parents continuously struggle for a living, their life is hard. It is not possible to afford private tutor. I've experienced the situation of paying fees, for them since they are extremely poor.

The opinion is commonly shared by majority teachers, though few admitted that very less number of children could opt for private tutor. She further added:

> These students are uncared ones by their parents, whether they are getting education or not, is their least priority; anyway, parents nowadays are educated unlike before. But, they are always busy in search of their food. Clothes worn by these children are unkept; neither mother nor father cares.

The brief narrations, as stated by the teacher, suggest that the parents of these students are incapable of thinking of their children's education, since they are primarily concerned with immediate issues of survival. Though survival issues remain crucial, the observation is to a large extent wary to be believed, since the idea does not correspond with the response and opinion of an overwhelming number of parents regarding the education of their children, most significantly, when the schooling norm in the region has acquired social dimensions. Another sociological dimension is: in majority households, the middle class value provides a reference group for poor households in terms of education, occupation and income. Parents, no matter from what economic background they hail, are always the main communicators to their children for such values.

Teaching Methods

Various resources of teaching/learning aids available in a school also imply pedagogy. A combination of correlated factors, such as effective use of teaching aids, preparation of lesson plans, supervision of class work, correction of homework, improves the method of imparting quality teaching in any school (Jalali, 2003: 116). Most common methods of pedagogy that the teachers used while teaching in the class are: textbooks study, verbal instruction, chalkboard, demonstration, briefings of the lesson to be taught, photo chart, plan book and group assignment. It was found that teachers, while using the above methods of teaching in the class, gave much time and took pains to make students understand what is taught in the class. Most teachers appear to be committed to their profession of teaching and making children gain from such efforts.

Innovative methods, such as the use of projector slides, are not used for want of regular electricity supply. All teachers did not have the opportunity to use demonstrative methods in science, or social studies classes except that one teacher was found holding up a torn chart while teaching geography of class VIII. Exciting and enriching study methods such as field visits are avoided due to security reasons as explained by the Hindi teacher, 'We avoid taking children to the field as it is not safe outside though few teachers manage, but hardly anyone of us can manage'.

The subjects taught in class VIII were Manipuri, English, Hindi, Social Sciences, Natural Sciences and Mathematics. Teachers were found committed to the traditional roles that practising teachers usually perform, but, are under severe constraints to deliver the much needed progressive education[9] to the deprived children since the much needed infrastructure and basic facilities are lacking in the sample school. However, all teachers were satisfied with the contents of course curriculum, arguing that these were designed locally suitable and relevant for children, though the English teacher of class VIII complained, 'The content is good, but the language is not up to the mark; but I believe it is ok since we aren't English-speaking community'.

However, the teacher complimented the content of curriculum as most relevant, since every possible local culture and literature is taken into consideration while preparing the syllabus. Famous local personalities, historical events and local festivals which are quite memorable for the people of Manipur are translated in Hindi.

While interacting with teachers as to whether children could understand what they were teaching in the class, it differed from individual teacher to teacher though majority agreed that children could understand what were taught in the class, as quoted by a female teacher who has been teaching English for class V:

> Almost 75 per cent of my students understand what I teach and discuss in the class. Those whose mental faculty is active don't find it difficult to understand my teaching.

Another female teacher who has been teaching Natural Science shared her observation:

> At least 80 per cent of my students understand what I teach; the remaining students can't cope up any longer despite my easy teaching method adopted in classroom interaction.

The teacher is resentful about the lack of science kits made for children because of which, no practical work can be done in the classroom. Like most of her colleagues, the science teacher was alarmed about the mismatch between what is to be taught, in what method and what kind of receipt the children will have. The mismatch in teaching/learning process can greatly discourage and undermine a child's learning capacity to comprehend about a particular topic.

Teachers Beyond the Territory of Teaching as a Profession

Majority teachers of the sample school consider the job of teaching as a serious vocation, since a miniscule of them cited convenient reasons for taking up teaching job as their profession rather than as a vocation. However, on the whole, as against the popular belief of teaching profession as lowly and underpaid one, there are individual teachers who consider teaching profession as rewarding. Thus, in the words of a female teacher, who has been teaching English:

> School children are like my own children and my children are always my priority, this is always there with me. School is an extension of family. We direct children since school is a second home for children.

A conscientious teacher, who is teaching General Science, shared:

> Teachers' training sensitises us to the extent that we're able to cultivate a sense of empathy for students as our own children. This really helps us in changing our outlook and attitudes. Teaching job is a huge responsibility. We can't think of our school children as other's children.

Drawn from this perspective, for some teachers, teaching could be treated as a vocation taken up for various reasons not solely for the comfort it gives but also the satisfaction it serves to the individual teacher. A male teacher, who is teaching Hindi, expressed similar articulation:

> Through teaching profession, one can help in building up of future generations and it is possible to spread the light of education through teaching.

Here, the role of teaching is viewed as overwhelming. Societal building through educating generations of children is considered the key role of a teacher. It also conveys how the job of teaching as a vocation, unlike those of others, is profoundly challenging since the destiny of a nation is linked to the vocation of teaching. This also views that teaching as a vocation is perhaps the noblest profession, as we traditionally look at it. Others emphasised the importance of the subject they are teaching in imparting knowledge to children; for example, a female teacher who is teaching Hindi of class VIII shared:

> I teach Hindi literature. Hindi as a national language and its usefulness particularly when one travels beyond Manipur is a known fact; it is an important discipline.

She seems to be delighted to emphasise the importance of Hindi language and to be a teacher of a discipline as important as the national language. Similarly, a female teacher, who is teaching Manipuri literature, expresses that the syllabus covers a good portion of the history of Manipur, sculptor of the region and updating the children with such background and knowledge is quite an amazing experience. Most teachers appear to have made good strides to make students feel comfortable, learn something of what they teach and also aware of their efforts. The head teacher is also vigilant about the teaching/learning process taking place in classrooms by observing while teachers are teaching in class, checking teacher's class notes, examining children's performance in test, etc.

All students found their teachers to be cooperative, understanding, loving and caring. The relationship between teachers and students in the sample school goes beyond classroom interaction. This could be noticed in the ways teachers pay extra attention to the students, both in material and moral aspects. For example, there were cases when teachers had to regularly pay fees or purchase stationery items for students who cannot afford to do so. Children do not want to be deprived of; but, to be comforted with necessary items of sufficient learning material aids. Often than not, the school faces shortage of stationery items since learning for children takes place randomly. In times of shortages of such learning aids, the teachers have to make up for such shortages. An extra activity that the head teacher initiates in the school is the conducting of quiz programmes. This, as she expresses, adds good taste to student life and relieve them from daily monotonous routine life. The programme is organised for every fifteen/twenty days. Any concerned teacher who is interested is involved and money is contributed by all teachers to conduct the programme. Winning prizes on such occasions is a great excitement for students. With delight, she continued proudly, 'Our students often win prizes at state-level competitions'.

As observed in the present chapter, the job of teaching is fairly seen from a social perspective, and hence teachers do not perform a mere classroom job that sees the immediate needs and the precedence of classroom situation of the students. They take into account of the students home background as well. This is more pronounced in a community where there is similarity of ethnic background, homogeneity and a sense of belongingness to a particular *leikai* such as the case of Manipuri society. Teachers of the sample school seem to be quite knowledgeable about home settings of students. Teacher's knowledge of the fabric of social life of the students is developed due to everyday routine face-to-face interaction and shared understanding what Harold Garfinkel terms as 'ethnomethodology'. It is this ethnomethodology which seems to be unimportant at first that turns out to be fundamental to the fabric of social life of the students, which teachers with a sense of humility cannot feign ignorance about their students' social background. It is this very micro-level fabric of social life of the students that is needed to be taken into account by policy considerations of macro-level institution such as the state while framing a policy for 'right to education', a radical education project.

Influenced by the poor economic condition of their students, it invokes a sense of empathy, considerateness and cooperation in teachers towards their students as the Social Science teacher narrated:

> When there is sudden strike in the region, we provide cycles to tribal students who come from a farther distance to ensure that

> they reach home safe. I remember, we teachers collectively pay school fees for at least about ten students every year; the school admits orphan students and students who top in the class without school fees; we sell stationery items at lower rates than those at market prices; say, the rate of an exercise copy in our school is sold at ₹ 7, which is ₹ 10 at market rate.

Though all teachers seem to be keen on promoting the welfare of children in their small ways, very few teachers stood apart from the rest in terms of compassion, sacrifice and commitment for their students. The overall observation finds the work of a school teacher as an arena where education and social justice condense when state accountability fails.

At one level the teachers thus command genuine appreciation for all the good strides and the sort of caring and permanent affectionate relationship they make with their students. But there is always the fear of what is transmitted in the minds of the students. The 'hidden curricula' that is taught by the school through different ways: the attitudes and values of the teachers towards the students, the atmosphere of the school, the building, the room layouts, the broken furniture, the damaged shabby school wall and the overall environment of the school, not just the formal official curriculum. To cite a concrete example, it could be said that lack of facilities and poor environment of the sample school are otherwise, conveniently used by the teachers to partly blame the students' home economic poor background that appears to be reinforcing for each other. On the one hand, the school fails to provide even the basic minimum teaching/learning requirements that are essential to constitute a school, leave alone quality education, and on the other, parents are blamed for their inability to afford even the necessary stationery items required for acquiring at least the basic skills of reading, writing and arithmetic, in a sense, functional education.

Thus, at another level, teacher like any other human being is unique to make massive use of symbolic communication with their students. However, the symbolic character of an attitude of this kind instils a sense of resignation, numb and submissiveness in the students, failing him to fully develop his own self. The idea is, the student, being a person, his sense of his own identity and his feeling that what kind of a place he has in the world depends on how he is being perceived and treated by others such as the teachers in classroom situation and his perception about self is the product of such interaction. The teacher as a powerful agency of school 'lives on' in the child. In this process, the child is a helpless lot, for he would not be what he is unless he does interact with such agencies. What is worrying is, therefore, the impact of the message a failed school transmits to its children. The failed school environment, which the child interacts every day, gets imprinted in the mind of the child unconsciously, and becomes a part of the self, affecting the perception of the child's self. The teachers' constant reference to children as impoverished ones, who are incapable of escaping from their socio-economic position, imposes defeating and negative images on the child's self. Self of the child is thus essentially a social product and this is truly an experience of disempowering the child through school processes. An oppressive school environment such as in the present case stands in sharp contrast to the liberating education agenda as Paule Freire would argue that schools through the banking system of education mirror oppressive society as a whole that can be analysed in the way teacher-students relate to each other. Here, liberative education (as the opposite to oppressive education), for Freire, acquires profound significance for children to make them truly empowered which children can acquire in their daily interaction with school environment.

On home front, parental support for children's education is indeed alarming. Two different home environments are created in different ways when one parent ignores the child's questions of studies but another parent makes a point of reading to the child every day or at least helping the child in completing home assignment. For a considerable number of children, parental support for children's education in the sample school is indeed fearful since majority of parents, despite having completed certain stage of education, continuously struggle for a living, and hence unable to spend time with children at home. Going by the occupational status of fathers of the students, it reveals that 20 per cent of them belong to service sector such as peons/chowkidars, clerks in government offices, 45 per cent are farmers, 25 per cent are construction workers/carpenters/brick makers, while the remaining 10 per cent are not engaged in any gainful occupation. Mother's occupation reveals that 15 per cent of them are engaged in farming or cultivation, 10 per cent in weaving, 5 per cent in business, 45 per cent are vegetable sellers while the rest 25 per cent are not engaged in any such activity. The educational status of parents reveals that 23 per cent of them are illiterate, 15 per cent have completed primary education, while the remaining 52 per cent have completed elementary education. While looking at study facilities available at home, 60 per cent students have separate rooms for study as against to the 40 per cent students who are deprived of such facilities. Most, i.e., 95 per cent do not have access to drinking water facility and fetch the same from nearby distance. In majority households of this type, there is no separate kitchen room and the degree of disturbance in the child's study is high since a child studies in a room that is combined with kitchen. About 35 per cent of children strongly dislike their home environment due to overcrowding, sibling disturbance and overall noisy and uncaring environment.

Therefore, presumably, children hailing from such background are difficult to handle. This makes the task of the teachers all the more difficult. Though most children are not first-generation learners, they do not seem to be academically helped by parents at home despite majority parents have completed certain stage of schooling and education. The fact is, most of these parents come back home after hours of hard and physical toil with bodies exhausted and minds dull and sluggish, with worries for the next day, leaving little possibilities to provide even the much needed moral support for their children's education at home. Coupled with the endless household chores children perform, learning difficulties for these children could also arise from cumulative factors such as poor nutritional intake and poor health, since some children admitted their inability to concentrate on studies because of dizziness caused by low blood pressure and anaemic. In addition, when there is dearth of supply of textbooks and stationery items at school, a child makes constant nagging to his/her parents to supplement his/her stationery items, school tuition fees and school uniforms. For example, a household makes yearly payment of ₹ 160 per child studying in class V, while it is ₹ 170 for children studying in class VIII. Yet, the head teacher shared about the plight of parental poverty:

> Some households still go hunting for schools that charge lower rate of tuition fees. We are charging minimal rate but they feel it is high. We provide stationeries at concessional rate too.

The reality is, there is no free education; schooling of children remains indeed costly and sometimes unaffordable affair for parents who are survivors or earning intermittent income. As is revealed in the present context, even despite their literacy and education level, parents due to their everyday engagement in survival struggle, fail to provide the much needed academic help and moral encouragement that a child can expect from home front. Poverty to this extent is certainly a real issue to reckon with. Everyday life for majority of these parents is dragged into making both ends meet, living from hand to mouth. An existential situation of this kind deprives their enabling opportunity to fight individually or collectively against the unjust treatment meted out to them, further rendering themselves virtually helpless and socially dislocated. This is amply demonstrated by the absence of effective Parent Teacher Association (PTA) in the sample school. All teachers were disappointed about their failure of instituting PTA. The school head shared her unhappy experience on the failure of forming PTA:

> With dogged perseverance, by using the mike, I tried to arrange a meeting by announcing and inviting the parents on the usefulness and requirements of forming PTA. My purpose of using the mike is that every parent in the nearby locality could hear my announcement so that they come together to form PTA.

The school head went a step ahead attempting to form PTA so that dialogue of sharing between teachers and parents could be initiated to help better understanding between them as responsible partners in school processes. Despite such efforts, no PTA meeting has taken so far since parents are not willing to spare even a few hours from their daily engagement of earning. But, the reality is that these parents are precisely the social categories to contest the views of the policy makers and implementers on the schooling of their children. This is a typical case of acute form of social exclusion faced by parents due to lack of income and other material assets.

In the context that several households are under the weight of severe economic constraints, greatly undermining their role in school participation, many scholars view the strengthening of school supply factors as most crucial that can positively impact on capacitating both parents and children in school participation. This leads to the more crucial issue, i.e., making basic education functioning for the system to deliver. Hence, a more meaningful debate could be on those issues of rights, obligations and duties of the state. Constraints due to poverty of children in school participation can be drastically alleviated by appropriate intervention, most notably by improving the provision of basic education facility that addresses the aspect of quality schooling. This remains crucial since learning capacity of these children takes place primarily in the school setting.

Accountability remains uncompromising number one factor that can effectively address quality of school education. Unfortunately, the sample school hardly meets the basic requirements of what constitutes quality aspects of school, if the physical aspects, ancillary facilities and teaching learning aids are taken into consideration. The dilapidated, school building, scarcity of textbooks and stationaries, extreme shortage of teaching/learning material aids of all kinds, and worst, is the non-functioning of basic convenience facilities such as the dysfunction of school toilet and non-availability of drinking water facility, collectively demonstrate the extent of impoverishment of the sample school. This further demonstrates that state schools persistently fail children in poverty, by experiencing a pattern of persistent deprivation in the quality of teaching/learning and depth of learning opportunities. This convincingly suggests reasons as to why children in the sample school who have completed basic education and who are currently at the stage of elementary education, have not been able to attain minimum level of functional literacy.

The extent of deterioration of teaching/learning standards in the sample school has gone far beyond what can be explained. Most children, who were interacted with, were inarticulate and lacked skills for comprehension. Hence, interaction was found to be tough, since most students were holding back, remained introvert while some looked on almost blank. Each student needed to be monitored individually so that some meaningful information could be sought from them. At the interval, the majority of the children looked up, completely blank, and needed to be monitored repeatedly with dogged patience. Even for the simplest and uncomplicated question, they were needed to be explained repeatedly, then, only could one gather some meaningful information from them. The process was assisted by the cook, since she was the last person who usually stays back in the school till the last hour. From the experience of interacting with the children who are studying in class VII and VIII, it is revealed that even the minimum level of learning has not been achieved, which should have been at the stage of the completion of class V. The more pernicious burden is that of non-comprehension. This may discourage children from attending school regularly. Irregular attendance, repetition and dropping out of school are a huge waste of resources, since the school is run through public funding and the children attending the school are also from poor background.

The foregoing discourse reveals that the sample school largely reflects the general failure of the state to deliver with startlingly naïve vision about the educational effects of this kind on the lives of those students who had experienced such form of schooling. Hopes and aspirations of these students to become a person of stature in their lives are crushed down during their early childhood period. They strongly feel that they have been treated unfairly and had suffered enough while they were in school. And, without suffering, there is no compassion. Their efforts of attempting to bring education reforms in the state is a sure sign that they are genuinely empathetic with children studying in government schools. A simple example will lend support to this argument. DESAM is a recently formed student organisation. Almost all the members of DESAM are government pass out students who are presently spearheading reforms in school education in the state of Manipur. Members of DESAM regularly check school registers to keep a track of absentee teachers, punish them after warning, and visit private schools suggesting them to maintain teacher-pupil ratio at 1:50. DESAM is also involved in transferring teachers to far off places in case a teacher consistently avoids their warning about regular absence from school duty. They are also involved in curriculum preparation by obtaining suggestions from serving teachers. Yet, DESAM is not in the good books of the public, since it is accused of being linked with an insurgent outfit, KYKL (though it strongly denies it), actively operating in Manipur. It however reveals that with lack of governance, there exists considerable vacuum which is being filled in by insurgents and earn goodwill from the general public. This experience is just one of the miniscule incidents, sharing how members of DESAM with support from KYKL actively intervene in school education to set the education trend right on tract.

Large-scale graft by politicians and high officials, which is spread downward to petty bribery, is a normal practice. It is strongly condemned by the general population but seems to be passively pardoned by the judiciary as the present judicial system in the state is infested with a high number of cases related to insurgency, arbitrary killings, kidnappings, arrests, leave alone looking into the development of educational entitlement for children. Corruption in the state is so deeply entrenched, to the extent that it is accepted as a rational way of unavoidable functioning as a social fact. Tarapot (2005) describes political masters in Manipur as utterly selfish, opportunists and self-centred, who are hopelessly corrupt, parochial and shortsighted with no principle or ideology but do whatever is possible to grab power and enjoy unbridled power continuously. Corruption and injustice that are interlocking constitute a twin set of values that systematically and criminally neglect quality education, because of which educational right of children in the state remains a remote prospect. This argument can be bolstered by ample evidences that are cited by both teachers and parents. Startling evidence is, distribution of dry rations to schools is almost crippled in the state since grains were reportedly transported to individual private homes of high ranking officials. Similar form of corruption also takes place in case of purchase of other necessary items such as school furniture, games, sports and siphoning of school developmental funds, etc. In the process the crucial issue of quality education is pushed in the backburner, while it should be the number one issue that could hold the future of poor school children in good stead.

Therefore, from all these aspects, unless the widespread corruption, playing the role of oxygen for black money in the state, is seriously addressed, its damaging consequences on children, particularly those of poor families and the society as a whole, are irreversible. When accountability fails, school children of poor households are the hardest hit since such action, by stripping of reasonable school facilities, denies them even the very limited options that are there for their social mobility through schooling. This also defeats the hopes and dreams of parents and eventually children themselves, who regard schooling as a key to higher income and status which is particularly crucial, for social mobility may mean difference between lifelong entrapment in poverty and decent living. If not immediately associated with status and income, an important reality is that exposure to qualitatively better school facility can have other psychological effects too on an individual student who delightfully shares about his/her day-to-day exciting school experience with his/her immediate society such as extended families, friends, neighbourhoods, etc.

School Children in the Crossfire and Violence

As discussed in the previous chapter, the present Manipur society is living in a nightmarish situation. School education is caught up like a cobweb in every social eventuality, at any given point of time in the state. Putting these issues into perspective, the main approach here is to examine what kind of impact conflict and violence has produced on the school education.

The school teachers unanimously agreed with the virtual seizure of regular attendance of children and normal school functioning by violent conflicts and other forms of trafficking such as *bandhs*, general strikes, economic blockade, etc., in the state. They were conversed with the issues of conflicts and violence as indicated below in Table 5.4.

Table 5.4 *Teachers' Opinion on the Impact of Violence on School Education*

It demoralises both the teachers and the taught	Yes
It undermines regular functioning of schools	Yes
School remains closed when violence occurs in the region	Yes
School infrastructure is destroyed	No
It affects transport and communication system	Yes
It creates a sense of insecurity among children	Yes
It forces young children to protest in streets	Yes
It creates psychological stress among children	Yes
It affects the general academic performance of children	Yes
Parents are apprehensive of sending their children to school	Yes

Source: Primary Survey, 2009.

Conflicts and violence ranging from ethnic clash, economic blockade, closure of National Highway 39, bloody killings, disappearance of individuals, general strikes, *bandhs*, to counterinsurgency movements by armed forces, critically sabotage school education in a variety of ways, as highlighted in Table 5.4. School teachers unanimously agree with how violence and conflicts can be highly disruptive for school community. When violence occurs, children have to naturally stop coming to school, experiencing a typical situation of education emergencies. Violence affects all those participants in school processes – the teachers, the students and the parents.

Violence is a big threat to anybody's life but young children are most vulnerable physically and psychologically. Most horrifying experience is, when children, on their way to school or back to home, encounter violence either in the form of gunshots or bloody killings or the sight of armed commandos or army personnel chasing suspected youths to be insurgents. If children compulsorily travel a distance of more than 1 km and the particular roadways the child is passing through, it becomes a matter of security concern by parents. Educational emergency destabilises regular school activity and is most damaging for children coming from poor households in unique ways. Firstly, when school is perhaps the only hope for the child to pick up certain skills of learning, its closure crashes this hope. Secondly, since the child is temporarily withheld from learning taking place, it becomes difficult for him/her to pick up afresh when he/she joins school after a time gap. It also becomes rather difficult and challenging task for teachers.

Sharing her experience, a female teacher, who is teaching English for class V, thus voiced out as commonly experienced by her other colleagues:

> During strikes and blockades, particularly *bandhs* imposed by factional organisations,[10] we obey their order, naturally, school is closed. We can defy government order but not the order of insurgent outfit or else we risk our lives. Such *bandhs* go on indefinitely for days together. Our children are worst affected. What they learn in school is the ultimate, since there is no academic help available at home. We, teachers have to try our best to revise in a manner they understand what they are taught earlier. The situation throws us in difficult circumstances both for teachers and students alike, since examination is always fixed on time and we've to complete our prescribed course.

Citing the most common form of trafficking in the state, the teacher who teaches Manipuri literature lamented:

> *Bandhs* are the most frequently observed form of trafficking for all of us. Observing *bandhs* can cause inconvenience for all. During *bandhs*, all important roads are blocked due to which offices and schools are closed. These cause major irritants and frustrations among general population. Another great obstacle faced by students hailing from far off places, mostly from Waraoiching hill area, is that they commute by Tata vehicles while coming to

> school. But suddenly when *bandh* is imposed, these students use bicycles arranged by teachers.

These reflect not only disturbances, frustrations but also concerns on the violent moments experienced by the teacher community. School closure, when it becomes a periodical experience, demoralises both the teachers and the students by obstructing regular, normal dialogical process and shared understanding that is cultivated over a period of time between them. *Bandhs* and strikes are symbolic to the state of Manipur and the education system gets jeopardised during such seizure of social life. *Bandhs*, strikes and economic blockades have become the most common form of protest to alarm the government. In the process, children are forced to reckon with an education emergency, which neither the state nor the civil society has attempted to address so far.

Academic loss for the students caused by violence in school operation is irreversible as lamented by the teacher community unanimously. Added to this, is the number of holidays observed by school as part of state holidays. State holidays cut down the number of days of regular functioning of school. In the academic session of 2008, for example, the school was closed for about 139 days including Sundays and holidays for harvesting, summer vacation and *yaosang*, Holi (festival of colour). Occasional *bandhs*, strikes and blockades accounted roughly for 28 days and permitted leave for teachers account for around 20 days. Another 25 days were spared for non-teaching duties at least for 2–3 teachers. As the head teacher of the school recollected:

> At a time when teachers are hard pressed to complete the syllabus, at least three teachers are compulsorily given non-academic duty for election duty which coincides in November–December months; any teacher is picked for the duty, this is most unfortunate, since final examinations for children start on the first of December every year.

The head teacher continued to lament,

> Engaging teachers for non-academic purpose has been in practice for the past twenty years and that too during the most crucial period when children require special attention. In addition, for every five years, our teachers are employed for non-teaching duty such as census; for about twenty days, at least three teachers under SSA were placed on duty to conduct survey on households

to find out the educational status of children which started in the year 2005–06 as per the directions of SSA authorities.

Therefore, the number of days the school actually works in a year is reduced to about 65–70 days. Secondly, on each of the working days, a teacher is supposed to spend about six to seven hours so long as the school timing is concerned. But arriving late and leaving early could be noticed. However, casual absenteeism, which is most common in government schools, was not noticed among teachers in the sample school. In fact, few teachers' sincerity and dedication to improving the state of the school has stood in good stead for the school and the children.

The emerging accounts from the present chapter indicate that there is a complete loss of political, bureaucratic and social will to repair the deteriorating government schools. In the state, equal educational participation and expansion of educational opportunities of government school children are critically constrained due to loss of right kind of vision for education, widespread corruption, insurgent violence, ethnic conflict, armed emergencies, etc. The existence of dysfunctional government schools, by default, remains justified so long as its pathology is internalised by government school children whose future prospects disappear in the void. This has, in turn, forcibly legitimised the status quo of highly fragmented disparity, discontent and disempowerment of these children. The prospect of educational right for these children continues to be elusive.

Notes

1. The Junior High School popularly known as Phoijing No. 6 school was established as boys' school in the year 1898 by the colonial government. It was first established as Phoijing Lower Primary school. At present, the school provides co-education starting from class I to class VIII.
2. The scheme of OB was launched in the year 1987 in pursuance of National Policy on Education, 1986 and Programme of Action, 1992 to provide minimum essential facilities to all primary schools in the country. These essential facilities include, at least one room for each class/section, a Head Master/Mistress cum-office room, separate toilet facilities for boys and girls, essential teaching-learning materials including a library, good working usable blackboards, maps, charts, toys, games and some equipment for work experience, one teacher for each class, contingency for minor/major repairs, etc. (Programme of Action, 1992, MHRD, Government of India, New Delhi).

3. In 1995, the United Front Government launched the centrally-sponsored scheme, the National Programme of National Support to Primary Education. The programme is specifically designed for children coming from economically poor households. Under the programme, cooked mid-day meals were to be introduced in all government and government aided primary schools within two years. In the intervening period of two years, state governments were allowed to distribute monthly grain rations to school children instead of cooked meal (Goyal and Dreze, 2003).
4. After successive education projects have been proved to be a failure in achieving Universal Education for All, the Government of India introduced the latest and the largest Education Project, SSA. The project was developed in conformity with the policy outlines of achieving Education for All by building partnership with state governments with a long-term perspective on cost sharing, with the aim to universalise elementary education by 2010. Assistance under SSA is on a 85:15 sharing arrangement between the central and state on its initial stage of IX plan, followed by 75:25 and 50:50 in the following plans (Sarva Shiksha Abhiyan, Manual for Appraisal of Plans, 2002, MHRD, Government of India, New Delhi). However, going by the nature of provisioning of schools in the state of Manipur, there is widespread disillusionment concerning the possibilities of achieving EFA within the stipulated period.
5. Even after six years, state governments failed to provide cooked meal and it was only after the intervention of the Supreme Court, in November 2001, that all state governments introduced cooked meal in primary schools within six month's time (Goyal and Dreze, 2003). However, some states complied, while some others have not. As there was so much corruption among politicians and the officials during the distribution of dry rations in the state of Manipur, the state has finally succumbed to the Supreme Court Order of 28 November 2001 and the programme was finally started during 2004 when SSA was launched in half haphazard manner.
6. When policy measures have been instituted, specifically aiming at ameliorating conditions for the lower strata, they have either not been implemented and enforced or have been distorted so as to favour the not-so-poor and to discriminate against the masses (Myrdal, 1970).
7. Concept of equality of educational opportunity, though a powerful one (if achieved, can act as a great equalizer), is a complex issue, particularly for a society where stratification based on various factors is high and rigid and when the state claims to be a welfare one, such as the case of India. In a debate revolving around justice as an integral part of welfare state, Gewirtz quotes Kathleen Lynch who asserts that equality of opportunity is viewed as being dependent upon the existence of equal formal rights, equality of access and equality of participation to ensure equal

rates of success for all groups of society through state intervention to prevent disadvantage. But the fundamental problems inherent in welfare state are the question of hierarchies of power, wealth and other privileges. Although a welfare state is a comprehensive set of institutional arrangement, such an arrangement is manned by social actors inescapable of attitudes, biases, prejudices and actors, and hence, the failure to realise equality of educational opportunity.

8. Most of the works of the sociology of education in the 1950s was concerned with the question of equality of educational opportunity within the framework of the structural-functional approach. The horizon, however, came to a rapid expansion with the accompanying of organisation theory, role theory, symbolic inter-actionism, phenomenology, etc.
9. Concept of Progressive Education and its application to school education is of extreme significance in making teaching/learning in classroom a meaningful and joyful learning experience. The process has powerful impact on young children since the main orientation of the curriculum in progressive education is focused on the needs and interest of the child, providing ample opportunities for children to choose activities and develop at their individual pace.
10. In Manipur when *bandhs* and strikes are imposed by insurgent organisations, it is bound to be compulsorily obeyed by the people since non-compliance to their order will necessarily invite trouble and threat to life. No one is held accountable in the court of law when insurgents take away one's life on flimsy grounds. This is precisely the reason why the lady teacher prefers to defy the legitimate order of the government but to obey the order of the insurgents.

CHAPTER 6

Civil Society Interventions

As argued in the introductory chapter, the emergence of various civil society movements in the education sector in Manipur is directly linked to the failure of the state in responding to the educational needs of children, particularly those belonging to poor, rural households. In Manipur it is common for communities to contribute to school education in terms of material, moral and human resources. Yet, these resources probably would be mobilised only when a number of individuals with a clear vision and passion, who volunteer to take up the challenge of providing schooling facilities to children at risk of exclusion due to the perpetual negligence of the state, would come forward. The aspirations of these leaders are mobilised with the support and solidarity of other like-minded individuals and social groups, including those based on kinship and lineage ties. Yet, the goals of civil society are self-limiting and are not accessible by all children in the light of various constraints and limitations. There is, therefore, every possibility that civil society movements will shift their interests and visions over time. The present chapter addresses some of these issues.

The legitimate and successful existence of these civil society sector depends on the acceptance of those whose interests are served. In this way, the educational project – curriculum, pedagogy, school environment, discipline and accountability of school authorities – must be pursued by private institutions to attract parents whose interests are similar. In the light of this observation, this chapter explores the role of such civil society institutions by examining the educational contributions made by Don Bosco, Bosco Mangaal and Bethel school. The success story of Don Bosco demonstrates the mutual articulation and consistency between physical and human dimensions of school resources. The case of Bosco Mangaal illustrates how the teaching/learning of children, when organically linked to their own community, can be most successful despite extreme resource constraints, such as the physical setting of learning environment. The study of Bosco Mangaal also highlights the significance of the joyous teaching/learning methods experienced by children and how such forms of pedagogy can be truly empowering for marginalised children residing in far-flung, scattered villages. Whereas the study on Bethel school mainly focuses on its humble journey of becoming a successful school. Various similarities can be observed between Bethel school and Don Bosco in terms of discipline, good feel factor of school environment, accountability, autonomy, etc. The success journey of each of these schools is indeed enriching and provides significant insights regarding civil society's role in the field of education in the state.

The Arrival of Missionaries in Manipur

Frederick S. Downs (1992) notes that the Treaty of Yandabo,[1] between the kingdom of Burma and the English East India Company on 24 February 1826, first linked the north-eastern region with the British India in a political sense. The history of the Christian missionaries' movement to northeast India was seen as an integral part of a larger process of political change. The Treaty of Yandaboo forced the Burmese to withdraw from Assam and Manipur and British sovereignty was subsequently established there. The initial British policy was to stabilise the buffer zone by installing rajas in the major kingdoms of Manipur, Cachar and the upper parts of Assam. Wherever the British administration found it difficult to rule, a policy of direct administration and economic exploitation of the Assamese plains was adopted within twelve years of the advent of British rule. In this process, various kingdoms of the north-eastern region were gradually annexed.

Still, the British kingdom found it difficult to control the warfare tribes, inter-tribal conflicts, inter-village feuds and conflicts arising out of British interference in tribal customary practices, such as head hunting and human sacrifice. Conflict also arose due to the forced collection of revenue by the government, the requisition of forced labour and the prevention of tribes from raiding the villages in the plains (ibid.). Finally, the warfare tribes were successfully subdued through direct and minimal administration. The policy of pacification at minimum cost to British government influenced the activities of Christian missionaries in the hill areas of the north-east. Downs quotes S.P. Sinha, who referred to missionary activity as an endeavour not designed to advocate faith, but for keeping imperialism alive. Sinha penned the often quoted statement: 'First comes the missionary, then comes the Resident, lastly the Regiment', implying common objectives between the missionaries and the colonial power (ibid.: 30).

The missionaries and the colonial government were thus mutually beneficial, in that, the government found the missionaries helpful in pacifying the hill tribes and providing education at minimal cost, while the missions found the government useful in underwriting their educational work and in providing security for both themselves and their converts. A similar observation was endorsed by Lal Dena, who undertook pioneering work in the field. Lal Dena argues, while the British officials looked at the introduction of western education as legitimising colonial rule, the missionaries used it as a vehicle for communicating with the natives. However, as Downs argues, the colonial government was more useful to the missions than vice versa, after the pacification of the tribes, the missionary education system was simply a convenient and cheap way of rendering a service that would otherwise have been the responsibility of the colonial government.

In *Christian Missions and Colonialism* (1988), Lal Dena argues that, at the core of the missionaries activities, evangelism seems to have been the primary objective but educational aims were also served, since reading the Bible was seen as a necessary precursor to worshipping God. This is how education and evangelism remained intertwined, and, hence, educational programme were seen as supplementary to the primary task of communicating the gospel to the people. This was further facilitated when the colonial government gave the missionaries additional responsibility for official duties in those regions where the missionaries had easy access for establishing schools and churches. For instance, Pettigrew's appointment as the census officer in the period 1910–11 enhanced his knowledge about many hill areas of Manipur, where he could open new schools. The missionaries and the colonialists were mutually beneficial to one another. Therefore, while the British looked at the introduction of western education as legitimising the process of colonial rule, the missionaries used it as a vehicle for communicating with the natives. Lal Dena (ibid.) notes that the mutual relationship between the missionaries and the colonial power arose out of conditional necessity rather than ideological confluence.

Americans and Welshmen were prominent among the Protestant missionaries, and German, Spaniards and Italians among the Catholics. Though it was the Serampore missionaries who had initial interest in the north-east, it was the American Baptists, who became deeply involved in Manipur. The missionaries' attempt to establish their influence in the state dates back to 1836, when the American Baptist Mission expressed its willingness to work in Manipur, when it was still a princely state. The strong opposition from the local Vaishnavite Hindus resulted in the postponement of the missionaries' entry into the state.

However, it was in the 1890s, when the colonial state had firmly established its power in Manipur by dethroning the then king, Surchandra Singh, that encouragement was extended to missionaries who showed a willingness to work in the state. The first missionary to Manipur was William Pettigrew, a member of the Arthingthon Aboriginese Mission Society, who reached Imphal in 1894 with the easy permission of the acting political agent, Major Maxwell. Pettigrew, being well versed with Meiteilon, opened a school at Imphal in the same year.

In an attempt to speed up his educational activities, Pettigrew compiled a Manipuri dictionary, an English-Bengali-Manipuri dictionary and a book of Manipuri grammar. Within a year, his school surpassed other educational institutions established by the British. An Annual Report on State Education from 1991 notes that his educational activities were extremely vast, which satisfied the British officials and the people at large. He was appointed as an honorary inspector of schools under the Education Department of Assam, though he was strictly prohibited from giving Christian instruction to the valley of the state. Thus, despite his interest of working among the Hindu Meiteis, Pettigrew was not allowed to teach Christianity in the schools of the valley. The policy of non-interference in the native's religious matters was a follow up to the precautionary measures adopted by the British towards the princely states, after the famous Sepoy Mutiny of 1857. Pettigrew was, therefore, directed to serve among the hill tribes, who were animists, and finally settled in Ukhrul, a Tangkhul Naga area.

By the end of the 19th century and in the aftermath of India's independence, when Christianity had gained a foothold in most areas of the north-east, the government took direct responsibility for education throughout the north-east. The practice of using Protestant missions for educational purpose came to an end, while at the same time, the Catholics began to establish an extensive network of schools. In the hills, Christian educational activity was much more extensive and carried a much greater impact, mainly due to the tribes unsophisticated background, with no literary tradition, as argued by Downs. Although the hills formed the main loci of missionary education, over time, missionary-run schools began to spread far and wide in various parts of Manipur as the people of Manipur steadily began to accept English education. The slow and steady acceptance of western education by the locals of the Third World countries was seen as an inevitable natural process. Pink and Noblit (1995) argue that, in developing countries, where the provision of education is executed by private entities (usually religious bodies), such bodies are more likely to act according to their own ideological mandates, making the guidelines provided by the state a secondary priority. The steady penetration of English education executed by Christian organisations in the state of Manipur was one such experience.

Don Bosco School

Don Bosco is the name of a holy priest of Turin. Don Bosco School, presently located at Chingmeirong, Imphal east, was earlier known as Don Bosco Youth Centre. The centre was opened in the year 1957. The school is located one and half kilometres south from the Zero Mile at Kangla, Imphal. The school was built by Salesian Fathers of Catholic origin. Fr. Aloysius Ravalico and Fr. Peter Bianchi are credited for establishing the school. They acquired the present site of Don Bosco, which was a low, marshy area, full of mosquitoes and frogs and was, in fact, considered a haunted place. The locals considered it to be the abode of evil spirits. The centre began with an unfinished residential building, where fifty male students of different tribes stayed. It was initially considered a tribal school, since the local Hindu population was not friendly with the missionaries, to whom they referred to as *mayangs,* while they referred to the tribal students as *hao machasing,* a name considered derogatory by the tribes. Occasionally, the local Hindu population disturbed them by pelting stones at their residences. In 1958, the centre provided facilities for classes up to IV level. The number of students kept increasing and there were about 200 boarders at this time. Most of the students were charged nominal fees or almost nothing. Interestingly, Fr. Ravalico, the head teacher, would give the students money for their journey to home and school during holidays as a form of encouragement to get them back to the boarding school.

Don Bosco School has a reputation of being a 'very good' school and is well established. It is indeed one of the most reputed and oldest Catholic missionary schools in Manipur. It is a three-storey building, with a residential complex located opposite the school building, separated by the main road. The premises of the school consist of four acres of land providing sufficient space for the children. The school has a cemented boundary wall across the building, with a huge iron wall, used as the main door to the entry of the school building. Almost 20 metres north from the middle of the school building, there is a well, where clean drinking water is stored. There are also 10 toilet facilities, all attached to the school building towards the end of the northernmost corner of the building, a little away from the classrooms.

The school is not only owned but also managed and controlled by the Selesian Fathers. It has a total strength of 33 teaching and two non-teaching staff. Of the total teaching staff, almost half are women. There are 15 female teachers, a number only marginally lower than their male counterparts, who are 17 in number. The teachers belong to different social categories, with Scheduled Tribes (STs) being five in number, along with one Anglo-Indian, while the rest are Meitei Hindus, who are from general category. There is a huge, separate room for the staff, with a sufficient number of tables, chairs, almirahs and shelves, with calendars and pictures hung on the wall. A white board is fixed at the centre of the staff room, to be used during teachers' discussions, workshops and meetings. The room is well lit, with sufficient ventilation from large, iron windows. Separate toilet facilities for female and male staff members are attached to the northern end of the staff room.

The head teacher's room is on the ground floor. Though separated, it is located right in front of the teachers' common room, near the stair case right at the middle of the entry of the school building, so that he can conveniently watch out for any happenings in the school from the centre. The head teacher's room is well lit. In his room, there is one main table with two subsidiary tables and seven chairs. There are three iron almirahs containing books, one shelf, a calendar, medals, globes, charts and pictures of famous personalities, such as Jawaharlal Nehru and Mahatma Gandhi, along with a calendar of the Virgin Mary. There is also a telephone connection, a wall clock, a dustbin and a blackboard, used as the notice board, in the head teacher's room.

The school has classes from grade I to X. There are 23 classrooms altogether: eight small-sized classrooms on the second floor, eight large classrooms on the first floor and seven large classrooms on the first floor. The floors and walls of the classrooms are well-built. The walls are neatly painted in a faded green colour and there are interesting pictures hung upon them. There is an electricity connection and one ceiling fan in each classroom, though the fan is not required very often, since the weather in the state is quite pleasant, even during summer. There is one table and chair made of iron in each classroom. Classrooms are well ventilated and large enough to accommodate sixty to seventy students. Not only that, the school has various physical resources, which are efficiently utilised. Basic teaching aids, such as globes, charts, maps, demonstrative materials, science kits, mathematic kits and audio-visual aids are not only available but regularly utilised in classroom teaching as and when required. There is one library, where books, newspapers, journals, etc., are available. Desks and benches are made of iron, painted in a light blue colour, while tables and chairs are made of wood, also painted in a light blue colour to protect from termites and general wear and tear. The school uses white boards for regular teaching purpose in the classroom.

There are pictures and writings about discipline and moral science hanging on the walls of almost every corner of the stair case leading to the first and second floors of the building. These writings and pictures are highlighted in bright colours to capture the attention of the students. The displays designed to discipline and sensitise the students regarding habits of cleanliness, punctuality, important announcements and the latest important news on events in the school. Thus, the school manages to create some kind of learning environment with whatever resources they have available to them.

Preparing for the Incalculable: The Youth Through Education

A crucial element in the modus operandi of the teaching system in Don Bosco School is the central focus on the welfare of youth. The teachings of Don Bosco emphasise the importance of youth development as a matter of principle. To achieve this goal, the entire school community, including the director, the Board of Executives, the headmaster and the teaching staff make every possible effort, as well as encouraging the healthy cooperation from parents. The functioning of this school provides an excellent illustration of how the organic relationship between the physical and human dimensions of school resources can harness maximum growth in children. Teachers certainly care about the school because they believe that it is also their children's school. There are pressures from parents to maintain high quality standards along with traditional value systems within the school and teachers have responded well to this demand. Parents come forward to cooperate in achieving the same goal by concentrating on their children's efforts to achieve cognitive learning, which is often reflected in the most visible outcome – examination results.

The Teacher: Myriad Journey of Dedication

The teachers were found diligent, knowledgeable, prudent and accountable. They consider themselves to be serious professionals. They were quite pleasant to interact with and intellectually stimulating too. Intense observation of the teachers in the school provides one with an insight to a teacher's vocation. They were always busy due to a myriad of tasks, particularly in the case of the head teacher, who has been working in the school for the past 20 years and is, therefore, quite an experienced teacher. His task begins before teachers and students enter the school and lasts long after the class hours are over, until the late afternoon, when the final bell has rung and the school caretaker attempts to repair the havoc that hundreds of walking, running and skipping feet have wrought in corridors, classrooms and staircases. Perhaps the tasks are too great to capture its 'felt' reality.

Such a task is multifaceted, requiring considerable flexibility of mind, spirit and great insight on the part of the teacher's personality. It suggests that a school teacher is not just a teacher, who engages in a vocation of teaching *per se,* but one who engages in professional readings, lesson plans and preparation, occasional participation in teacher training courses, examining and assessing, maintaining discipline and order, imparting knowledge, administration, field trips with pupils, sports and games, organising extra classes for weak students and organising all kinds of activities for the holistic development of their students. In the school, it was found that, even during holidays, teachers were assigned responsibilities around the clock for student welfare (e.g., providing free teaching for weak students of class X, who were appearing for the High School Certificate Examination conducted by the Manipur Board of Education). The Salesian Fathers assigned such duties even during unsociable hours and all teachers complied as a matter of duty and principle. In all these situations, the head teacher is careful to create conducive conditions for teachers to help remain spirited and acknowledges their efforts and innovative suggestions. No teacher seems to have major grievance about any extra responsibility shouldered on to them on top of their usual workload.

What is truly remarkable and inspiring about the teachers of the school is their commitment to their duties, which can perhaps be traced to the autonomy and accountability of the school's organisational structure, directed by the Salesian Fathers. This best illustrates that the functioning of the sample school is free from the myriad of bureaucratic problems that beset government schools, which allows the teachers to accomplish their goals with minimum interference and misuse of school resources. The school finds itself in a favourable environment that can insulate the system from bureaucratic interference, allowing it to establish and accomplish its goals. By adopting its own internal mechanisms, the school establishes their own goals. The inward focus encourages greater goal clarity and consensus. Not a single teacher was found involved in government activities outside school, such as assignment for surveys, election duty, census collection or any other such assignment, which are common occurrences among government school teachers.

Thus, unlike the various layers of administration controlling government schools, more often than not, the responsibilities lie in the hands of the school head teacher, often in consultation with the Fathers, who are readily available. The head teacher is not only an instructional leader but also plays a watchdog role. When asked about the inspection system in the school, the head teacher firmly responded:

> We don't have an inspection system. I myself monitor regularly; I sit in classrooms like a student to observe how teachers are teaching. I also check student class notes. I walk around the school verandah to watch out what's happening in classroom teaching. There is constant watch while teachers are teaching and interacting with the students in the class. Not only that, it is my responsibility to examine lesson plans and it is mandatory that all teachers submit their lesson plans before hand. We aren't a part of any Teachers' Association. We don't invite outside agencies because we are under Selesian missionaries. So, we have our own internal system of management; every now and then, we interact

> with the Fathers to discuss school-related issues. We get our things done in our own ways, without any help from government, since we don't want any interference from them.

The absolute autonomy in school organisation was also observed in other spheres, such as the recruitment process for teachers, training of teachers, orientation courses, curriculum formation, etc. For example, unlike in government schools, the recruitment of the headmaster and his induction in the sample school was done by the Board of Executives of Selesian Fathers. The appointment of the rest of the teachers was done through written tests, viva, interviews and demonstration methods of teaching in classroom. The selection process was rigorous and tough, as narrated by teacher themselves. For instance, the teacher who is presently teaching English literature, recollected:

> While recruiting for my job, there were more than sixty candidates who applied for two posts. Ten candidates were selected through demonstration methods in classroom teaching and then three candidates were called for interview. Finally, two of us were selected. The entire process was tough and done through a series of filtration.

Similar norms are followed in the selection process of other disciplines as well. A teacher who is teaching Manipuri literature shared delightfully, 'There were thirty candidates for the post I am teaching at present, but only one candidate was selected to teach Manipuri literature'. The same recruitment rules apply for other posts, such as in the disciplines of Mathematics, History, Geography, etc. While sharing their circumstances, teachers honestly admitted:

> My life started with struggles. As a child, I faced grinding poverty; we are ten siblings. My father was a driver and my mother was a weaver, but we couldn't afford much. With so many struggles, gradually, I completed my Master's degree. This was the time when I started thinking seriously about helping and assisting young people by educating them. Ultimately, I took up teaching.
>
> I am a graduate in Social Science. I took up teaching as my profession because unemployment problems in the state are extremely acute and I needed an income, I joined teaching due to financial strains in the family, but now, I've developed a sense of passion for teaching young students. Today, I am a dedicated teacher.

> By circumstance of family poverty, I took up teaching job; but now, I am willing to take it as a profession. I honestly like the idea that I am guiding my young students.
>
> I am a postgraduate in English literature. Since my childhood days, I used to dream of teaching and becoming a teacher. On the financial side too, I had no alternative. I took up teaching both by choice and compulsion, since other options are also quite constrained. Nowadays attempting to get a government job is just like chasing a wild goose.

The salary paid to the teachers ranges from ₹ 3,450 to ₹ 4,393 per month, which is quite low compared with their counterparts teaching in government schools. Teachers unanimously agree that the salary paid to them is much below their contribution and the amount is extremely marginal when compared to government teachers. Despite such a low salary, there is huge competition for getting a teaching job, which is also indicative of the critical situation of unemployment problems in the state. This was commonly lamented by all teachers, while citing reasons for taking up teaching as a profession.

As such, reasons for joining the profession of teaching cannot be divorced from the acute situation of unemployment in the state. Despite the fact that the teaching profession was not the first choice for some of these teachers, once inducted in the profession, either by compulsion or choice, they were found to naturally cultivate a sense of satisfaction and commitment to the vocation of teaching. For example, a teacher who has been teaching Mathematics and Science, claimed:

> Truly speaking, we can mould children in any shape; they are just like clay. We can impart them with true knowledge and this is possible through teaching – it is a great opportunity. Children are the pillars of a nation; it is most important to build children, rather than building concrete buildings.

Emphasising the role of formal schooling, he further added, 'Building children in this manner is not possible through any other means, say media or other institution'. Just like the concept, *Tabula Rasa,* first introduced by John Locke in 1693, when he compared a child's mind to a completely blank piece of slate, on which adults provide information. In this way, teachers are looked upon as key player in the nurturing of a child into a pupil who comes to school to acquire certain skills and knowledge. School teachers are very pleased with the idea that it is in their hands to cradle a child. A child is a person who is endowed with certain inherent qualities, which he develops in conformity with his environment.

It can rightly be argued that all teachers are recruited by virtue of being meritorious in their own disciplines and for possessing teaching skills as well. They enjoy permanent position in their jobs and receive their salary on time, i.e., on 1st or 3rd of every month. All were given the opportunity to attend orientation and teacher training programmes, organised occasionally by Manipur Board in Manipur, Selesian Fathers at Guwahati and sometimes in collaboration with other corporate sectors. The content of training programmes was mostly oriented towards progressive pedagogy in classroom teaching, after which the teachers effectively utilised their new skills in classroom teaching and interaction with students.

When asked about the training programmes and their usefulness, all teachers agreed about its benefits. Thus, quoting a teacher who stated:

> Yes, I've attended many educational seminars/workshops/ training programmes under Manipur Board and, sometimes, the ones organised by Fathers. I attended an orientation programme on methods of teaching, how to make lesson plans, how to guide students and how to punish naughty students. There were also courses on how to make questions. There were trainers for different disciplines. For example, I teach Poems and Poetry; these disciplines are under Manipur Board. Most of these trainers are lecturers and professors. I believe this is the same for other disciplines as well. In a year, three days are held for training programmes, for a period of six hours.

However, despite such usefulness, the course was not without its deficiency, as the teacher further pointed out:

> Time was short; the course could have lasted eight months, but it was completed in three days. It is not fully satisfactory because there is only one trainer for forty trainees and so they are overcrowded, but I can say there is at least 80 per cent benefit. Teachers from surrounding schools also joined the courses and we were assigned an activity to test our understanding of the course taught to us; but at times we don't get head or tail of the course due to shortage of time period.

However, for some, teacher training was purely on progressive pedagogy, where teaching orientation attempts to focus on the practical areas of students' lives. A teacher who is teaching English literature shared:

> I've attended many seminars, one was held at Silchar in Assam from 1 July to 9 July 2006. This was a most exciting and enriching experience. The programme was organised by an insurance company and Christian missionaries, Don Bosco, Silchar. Two of us were sent for the training. The approach of the training was for not teacher-oriented or teacher-dominated, but how to draw constantly from the students' own experience, learning by doing, development of democratic attitudes and how to deal with weak and shy students. Sometimes in classroom interaction, when a student suffers from low self-esteem, while speaking or talking to the teacher, he or she is withdrawn. So, during the training, we are taught how to deal with students who are shy and withdrawn during classroom interaction. To deal with the situation, I was trained to place myself just at the level of the student by being in the students' position.

Pedagogy in and Outside the Classroom

Teaching methods in the sample school are, by and large, qualitatively different from those followed in government schools and other lesser-known private schools, though certain parameters remain similar, such as reciting numbers and memorising texts, as well as classroom and homework assignments. In the sample school, teachers closely monitor the students, pay close attention, and study the psychology of children in classroom interaction. A teacher who has been teaching English literature, shared his enriching experience:

> We make a point that our teaching methods are multifaceted to take care of children's psychological needs. If a student suffers from low self-esteem, he surely feels uncomfortable to look at the teacher and remains shy and withdrawn. Whenever we find a student in this position, we stoop down to the student's level for interaction. This gesture symbolises an equal or democratic relationship between the teacher and the student. We don't just have to think about completing the syllabus. Taking care of the psychological needs of our students is of utmost importance. In classroom interaction, disobedient and naughty students don't

> want to follow the instructions in the class, rather, they want to distract by not following the instructions. In that case, we adopt a different approach. Simple corporal punishment on a student does not work; it doesn't help. Here, maintaining eye contact with the students is very important. Sometimes, simply teaching in the classroom does not work. Then, we narrate stories about a particular event and make them understand about the particular episode. My teaching must arouse curiosity in children about learning to make it more enriching and exciting.

Thereafter, he narrated:

> If I am teaching poems to my student, I have to relate the insights, the history, and the background of the episodes of the poem.

Interestingly, he talked about one of his favourite poems 'The Charge of the Light Brigade' by Alfred Lord Tennyson. To make the poem interesting and enjoyable, he narrated about his truly enjoyable method of teaching:

> I have to be well informed and knowledgeable about the war fought between different nations; what type of war it was; incidents behind the war and its causes; why the war remains mortal; reasons that inspired the poet to make a tribute to those British soldiers and how each stanza yells a different part of the poem, with a delicate balance between celebration of nobility, brutality of war and heroic death.

Further, he continued:

> Even the rhythmic expressions while citing the poem make them completely involved. Then, last but not least, is to let children know that the poem is not merely the poet's ode to the brave six hundred soldiers of his native country but it holds profound historical truths about man, warfare, defeat and victory; a timeless living truth of our existence.

The teacher further highlighted the significance of demonstrating such historical events with the help a world map.

Apart from this, all teachers use teaching methods, such as textbook study, verbal instruction, white board, demonstration, field visits, briefings of the lesson and sometimes audio-visual methods when there is electricity. It is compulsory for all teachers to make a lesson plan and to share it with the head teacher, teachers committee and Catholic Fathers. Fathers verify the lesson plan and then return it to the concerned teacher.

The use of textbooks and verbal instruction in classroom interaction is also different from other schools, as the experience narrated by a history teacher reveals:

> While teaching history, I simply can't have knowledge of history alone; I must be equally aware of anthropology, or at least its fundamentals such as the different stages of culture, races of mankind, their geographical distribution, etc. Having knowledge is not sufficient; my attitude as a history teacher must be oriented in such a way that I am capable of maintaining an objective spirit. For example, while I am teaching about nationalism or religion, I can't be biased or dogmatic or fanatical. In the same way, I am a Christian, but I can't just emphasise Jesus as the most important historical figure. Rather, I equally highlight Akbar, Bir Tikendrajit or Hindu kings in equal measure as the heroes of history.

Audio-visual methods are also popular in classroom teaching. Highlighting the importance of this method, he shared:

> While teaching about the ancient civilisation of Egypt, I use a pyramid made of clay and ancient antiques for my students to observe during classroom teaching. A fairly large globe that is also used in class and a historical chart showing the rise and fall of dynasties is nailed to the wall for demonstration purposes, so that my students can easily recall what happened what, when and where. In this way, their learning lives in their mind very clearly.

Another teacher, who is currently teaching Manipuri literature, stated:

> I was teaching about culture and ideas of the 'modern' and 'traditional' the other day. I demonstrated the various shapes of houses, indicating both modern and traditional house types and shapes. The children found it very engaging. Children thoroughly enjoy such methods; their participation was amazing.

In *The Art of Loving,* Erich Fromm talks about the art of learning in two ways – the mastery of theory and the mastery of the practice of the said theory. He states, 'If I want to learn the art of medicine, I must first know the facts about the human body, and about various diseases. When I have all this theoretical knowledge, I am by no means competent in the art of medicine. I shall become a master in this art only after a great deal of practice, until eventually the results of my theoretical and the results of my practice are blended into one – my intuition, the essence of the mastery of any art' (1956: 5). Drawing inspiration from such methods, experience and field visits remain at the core of the teaching in the school. A geography teacher explained the importance of learning from exposure in the field. He narrated the delightful experience teaching children about a species of deer, known locally as *Sanghai:*

> As a part of an interesting exercise, I asked children to give a description of the animal, its habitation, surrounding environment, its culture, etc., and then I took them to see the deer for themselves.

Many teachers shared their belief that children learn better through seeing and observation. For this purpose, they are taken to interesting sites, such as the polo ground, the zoo, various museums, as well as Singda dam and historical places like the Khongjom War Memorial, the Indian National Army (INA) museum at Moirang and the Andro, Dzudko valley, etc.

The teacher further explained:

> When we teach children, sometimes we go beyond everything in geographical terms and knowledge. Dzuko valley, for example, is one of the most beautiful valleys and picturesque places in Senapati district. A few years before independence, it was an apple of discord between the two states of Nagaland and Manipur. So here we go back to history and learn about why it became a bone of contention and the events that took place there, because children's curiosity must be supported through facts and observation.

The opportunity for field study is, therefore, made available to all students. After their exposure to the field, students are asked to write reports and descriptions about what they saw and observed during such visits. As such, teachers make field learning a truly enriching and enlightening experience, by empowering young children to reflect about the real world and objects they constantly interact with. It empowers children to enter into the creative power of dialogue and clarification of vague ideas and knowledge that they previously held, after which children feel closely rooted to the very soul of the objects they are studying.

Interestingly, debates on the sociology of knowledge propound that the social origin of knowledge is related to the possibility of grasping truth. For example, Durkheim would argue that social knowledge is based on the observation of universal structures, which can be uncovered by scientific knowledge. His sociology of knowledge postulates that man's thought, such as his ways of conceiving space and time, for example, can be traced to his mode of social life. Durkheim discusses this in one of his most celebrated books, *The Elementary Forms of Religious Life* (1912). Referring to the religious organisation of the Australian Aborigines as a case study, Durkheim argues the basic mental categories by which we order the world are rooted in the way we organise society, i.e., the underlying social structures of society. Temporal divisions into days, weeks, months and years correspond to periodical recurrences and celebrations of life-cycle rituals, rites, feasts and various other ceremonies. A calendar expresses the rhythm of collective activities, while at the same time its function is to reassure their regularities (Coser, 2007: 140) and maintain social order. Durkheim's observation provides insights about specific systems of thought and systems of social organisation, but he remains vague on his epistemological proposition. For the Marxian tradition, the basis of truth is the content determined by material conditions, such as the economic position of the bourgeoisie and the proletariat in the capitalist mode of production. Marx was a witness to the wretched reality of the working class, with workers being trampled down by the ruling classes, causing streams of stormy upheavals in Europe, including France, more than anywhere else.

The scene was a ghostly spectre, which deeply inspired Marx to eventually challenge Hegel's teachings, the most dominant German philosophy of that time. Marx argues that the human mind and spirit must be derived from nature, i.e., the matter. Marx perceived that, just as material causes underlie all natural phenomenon, the development of human society is conditioned by the development of material forces or, in other words, the productive forces. Marx further argues, men naturally enter into a relationship with one another in the production process and it is in these relations that the explanation of all the phenomena of social life, human aspirations, ideas and laws, etc., can be found. As the development of productive forces grows phenomenally, it leads to the creation of a social relationship based upon private property (Marx and Engels, 1968: 17), by depriving the proletariats of their property and concentrating it in the hands of an insignificant minority – the bourgeoisie. The bourgeoisie's world view is oriented towards individualism, competition and survival of the fittest, while that of the proletariat is in opposition to this, stressing cooperative enterprise and mutual support. The bourgeoisie's main preoccupation remains with the development of material forces, the establishment of factories and industries and the development and expansion of markets, cities and roads for their own benefit, while the proletariat live in destitute circumstances. Marx thus takes this position – that the categories of class emerge from their own experience of the relationship entered into during the production process. Marx has, however, been challenged for apparently reducing knowledge to an ideology that is purely economic in nature, determined by materialism, which was indeed at the heart and soul of Marx's philosophy.

Karl Manheim's contribution was most influential in shaping the dominant tradition of the sociology of knowledge by proposing to replace all forms of knowledge with a direct grasp of living reality. He established the foundations of a more rigorous sociology of knowledge, as an analysis of how social groups construct systems of knowledge based on existential conditions, by rejecting phenomenologists' theory of an objective, absolute knowledge of values (Manheim, 1952: 8). Along similar lines, Michel Foucault suspects social scientists of not knowing what they are doing. Social scientists, he claims, suffer from self-deception because their methodologies purport to produce so-called objective knowledge about society. Manheim argues, all knowledge and ideas are bound to a location, though to different degrees, within the social structure and the historical process and, hence, human thought is perspectivistic, like the proverbial seven blind men trying to describe the properties of an elephant. It views that persons, viewing a common object from dissimilar angles of vision rooted in their different social locations, are apt to arrive at different cognitive conclusions and value judgements. Human thought is, thus, 'situationally relative' (Coser, 2007: 432). Manheim's discussion is favourably oriented towards historicism, with a tinge of sociological flavour. This is clear when, like his predecessors, he naively describes the types of relations between social structure and knowledge. Secondly, his historicism succeeds sociology of knowledge. In his discourse on sociology of knowledge, Manheim argues, the subject who knows history is the subject who participates in history; he is an active being, sharing in the dominant social aspiration of his epoch. There is an inner link between aspiration and knowledge. Historical knowledge is bound to a location within the historical process, the claim to 'self-evident' knowledge of 'absolute', proposed by the phenomenologists, is nothing but an illusion. In reality, there is nothing 'absolute' about such firmly held value positions: they too, merely reflect a 'standpoint' resulting from the interplay of historical, social forces (Manheim, 1952: 14).

The debates on the sociology of knowledge no doubt make relevant appearances in academic areas, such as the present case study. Returning to the study of Kangla, as also addressed in Chapter 3, Kangla symbolises many sacred meanings to the people of Manipur. Its study opens up the history of the social formation of its own society, a timeless living memorabilia in the hearts of the Manipuris. The history teacher thus shared his emotive reflections:

> It's important to make children aware about what Kangla symbolises; its occupation by the Assam Rifles is the very thing the Manipuris despise most strongly. People of Manipur, due to their continued protest to hand over Kangla to Manipur state and to restore its sanctity, finally freed Kangla from the security forces of the Assam Rifles. Kangla is a sacred zone, it can't be misused by profane forces.

Thereafter, in a thoughtful gesture, he continued:

> Almost 57 years down the line of history, Kangla was freed from the occupation only in 2004. I know why I choose to take children to such an important place like Kangla. It has been a part of our own life and history since time immemorial. with its ups and down in its making, its destruction and reconstruction. In ancient Manipur, Kangla was the capital of Manipur and it then became a palace and the most important abode of successive rulers in Manipur. Interestingly, it was also the ancient University of Manipur where the king permitted the Meitei Pundits to impart education to their subjects free of cost. For the Manipuris, it still remains a sacred place, where even rituals and prayers are performed to ward off calamities that had befallen the people Manipur. While walking around inside the Kangla Fort, children were exposed to the rich historical royal chronicles and archaeological sites, as well as the political, religious and holy symbols of Kangla, which successive invaders, including the British, failed to destroy with their mighty power. Within the Kangla, there are 360 important sacred places; the Kangla is the very soul of its people. We have a folklore explaining why Meiteis worship the snake, the symbol of Pakhangba, the Almighty from whom our ancestors are believed to have descended; our basic instinct is to kill the snake at its sight because it is dangerous. Yet, we offer prayer when a snake crosses us.

Each class teacher is responsible for taking children to field sites for the whole day. This form of pedagogy draws closer to Manheim's vision, when his sociology of knowledge suggests making education as relevant to the social environment as possible, since one must be prepared to live in that environment, so that one is not taken hostage by the storm of life (ibid.). Manheim's observation makes all the more sense when teacher themselves exercise a certain amount of autonomy in contributing to the making of the curriculum, as revealed in the sample school. All teachers were satisfied regarding curriculum content of different grades, since the official curriculum is made locally relevant.

Thereafter, the school head teacher added,

> Besides field education, every week, there is a counselling session for classes VII, VIII and IX. This provides better scope for parents, teachers and students to interact, and, most importantly, we teach practical moral science to our students up to class X, whereas it is taught only up to class IV in other private schools.

The dedication and commitment of the school to the cause of students' moral well-being is thus reflected in the pedagogic content of the practical moral science. The textbook on practical moral science is compiled by collecting accounts of true personal lived experiences of individuals that are brought out by local media time and again. For example, while giving value and peace education as part of practical moral science lessons, Father M.C. George, the then director of Don Bosco School, compiled materials about violence, substance abuse among the youth, as well as about HIV/AIDS. As the school head said:

> The real story is there in the newspaper reports, but we change the true identity of the youth. The moral message is to sensitise adolescents about the vulnerabilities of youths and crimes and its harmful consequences on the health of both individuals and society. The interesting venture of this exercise is that these lessons are prepared with pictographic highlights that are quite appealing to the imaginations and sentiments of children. This method is considered most effective in preventing children and adolescents from being trapped in risky habits. What makes these students stand out in today's chaotic Manipuri society is that these students have an edge over their peer groups studying in other schools in terms of moral and character formation.

As observed from the above narrations and the foregoing discourse, teachers of Don Bosco School are committed to the overall well-being and academic achievements of their students. Yet, teachers themselves unanimously admitted that 90 per cent of children opt for private tutors, especially as a trend. Teachers unanimously agreed that the concept of hiring private tutor was started by rich and affluent parents for they believe that hiring private tutor will enable their children to clear technical and tough examinations such as engineers, doctors, administrative civil services, etc. In the past children opted for private tutor to clear about doubts they could not clear in class room teaching. Educational emergencies due to violence have also caused private tuition to flourish since teachers are not able to complete the full course in a year due to sporadic school closure. Whatever the reasons could be hiring private tutor has become a trend in present-day Manipuri society as unanimously expressed by majority teachers. Thus, in the words of a literature teacher:

> With private tuition, the child can clear up his/her weak points, but now, hiring tutor for all subjects has become a fashion. In the classroom situation, children learn so many things continuously, which may mean a plethora of information gets stored in the subconscious mind of children, whereas, during tuition, specific areas of the information gets cleared and filtered. Through tuition, what exists in the subconscious mind of the child can be transferred to the conscious mind. In a classroom, out of a total of students, say, 60 students, 30 of them are really good, even without getting the help of a private tutor. However, as I said, going to a private tutor has become a trend. The tuition system is for status enhancement. When I teach students in the class, they seem to understand what I teach, but, most children opt for private tutor. My students are free to ask about any problem in class, but parents initiate tuition for children. On our part, we even give extra classes to complete the syllabus and, in most cases, complete course on time because of strict order from the Catholic Fathers. We devote extra time for children, so I don't understand why any student should be facing problems when we are always there for them.

These were some of the concerns raised by teachers of Don Bosco School while citing reasons for students fathoming for private tutors while they remain committed to their teaching vocation and welfare of students.

Discipline, Examinations, Ranking and Grading

For the enforcement of discipline in the school, the school operates like a laboratory, where students are meticulously observed for their habits, walking styles, rules, examinations, their rankings and, ultimately, the preservation of the school's reputation. The students are under constant surveillance through discipline and moral order by teachers who strictly enforce the moral order outlined by the Salesian Fathers. The pioneering work of Michel Foucault, who examined the origin and development of the processes of discipline beginning in ancient Europe, has provided interesting observations regarding discipline in schools. Foucault's analysis of discipline and punishment in schools is traced back to ancient regimes, where visible power was placed on the offender as retribution for trespassing against kings.

In *Discipline and Punish* (1977), Foucault writes that the mechanisms of discipline prevalent today in schools, monasteries, military institutions and hospitals, etc., can be traced to the period of 1760–1840 Europe, where penal detention in various forms replaced public execution as a brutal technique, with the aim of altering individual behaviour. Foucault details how torture of bodily inflictions (with the body as the major target) during public execution and punishment as an exciting spectacle was replaced by the penalties of prison. While highlighting this shift, Foucault documents in detail the stricter method of surveillance and the dying out of penal repression whereby the body was targeted as a sort of gloomy spectacle, with the tortured body symbolising an object of pity or admiration by the end of 18th and beginning of 19th century, say in France in 1789, and in England in 1837. Equally significant is that it marked the slackening of hold on the body to be condemned and mocked. With the disappearance of punishment through bodily condemnation, he argues that the mechanism of discipline underwent change, i.e., from being an art of unbearable sensations, punishment has become an economy of suspended rights. If it is still necessary for the law to reach and manipulate the body of the convict, it will be at a distance and in a proper way, according to strict rules, and with a much 'higher' aim (Foucault, 1977: 11). As a result of this new restraint and the establishment of strict rules, a whole army of warders (wardens), doctors, chaplains, psychiatrists, psychologists and educationists gradually took over from the executioner. The movement as discussed by Foucault affected the various legal systems in Europe.

Following from the above discourse, Foucault related school as a disciplinary and grading mechanism through the organisation of space and time. He argued that in schools, discipline proceeds from the distribution of individuals in space and that discipline requires enclosures. It made the educational space function like a learning machine, but a machine for supervising, hierarchising and rewarding, just as we do in a factory, where production is divided up and each variable of the workforce, such as strength, promptness and skill is observed, assessed and computed. The concept of economising time emerged, which can be most visibly seen in schools through the gradation of time table according to which the use of rhythms and regular activities are meticulously followed.

The division of time and activities of students and teachers alike are governed in detail by orders to be obeyed immediately. For example, as the head teacher narrated:

> At 8.30 a.m., all students must be present within the enclosures of the school complex, at 9 o'clock, the school bell rings and all students rush to the morning assembly ground, where they line up and observe silence, keeping their body facing forward, with full concentration on the moral education and announcements being given by the Catholic Father. This is followed by prayers and songs in praise of the Lord, while all teachers standing behind the students bow their heads down in silence. After the assembly is over, students move in an orderly fashion towards their respective classrooms. By 9.30 a.m., they occupy their benches and keep their books and exercise copies ready on their desks.

Teachers try their best to assure that time is not wasted, to the extent that even the request of a child wanting to go to toilet is suppressed. As noted by Foucault, it is a question of constituting a totally useful time, with precision, application and punctuality-the fundamental virtues of disciplinary time.

While narrating his stance on the distribution of individuals in space, Foucault relates it to the ranking that defines the great form of distribution of individuals in educational order: rows or ranks of pupils in the class, ranks attributed to each pupil at the end of each task and each examination from week to week, month to month, year to year, and so on. Similar patterns, such as the ranking of students as the most cherished value, is visibly noticeable in the sample school. In the words of the school head teacher:

> We conduct class tests, weekly tests, monthly tests to determine the students' ranking after the final examination. Making an effort to increase the number of top-ranking students is our endeavour. Indeed, rank holding by students of Catholic schools is prescribed as a matter of principle. Our school is very good because we take out only the cream. Every year, students are ranked. Ranking of students is good; they bring prestige and reputation to the school. Teachers and committee members always consult each other for the welfare of students and student ranking.

It seems that obeying the orders of the Catholic Fathers is a norm not to be violated. As the head teacher described in our discussion:

> The Catholic Fathers are quite concerned and serious about students' results in Board examinations; it is a matter of principle. Teachers are asked to teach weak students even at night by assigning duty to teachers and no teacher refuses. We are under constant scrutiny by the Fathers. Our teachers are not only committed, but very committed.

A similar view was endorsed by another teacher who has been teaching Manipuri literature:

> The general reputation of the school is very good. The staff members are very hard working and disciplined and the relationship between teachers and students is very cordial. Senior staff members form committees in the schools are concerned with assigning roles such as examination duties, duties during sports, festivals, field visits, etc.

In a confident and spirited tone, he continued, 'Very often, we, advise students to be the winners in any competition such as examinations'.

Another teacher who has been teaching history expressed appreciation regarding the performance of the school in terms of performance by making positions by students in examinations every year. Thus, in his words:

> Our students come out with flying colours. Most students clear examinations with first division, apart from holding top positions in Board Examinations. We are equally committed. Our school reputation is extremely good. Yes, result and ranking really matter to us. The Catholic Fathers are very particular about our students taking top ranks in examinations. We discuss student performance every time, in our meetings.

Another teacher who is teaching Science complimented Don Bosco School as one of the best missionary schools in Manipur. He thus reasoned:

> Meritorious students and teachers' commitment to students' well-being are contributory factors for the success of the school. Our Fathers are very strict with our responsibilities for children, constantly reminding us that we should be role models for our students, so we naturally become conscious.

Competition among students at Don Bosco is so intense that students are divided up into different houses such as Red, Blue, Yellow and Green. Each student is identified with one of these colours. Once accorded a particular colour, the symbol remains permanent. The house system is usually followed in debates, sports, quizzing, charity drives, etc. Merit points for good behaviour, discipline and academic achievement are also totalled up for comparison between houses. A teacher explained:

> Students are assigned to houses randomly, according to their first or last name and based on ability, with the aim of balancing the houses in order to increase competitive spirit in the groups and to foster the spirit of leadership, by choosing a house captain.

As seen above, what lies at the core of the totality of the performance of the sample school is discipline – a technique that draws up everything so minutely such as time tables, prescribed movements and dressing codes, behavioural patterns, punctuality, performance and a permanent state of competition among students. Foucault further argues that discipline in schools presupposes a mechanism of coercion by means of observation, which is found in the construction of the school building such as confinement and the construction of enclosures like thick walls and heavy gates preventing the entry or exit of students in an attempt to discipline them. The functional surveillance, as argued by Foucault, was decisively extended to a whole micro penalty of time in school such as lateness, absences, lack of attention, negligence, lack of zeal, idle chatter, insolence, incorrect attitudes, unhygienic practices and so forth. It is through this discipline that the power of 'the norm' appears, in which the normality is established as a principle of coercion. According to Foucault, the technique of normalising judgement is through examinations that determine averages, hierarchies and notions of the good and the bad, which, in doing so, also punishes and rewards. Thus, according to Foucault, the examination is another new form of modality of power regulated by the mechanism of discipline. Therefore, discipline for Foucault, is an instrument of power, and also a means to normalisation, control and surveillance.

For Durkheim, discipline takes a metaphorical departure from its role and functioning described by Foucault. In his book, *Moral Education*[2] (1961), Durkheim analyses discipline as a *sui generis* of education and the first and foremost element of morality. Durkheim's analysis of discipline seeks to understand morality as a social fact, which is to examine the way in which it serves the needs of social organisms, in that morality is binding, coercive, external and general to the individual members in society. His argument essentially reflects social determinism of moral education.

According to Durkheim, when a child is in his elementary stage of schooling, it is a period when he or she is most in need of moral education, which schools must take up as the greatest challenge as a matter of necessity. He further argues that morality consists of an infinity of special rules, fixed and specific, which not only regulates a man's conduct but also allocates rights and obligations in as much as the domain of morality is the domain of duty. Most importantly, Durkheim argues that if the foundation of such morality has not been laid at the elementary stage of a student's life, it never will be.

Discipline also helps one to exercise self-control. For Durkheim, discipline is indispensible in schools since it trains individuals to master one's thoughts and is, therefore, a means towards emancipation and freedom, while Foucault necessitates it as the most torturous, exploitative and brutalising technique. According to Durkheim, it is up to the morality of the class to maintain peace, allowing the classroom to roll on tranquilly. For this, necessary authority must develop in a teacher who must resist arrogance, vanity or pedantry to the extent that a student obeys his authority without questioning it. Durkheim argues that the punishment coerces the child to obey the authority of a teacher but to punish is not to make the child suffer in body or soul; it is to affirm in the face of an offense, the rule that the offense would break.

Durkheim thus condemns brutal and dehumanising corporal punishment to a child because the chief function of moral education is to instil humanistic morality, 'to give the child a feeling of the dignity of man', raising an important issue that disciplining with humanitarian feelings forms an integral part of pedagogy reforms and educational rehabilitation, in as much as educational issues and problems cannot do away with it (Allen and Alberto, 1995). For Durkheim, punishment is a symbol through which the inner state of the child and the teacher is represented; a language, through which either the general social conscience or that of the school teacher expresses the feeling inspired by the disapproved behaviour. The emphasis is on the social character of the discipline that prevails over and above individuals. As such, punishment in schools bolsters the authority of society's moral form of life by confirming that social ideals and practices cannot be encroached without proportionate repercussions. It is through punishment that society's collective representation is strengthened. Despite such startling contrasts between the two propositions, there is also an interesting convergence between the two. Both Foucault and Durkheim, thus, treat 'discipline' as an instrument that reigns in society as a whole. Both agree that the authority of social norms is not only instilled but also secured through educational institutions. However, Durkheim has been criticised for placing teachers as the sole moral custodians of children in school, despite the possibility that some teachers may suffer from moral bankruptcy. Durkheim's teleological approach to discipline and punishment remains unbridgeable to those of Foucault, who first unearthed the buried horrors of bodily torture of punishment and discipline and has shown how the modern world has evolved and managed to change its form, which is now seen prevalent mostly in total institutions.

School Children in the Line of Crossfire

The most unimaginable experience for the present generation in today's Manipuri society is their being accustomed to living with constant outbursts of unanticipated sporadic violence in the state. An experience that none had thought possible has become a true nightmare for both the young and the old. This tragic experience brings despair and disillusionment for one and all, but exerts its greatest toll on children and youths more than any other social category. This assertion was reflected in the study of the sample school.

Regarding the alleged killing of school children from Don Bosco School in Senapati district, the school head shared his grief in a low tone, as if the present crisis of violence is non-corrigible. He recounted:

> Pictures of those children murdered are flashed in the media and we are extremely sorry and pained within. We always pray that such tragedies don't befall our school children. During school assemblies we pray for them.

The teacher expressed both admiration and regret regarding the school's efforts to continue functioning despite strikes and *bandhs*, claiming:

> There is some peculiarity about this school, even if there are *bandhs* and strikes, we always arrange vans to pick up children, but when the van fails to turn up with children, the class strength is diminished and ultimately school is closed.

Another teacher, who is teaching English literature, recounted:

> Given the climax of violence, I always start my classes with peace education and practical moral science lessons; it's necessary. Depending on the nature and degree of violence, the school remains closed. If the violence occurs at a far distance from the school, the school remains open or else how will children come to school? Most children come to school by van. Yes, in the case of general strikes, children feel extremely uncomfortable. The murder of Lungnila Elizabeth, students of Don Bosco, Senapati frighten our children.

The teacher further lamented:

> Apart from these disturbances, we have so many irrelevant holidays such as *Yaosang* (Holi), which is observed for four days and after *Yaosang*, many festivals follow, such as *thabal chongba* (the moonlight dance), which goes on for months. Such celebrations are during the peak time of final examination for children. Celebrations with loud music creates nuisance for children's study.

In an assertive high pitched tone of condemnation and concern over the growing violence in Imphal valley, a literature teacher observed:

> More than anywhere else, Imphal valley is gripped by violence all the time. It is very important to give peace education to students in the light of violence in the state, especially in Imphal valley. In the year 2004, a student, Lungnila Elizabeth, of Little Flower School, was killed. Immediately after her disappearance, all children observed sit in protest march. After disappearance for 14/15 days, her body was found in a big sack. Such a case occurred three times in the recent past as the students are soft targets of violent insurgents when they fail to attack their parents or fail to get their demands fulfilled by their parents. Elizabeth's killers have not yet claimed responsibility for the murder. Two young male students disappeared from our Don Bosco School mysteriously and, later on, they were found dead. Every time our students

> protested against such acts of violence by putting up posters. We select the grown up students to join such protests.

Another teacher voiced out:

> Frequent violence has a greatly demoralising effect on both teachers and students; it jeopardises transport and communication system, as well as the general academic performance of children. Gun culture was an alien thing in the past. We are peace loving people. In today's situation, our life is always in danger; we adults are so affected. Nowadays, small children don't ask for toys but for guns to play with. The continuity of violence certainly creates psychological warfare in children. Very often there are barbaric killings both by insurgents and commandos and armies. Then, there is a sudden closure of school due to strikes and *bandhs*. We are just operating within a cruel system hardly accountable to our lives.

Another teacher condemned the violent acts, claiming:

> Time has never been a great healer; we have never forgotten the unforgettable horrors of the murder of our young students by insurgents, even with the passage of time. Whenever violence erupts, students are used as tools of protest. In case our children refuse, these insurgents dictate us to close the school or pay a fine to them.

While interacting with students of class VIII about their participation in protest marches, 70 per cent of them admitted participation in protest marches due to the killing and disappearance of their fellow students, while all were disgruntled and condemned the great social unrest and trafficking faced by them in the heart of Imphal. All students agreed that social unrest in the state is a cause for occasional stress, anxiety and restlessness, greatly affecting their concentration on studies and the normal functioning of school. Students also expressed distaste regarding the MSU and DESAM[3] for brutally misusing them and coercing them to often participate in protest marches on almost all issues in the state. These organisations have often been accused for their alleged nexus with some of the banned insurgent outfits in the state. As narrated by a teacher above, it is also true that Imphal valley has been the focal point of violence, since as many as 70 per cent students of Don Bosco were found participating in all forms of protest demonstrations against violence in the state. This was again a huge number as compared to the 5 per cent of children who joined such protest marches from Bethel School and Phoijing

Junior High School. This further indicates that, though violence has affected students all over, it is impossible for children studying in schools located in Imphal to escape from the wrath of the many forms of violence that erupt in Imphal, since they are compulsorily forced to be a part of it in the form of protest demonstrations.

Violence and conflict greatly affect the regular functioning of schools, such as conducting examination on time, completing the syllabus and even celebrating school related functions like sports, cultural programmes, etc. Teachers and students alike are demoralised. Teachers also alleged how violence in the region has encouraged the private tuition system, which was previously a culture of rich families, but has now become a norm among almost all families. Violence has demoralised students maximally, since their future hope is often crushed as they cannot hold any expectations from a violent state.

While conversing informally with the then director, Father George, about the vision and mission of Don Bosco, one striking issue emerged regarding the educational concern of disadvantaged children hailing from destitute families and their opportunity to access schooling facility in Don Bosco School as one of the elitist schools in Manipur. To this, Father George admitted honestly the difficulties of admitting poor children in Don Bosco, since the operation of the school depends on the contribution of the students. It suggests that almost all students of Don Bosco School belong to relatively well-off middle class and affluent families. The monthly school fee is ₹ 260 per month for all classes starting from nursery to class X. The amount is almost 24 times more than that paid by a student studying in a government school. Apart from this payment, there is a system of instalment payments for fees, three times a year. The fee for the first instalment is ₹ 1,200 for the old students, while it is ₹ 1,400 for the new students. All those students who join computer classes pay an extra amount of ₹ 500 per month. The study also reveals that 55 per cent children had parents who are salaried, 35 per cent belong to business class while 10 per cent belong to a class of farmers. Similarly, 65 per cent of these students enjoy better housing facilities such as well-built houses and more than 60 per cent of them commute to school by van.

Despite the expensive and elite status of Don Bosco School, any orphans admitted to the school are naturally given free education. Apart from this, the school authorities including teachers have been identifying the poorest students from the classroom itself, in order to support them with free education. Due to their proximity with students in classroom interaction, teachers are given the responsibility to identify two of the poorest students from each class in case there are not orphans. Father George, sensing the precarious condition of many destitute children being deprived of literacy and educational opportunity, strongly felt the necessity of opening mobile literacy centres to spread literacy and education far and wide in the state of Manipur. This idea gave birth to establishing Bosco Mangaal in 2002, an NGO operating with a special focus on literacy and the education of children and youths, along with awareness education about HIV/AIDS and creation of women Self-Help Groups (SHGs) for generating income among rural poor women folk. However, the present study focuses on the literacy and education mission of the organisation. Bosco Mangaal provides the opportunity of alternative schooling to children of parents who are unable to send their children either to private or government school.

Bosco Mangaal (Bosco Light)

Deeply influenced by the ideologue of Bible philosophy (Biblical teachings) to care for the poor and the needy and to discover their identity as being created in the image of God, Father George ventured into the pioneering works of educating destitute children by establishing Bosco Mangaal on 12 October 2002. The focus of the programme is youth oriented with a vision of 'Youth Friendly Manipur'. Youth-friendly programmes are conducted due to the felt need of youths who are at great risk in Manipur for several reasons.

The programme was initiated by M.C. George, who was the director of Don Bosco School, Chingmeirong, Imphal. Father George described his passionate work as:

> In the context of their destitute existence, poor children can't get education from missionary school, which is why I started mobile literacy centres for the poorest children of Manipur.

Father George, at the risk of his life, being under constant threat of kidnapping by local insurgents, has sustained himself in his noble cause of empowering children and youths through educational programmes. When asked about the threat from local insurgents, he said:

> It is the support of *Ima Meira Paibis* (Mother Torch Bearers), teachers and local youths that has sustained my mission despite

continued threats of kidnapping and killing by local insurgents who engage in extortion.

Today, Bosco Mangaal has become extremely popular among many poor households, whose hopes can move from the zone of despair after being provided literacy skills and education.

The main office of Bosco Mangaal is located at Chingmeirong, Imphal east district, within the residential premise of the Salesian Fathers who are looking after the function and administration of Don Bosco School. The NGO works under the supervision of the Salesian Fathers. The staff carry out all directions given by the Selesian Fathers. There are different divisions of the NGO whose members are delegated with different activities. Among these members, there is a core committee group, the teaching staff, the administrative staff and two office assistants. The core committee consists of two programme managers, two assistant programme managers and two coordinators.

Opening of Literacy Centres: Modus Operandi

Literacy campaigns under Bosco Mangaal are spread over greater and east Imphal and beyond Imphal, covering Moirang Kamphu, an area that falls within Bishnupur district. In Imphal district, there are 32 such educational centres in 23 *leikais*. *Leikais* are selected on the basis of availability of 20 children, who are in the seven years age group and who have never been enrolled in school. The presence of never enrolled children in this age group in any *leikai* is a prerequisite to open a centre in that particular *leikai*. The staff members prepare and compile data on the actual number of children sent to school to identify the number of children who have not been in school.

Bosco Mangaal does not take care of children below six years. According to Bosco Mangaal, their main aim is to provide bridge education. Bosco Mangaal argues that, in the village, it is the responsibility of *anganwadi* (pre-primary school) teachers to teach all children at least upto six year of age. Angawandi centres (pre-primary school centres) have operated in the hands of the government since the year 2002. Bosco Mangaal staff initially used to campaign a lot to mobilise about the basic education programme, by selecting villages where there is no government school and villages which are extremely under-developed. Household surveys were conducted through the help of village heads or *pradhans*. They examined the number of illiterate children in the village followed by household visits to discuss with parents if their children can be sent to the literacy centres. The profile of children includes sex, age, name and parental occupation. The survey of identifying these young children was assisted by the teacher himself/herself who has completed either class X or XII from the same *leikai*. This method is similar with the famous Lok Jhumbis model of Rajasthan, where identification of needy villages for opening of literacy centres are done through micro planning and school mapping, using a participatory appraisal method.

Staff members of Bosco Mangaal choose the potential teacher while organising sensitisation programmes related to drugs, substance abuse and HIV/AIDS in the villages of Manipur. During the programme, if the organisers spot suitable candidates, they approach potential candidate to become a teacher. Choosing the teacher from the same locality ensures that he/she will not be absent and will be useful in discussing with the parents or guardians about children when they face problems. The literacy centre can be any place that is comfortable and convenient for the children. It can be, for example, a *Sanghoi* or a verandah, or a place under a tree or school building that can be used after regular classes are over. Both boys and girls freely mix since they are from the same community and parents need not fear sending their daughters, since the literacy centre is located in the same *leikai*.

In the initial stage of its operation, there was strong resistance from parents and guardians belonging to certain community such as the Muslims. In the process of spreading literacy campaign, these communities got upset about a song that goes, 'If I have a white little box, I put Jesus in it'. Children who come to the literacy centre usually sing the song and when children started singing the song very often, even outside the class, parents and the elderly in the village started feeling worried that baptisation among the children might be underway. Because of this suspicion, children failed to turn up for classes on the following day. Worried over the development, Bosco Mangaal staff visited the households and made them understand. After understanding their sentiment, the verse of the song was changed to 'If I have a white little box, I put Allah in it'. Today, children are benefited by the education they have received. Village elders have come forward and have requested the staff of Bosco Mangaal to open more such centres. Today, there are 39 existing centres, with a total number of 899 students, of which 417 are boys and 482 are girls.

Changes started in the year 2004. It was no longer necessary for Bosco Mangaal to popularise or publish any advertisement relating to its basic education programme since the programme became very popular in a short span of time. At present, changes are being introduced in the method of choosing teachers and students. Selection of teachers is done through the written test for candidates with minimum qualification such as class X pass or XII pass. The teacher's basic skills in English grammar and the structure of written English is tested. These teachers are not only responsible to identify deserving, illiterate children for enrolment in Bosco Mangaal centres, but also verify student's family backgrounds with regards to income and their parental and household profile through observation and interaction to ensure that these children are from below poverty line families. Identification of poor families can include how well a kitchen garden is maintained and possession of other household items of the family.

At present, a teacher is paid ₹ 700 per month and the duration of teaching is only two to three hours per day, say from 6.45 a.m. to 8.45 a.m.. The time period is chosen so that children are not taught at a stretch without a break. Moreover, there are no toilet or latrine facilities available, making longer teaching hours unfeasible. Classes are conducted six days a week. There are no long holidays so as not to risk the learning continuity of children but classes are not held on three national holidays and a few days of religious importance for the community to whom these children belong.

Teaching/Learning Material Aids, Pedagogy: A Joyous Experience

The teachers are provided with in-service training every month at the time that they collect their salary to ensure their attendance, but quarterly training is also provided continuously for three days. Training is imparted by focusing on weak areas of a teacher. Training orientation covers issues of how to teach children who have no textbooks, skills of multi-grade teaching system, class management, discipline, child psychology, teaching through games and songs, making teaching aids and creative activities (soft toy making, and pictures with sand, leaves, flower petals, seeds, match sticks, etc.). Games, action songs, rhymes, etc., play an important part of learning. Non-Hindi speaking children such as Christians, Muslims and Meiteis are taught Meitei *mayek* and Hindi is taught to Hindi-speaking children such as Nepalis and Biharis who are residing at Mantri Pukhri, Imphal. Therefore, the instructional language used depends not only on the location of the place but the language commonly spoken by the children. Teaching Mathematics and English is compulsory with the ultimate aim of sending them to regular schools. Teachers are encouraged to be innovative and evolve interesting and pragmatic topics to be covered for teaching children. Teacher-pupil ratio is usually 1:20 or 1:30.

Every class at literacy centres begins with a citation of prayers. Muslim children will begin in Arabic while Christian children will pray in their own style, depending on the community to which the children belong, for instance, for Christian children, the class begins with a prayer such as:

Dear God, we thank you for this day
And also for giving us a good teacher
Help us to learn new things each day ...

While a Muslim prayer begins as follows:

Bismillah ar-Rahman-ar Rahim
(In the name of Allah, the most beneficent and merciful)
'Rabbi Zidni Ilma ya Fa' tahu
(Who enhances the knowledge).

The class comes to an end with a song. The lyrics of the song are as follows:

School is over, school is over for today,
We will come tomorrow, we will come tomorrow,
Bye bye teacher, bye bye friends,
Thank you teacher for your love,
We will come tomorrow.

Though the wording is simple, the songs that the children sing are quite attractive through dance and body movements, with tiny hands swinging according to the rhythm of the song. Children enjoy singing the song with actions, arousing a sense of belonging. This enjoyable method motivates them and prepares them to be in school the following day. Teaching/learning in all literacy centres has been made child-centred and activity-based. As such, the potential de-motivation caused due to lack of facilities is compensated to some extent through such methods of joyful learning. Secondly, the learning process has been made community-specific so that students are readily able to relate themselves with the teachers who are in everyday interaction with them.

While visiting a Bosco Mangaal centre, established in January 2008, at Kairang Umang Leikai, literally meaning Kairang Forest Leikai, Imphal east district, a young female teacher was found teaching the students how to sing certain rhymes. There were 23 students present while visiting the centre. While interacting with them, children were found to be articulate and interactive. The children naturally assumed that I was from Bosco Mangaal and welcomed me with a song in Hindi which begins as follows:

Mere Liya Ek Dostic Hain
Bosco Se Aaya Hain
Dost Ke Sath Chalte Rahe To Kitna Accha Hain
Dost Ke Sath Khate Rahe To Kitna Accha Hain
Dost Ek Sath Sote rahe to Kitna Accha Hain ....

Despite their uncomfortable sitting arrangements and lack of basic facilities, the children did not show any signs of fatigue or disinterest, rather they were found to be quite enthusiastic and most children displayed smiles on their faces.

There is no prescribed rule of teaching and no system is imposed on the teachers and the taught. The teacher prepares teaching aids on his/her own. Mobile textbooks and other related books are provided to children in circulation among centres. These mobile books costing ₹ 3 lakhs are mostly textbooks such as English, Mathematics folk tales, moral education, etc. Most of these are taught with pictures and diagrams, for example, letters such as A, B, C, are printed on handmade cards with different bright colours. All are taught in a joyful learning style, through counting papers, demonstration, rhymes, conversation, etc. Learning general knowledge at literacy centres is compulsory. Concerned individuals donate teaching aids such as balls, numbers, cards, charts, blackboards, etc. There is no sitting arrangement made, but children naturally come. During creativity periods, children develop the art of making mats and other items, developing skills which may be useful for future income-generation opportunities.

A multi-grade teaching system is adopted, since teachers cannot teach all students of different classes at different timings, owing to time constraints and limited resources, both human and physical. For example, let us analyse a situation such as the study of a bee. To identify the bee, it is drawn in a colourful picture and the different bodily parts of the bee are highlighted. At the nursery level, the teachers identify what a bee is; then in the next stage, teachers make the students acquainted with the bee by asking them to describe the functions of a bee. At group III level, children are taught whether a bee is an insect or a mammal, etc. At the higher level, children are taught how many wings, legs, eyes, etc., bees have. As children move on to a higher grade, say at level IV, children learn details related to the functions of bees, what they produce and how honey is produced. In this way, children will develop the art of knowing about bees in different forms. This method of learning is also used for other objects, to learn about a banana, balloon, book, etc. However, the multi-grade teaching system has been heavily criticised as an extremely poor quality form of instruction, since a single teacher must manage students learning in different grades.

In every literacy centre, both boys and girls attend the centre in equal number. However, when it comes to retention, a higher number of girls continue to study in the centre until class X instead of attending regular schools because of the flexible timings at the centre, which allows them to attend to household chores on top of their studies. When they reach 17–18 years old and do not want to go to regular schools, they are provided with vocational education.

Literacy Campaign: Reaching the Unreached Children

The concept of mobile library facilities is excellent to meet the demands for books at various literacy centres. Children at literacy centres are deprived of books and printed materials. Since children are too poor to afford textbooks, Bosco Mangaal makes a point that they do not need textbooks, instead provides one copy only to the teacher. Therefore, children learn whatever a teacher teaches them through chalkboard and what they themselves copy out in their books.

Library books costing around ₹ 3 lakhs are distributed to all literacy centres and after a period of two months these books are collected back to ensure that each centre gets new books on rotation. Books are distributed to teachers of each literacy centre. To avoid the cost of transportation, teachers themselves pick up these books by visiting the literacy centre once in a month. These books are used while teaching or sometimes children are allowed to take them to their homes for a day or two. Each centre has only 50 books. The content of the books is so good that even regular students are not privileged enough to access such information.

Trained animators visit the literacy centres regularly. The frequency and the length of the animator's visit can be reduced as the teacher steadily gathers experience. An animator has to be well qualified and trained enough not only to guide a teacher but also to motivate him/her. The animator signs the register after each visit and it is countersigned by the teacher. If a student is continuously found to be absent, the teacher visits the parents and inquires about the problem causing the child to stop attending the centre. In all possible ways the animator and the teacher encourage the parents to participate regularly. These animators inspect the teaching of the teachers and students. An animator visits one centre four times a week and examines the progress of that particular centre, checks the attendance sheet, enquires from the teachers about their progress weekly and gauges the responses from the students as well. An animator must be highly self-motivated to be of immense help to the teaching programme and overall motivation of the teachers.

Another important dimension of the educational programme at Bosco Mangaal focuses on the health and hygiene of children. A teacher creates health awareness among children by stressing the importance of personal health and hygiene and by sensitising them with advice like 'if you fall sick, you will not be able to study'. To motivate the children to maintain health and hygiene, they are asked about basic hygiene issues and whosoever responds positively is rewarded with a small prize. It is a normal routine that the nails and hair of the children are checked. In the centres visited, children were asked to show their nails and teeth. If any child was found having long or dirty nails, they were strictly sensitised about possible infection and falling ill, because of which they would fail to come to centre. This was communicated in a light and warm tone with smiles on the face of the teacher, while the children listened keenly. Parents are also sensitised about the importance of health and hygiene for their children during meetings with them once a month. During the meeting, teachers communicate with parents about what they teach children regarding behaviour, bathing, cutting nails, trimming and combing hair, wearing clean clothes, etc. Parents are also told to ensure that their children study at home even if they themselves are illiterate.

Examinations are held three times a year. These are both oral and written. Students who perform well are rewarded with learning aids, such as pens, pencils, paper, etc., in order to motivate and encourage them. After completing a certain stage of education, if a student wants to attend regular school, the arrangements are made for admission in a mission or government school. The skills and aptitude of the children are also tested. Quiz programmes, song competitions and story-telling are some of the programmes children celebrate in addition to normal classes. Once a year, children from all literacy centres get together. They organise a cultural programme, play games and enjoy a good meal together. Apart from this, they are given an opportunity to watch exhibition shows and other entertainment programmes. During the gathering, children from all centres have an opportunity to meet other children in circumstances similar to their own. This exposure boosts their moral confidence.

The staff of Bosco Mangaal is quite encouraging so that children are motivated to join the regular school system. In the monthly meeting of parents, Bosco Mangaal gradually introduces the issue of sending children to a regular school. In case they are unable to send them due to financial constraint, Bosco Mangaal invites the parents to join an SHG and discusses about internal loaning and income generation activities, etc. Bosco Mangaal requests the head teachers of private schools to admit the children into classes according to the level they have reached. There are as many as 2,344 students who enrolled in regular schools. In 2007, there were 14 students from the centre who were enrolled in regular schools and achieved a high rank in class V examinations. So far as the number of failed students is concerned, until now there is only one student who failed.

Parents, local clubs, *Ima Meira Paibis*, Women's Committees and Children's Home are the main supporters of the programme. With the help of these groups, Bosco Mangaal is able to organise programmes and sponsor children who are deprived of education and who belong to families below the poverty line. State Children's Home have special demand for such education centres, while even individuals including government functionaries have realised the goal and vision of such education centres and started supporting the programme by distributing clothes, eatables, stationery and other items. The closing down of centres in particular localities indicates the successful completion of programmes. So far there were as many as 38 centres which were closed down and these centres sent children successfully to regular schools.

Bethel School: Its Inception and Rough Journey

The case of Bethel school illustrates another interesting experience of civil society participation in the educational development of the state. It also demonstrates that in any given community there are a few people who are quite voluntarily capable of contributing to the welfare of society. The school is illustrative of a model that can provide schooling for children who have no option either to join a failed government school or an elitist missionary school, such as the Don Bosco School.

The inception of the school began way back in 1985, when government schools started declining steadily in the state. The school had an extremely humble beginning, with a mission to serve poor village children, who, despite being talented, are deprived of schooling facilities. After having evolved for a period of 15 years, the school today has become the most sought after school for local parents in addition to students coming from relatively distant areas. In the words of the founder of the school:

> Just for the sake of future generations, I felt lots of responsibility, since I witnessed many young children deprived of educational facilities in my village, Langpok, about around 4 km away from Nambol Keithel.[4] These children are very talented but illiterate. Since the government has failed to establish schools in this village, I decided to establish one school.

The school secretary, who is popularly known as Oja Tomba, recounted that it is his humility, courage, unfailing faith and discipline that helped him achieve his burning desire. Since his childhood days, Oja Tomba was deeply concerned about the non-availability of government schools, due to which his own village children remain beyond the reach of schooling facilities. While conceiving the idea of establishing the school, he was in a sorry state. He narrated:

> I was very poor and lived from hand to mouth. I was only 25 years old then and lived in a broken family. My father lived with his second wife and my grandfather took care of us. My mother was illiterate, working only in gardens and paddy fields for our living. My grandfather was a constable in the police and, being posted everywhere, I had the chance of meeting many people while accompanying him. My grandfather was posted at Kabiri. My

> village and Kabiri village are not very different in terms of eating habits, lifestyles, etc. That way, we were freely interactive. The villagers were always in search of Chengkup (particles of pounded rice grain) to feed pigs and we were always asking for vegetables like cabbages. So we had economic interdependence. In this Tangkhul village, I came across two evangelists named Ibobi and Kumar, who came to my village for mission work. These were the people who strongly felt the need to establish a school in the village and provided the ideas, but they themselves did not know how to implement their ideas.

Oja Tomba received both moral and material support from them, although in small measure. As he was already so passionate about establishing a school, Oja Tomba started working towards the same idea that could serve to the needs of local children. He shared his interesting venture with great zeal:

> Since my childhood days, I was quite aware about educational problems and issues in the state. I was passionate to establish a school so that children in my village would not be deprived of schooling facilities. In the entire village there was one government school which was no longer functioning. My faith in God has motivated me to go on this mission. On a personal level, I suffered a lot during my childhood days while attending a government school. The government school I used to study in had no building, no benches and I had to spread a big sack for myself while attending the school. There was no building and we had to sit in the open space. I studied this way until the end of primary stage. After primary stage, I had to walk more than three and half kilometres to join the Junior High School, Nambol. Any student who was travelling to the school was bound to bear the brunt of any unforeseen natural calamity, such as a sudden storm on the deserted road between school and home and that too in the absence of any place to shelter in between.

Despite formidable difficulty, Oja Tomba established a primary school in his native village, Langpok, in the year 1990. However, the most difficult part was continuing the school as he recounted, 'I am alone, so I needed the help of other like-minded people because it is a private school'. Unfortunately, the school could not operate in his own village due to the non-availability of qualified villagers who could contribute not only as a staff but also to the overall development of the school. In early 1993, the school got shifted to Nambol Bazaar on rent. Building a school of a generally acceptable standard was a herculean task for Oja Tomba as it required lots of hard work and sacrifice on the individual level.

He thus narrated building the school block by block:

> I built the school with wood supported by bamboo. My family arranged these materials from my own homestead and I made benches and chairs with my own two hands. Slowly, my school became very popular and lots of volunteers came forward to contribute donations. In the process, my hard work and sincerity paid off. There were friends and students' parents too. I got tremendous contributions from them such as stationery items, school blackboards, etc. I am particularly indebted to Kumar and Ibobi who are no more.

It was during this period that lots of resources through voluntary help came to his school in the form of cash, school materials and other forms of donations from friends and his kith and kin from far off villages. The school operated on rent for seven years from nursery to class VII with the help of seven staff members.

In the meanwhile, it was deemed necessary for Bethel School to be shifted from the market area at Nambol *keithel* to Phoijing, just near *Khoriphaba* hillock,[5] behind State Highway 150. The area of the plot, which is more than one and half acres of land, was donated by a local physician. The school site was formerly a paddy field. Presently, the school is a one-storey building standing in the middle of a large paddy field. The location is about 13 to 14 km southwest from Keisampat, Imphal. Having decided to build the school on the chosen site, a loan was procured and the school was built. Today, Oja Tomba is looked upon by others as an ideal man, whose zeal and spirit can do great service to his people, though he quite humbly admitted, 'I am neither trained, nor qualified. I am just a graduate. Like a child, I always dream when I sleep. I plan everything during the night time'. At present, the school is owned by Oja Tomba. The school provides education to children starting from nursery to class X level for both boys and girls.

The School Building and Infrastructural Facilities

The school is well-built and is one-storey high. The school is in the process of expansion and is under constant renovation. The location of the school is ideal since it is built on the side of Tidim Road, which is easily accessible from all roadways. It is also free from noise and other forms of disturbance. There is sufficient natural light in the classrooms. Windows and doors are made of wood and are large enough for sufficient ventilation. The building has one big staff room, which is partially partitioned from the administration room, where the headmaster and the secretary sit in separate rooms partitioned by wooden walls. There are shelves, where teachers keep students' note books. The staff room is separated from the head teacher's room, which is adjacent to the secretary's room. The secretary's room has a big table, where lots of books and one laptop are kept. A calendar and pictures of geographical importance are hung on the wall. In the secretary's room, the administrative and teaching staff also sit but the room is half partitioned so that he can monitor and watch over their work. In the administration room, there is one computer and some tables and chairs along with laboratory and science kits for science students.

The staff room is located in the passage leading from the secretary's room. In the staff room, there are strong wooden desks and chairs, sufficient enough for the 24 teaching staff. The room is relatively large with basic amenities, such as drinking water facility kept in a filter container, shelves, calendar, fan, etc. It is also well ventilated with large wooden windows on all sides. Recruitment of staff is done on the basis of oral tests and classroom demonstration. The method of selection is based on one's ability to speak English, since English language is the medium of instruction. Hence, subject specialisation was not found to be the only criterion of selection. Of the ten teachers interviewed, only one was trained with a Bachelor's of Education – a formal requirement of teaching eligibility in schools. However, all teachers were found to have completed a certain degree of qualification and five of the teachers had completed post-graduation in Mathematics, English, Manipuri Literature and Science. One teacher was a Ph.D in Social Anthropology from Delhi University, teaching Biology, while the rest of the teachers were graduates.

In our discussion of teachers receiving training programmes, it was found that only two had attended workshops and seminars on teaching skills, while the rest were deprived of such trainings. Six of the teachers were on a temporary contract, two of them were appointed permanently and two were given teaching assignment against leave vacancy. The salary structure ranges from ₹ 1,700 to ₹ 2,400 per month and all teachers had huge complaints against the low salary paid to them, though it is paid on time. Hence, although there was widespread dissatisfaction among teachers over the pay structure, one teacher distinctively argued that teaching is a profession of commitment that should not be compromised by pay structure. Despite grudges against the low salary structure, these teachers were committed to their profession with a clear-cut goal of leading the young generation to the right path.

The school has students from nursery to class X. There are 20 classrooms in all, whereas the total number of students from class I to VIII is 943, making the classrooms overcrowded. There are three sections in class VIII alone. The teachers' priority in such situations is to maintain order to avoid disruptions and troubles while teaching. The problem of overcrowding in well-performing private schools has become unmanageable that the outside agencies such as DESAM intervenes in reducing the number of students to just 50 in one section, which has to be followed as a matter of rule in all private schools. Pictures of demonstrative handwritten and cleanliness are hung on the walls of classrooms to deter the students from dirtying and littering the room. Classrooms are separated from each other by constructed walls and hence noise and disturbance from the other classes are not audible.

The physical and other infrastructural facilities are of moderate quality, but the overall school environment is pleasant. Likewise, teaching/learning facilities in the school are also of average status. Tables and usable blackboards are in good condition with sufficient chalks available. However, there is no mathematical kit, children's book bank, school textbooks or audio-visual aids. There are science kits but are inadequate. The facilities are not excellent, but the infrastructure and resources available are used judiciously. There is a small library facility, containing 4,000 books of Manipuri, English and Hindi literature, kept in almirahs since there is no separate library room. There is a regular supply of newspapers and journals in English and Manipuri language. The newspapers are distributed in classrooms before classes begin. Teaching methods include verbal instruction and use of blackboards, though sometimes the demonstration method is also used, especially while teaching geography.

Basic conveniences, such as separate toilet facilities for girls and boys, drinking water and electricity connection, are available. First-aid kits are readily available in the school. One nurse is also deputed for attending to the students as and when required. There is a regular medical check-up for resident students and immunisation facility for non-resident students.

Discipline, Obedience, Moral Order, etc.

In the sample school, there are no exciting and innovative teaching/learning methods such as audio-visual aids and field visits. Yet students were found attentive in classroom interaction with teachers. This indicates observance and maintenance of discipline in the sample school in great measure that norms of discipline are strictly followed. There are prescribed rules pertaining to sickness, irregularity, weak performance, juvenile delinquency, obedience, punctuality, performance of home work assignments (whether they are correctly done or not), punctuality, discipline, moral foundation, health and hygiene, which are strictly followed in the school.

Obedience and discipline occupy top priority among the above traits as the secretary said:

> Once students start listening to what is routinely prescribed for them by being obedient, then not many problems are likely to occur in future.

Discussing the most prevalent crisis faced by adolescents in Manipur, such as the case of drug addiction, he shared his concerns, stressing what could hold good for students by being obedient:

> To prevent addiction, it is always better to guide our young students. Our motto is to learn to live responsively in family, society and the country; these attitudes are built into them only when they inculcate the value of obedience and discipline. As elders, we guide them.

There is a huge demand for children's admission to Bethel school from local parents. In the year 2007, it was found that there were as many as 717 students at primary level starting from class I to class IV and 442 students at elementary stage. One feasible reason for the Bethel school to be famous and also a desirable school for children as perceived by local parents is the successful performance of students and their ranking in final board examinations. Parents consider this one of the most successful parameters of a school. Secondly, the school provides the best model of a flourishing school where management of school affairs, norms and discipline are almost on similar lines adopted by elite schools such as Don Bosco School. Hence, Bethel school provides an alternative choice for parents whose children either fail to gain entry or cannot afford to study in reputed private schools charging exorbitant fees. Lastly, parents increasingly notice differential socialisation patterns of children in such well-managed private schools. Therefore, parents do not perceive result and examination performance as the only reason to choose a private school.

According to the secretary, the cultivation of holistic development is another attractive factor:

> Results in examinations are not the end of the story. Moral foundation is the main issue. We sometimes use corporal punishment and repressive action. I experienced a child of class IV stealing money (meant for tuition fees) from his friend. I asked for the money to return but he refused. The child confessed only when I threatened him. The child spent one hour with me. All our efforts will not help children unless they are self-corrected. Counselling him not to repeat such wrong doings is my responsibility. Later on, I found him improving in his grade tremendously and we make counselling an integral part of dealing with children. I also visit psychologists to discuss dealing with students' problems when required. In the last three years, we have changed from corporal punishment to psychological counselling. Our objective is to deal with students with affection and cooperation in an honest manner. My fellow teachers are extremely cooperative.

The affectionate and cooperative nature of teachers was reflected during the conversation with students, when 65 per cent of students interviewed claimed that their teachers were quite helpful and cooperative, while 30 per cent found the them to be quite loving as against the 5 per cent of students who found their teachers quite authoritarian.

The concept of discipline and moral foundation as the prime criterion in the school can be observed at the time of school assembly and is extended to every move the students make, whether in classroom interaction or taking a stroll during lunch hour. During morning assembly hours, students are under intense observation by 4–5 teachers, who check their dresses, shoes and socks, hair, nails, etc., to ensure that students remain neat and clean and in proper order. The school premises are neat and clean and children do not litter. There is a boundary wall with proper concrete fencing and a small iron gate, always guarded by a watchman, controlling one's entry to the school. There is a playground facility, though quite small. Still, it is sufficient enough to accommodate almost one thousand students during morning assembly. Annual sports and games are also held here every year at the end of March. In admiration of the spirit and zeal of his students, the secretary expressed his happiness delightfully:

> There are 10–15 types of sports, including martial arts, football, chess, tennis, and other cultural items like singing, debating, poems, etc. During such competitions, I've found young children, even students of class IV or V, very fearless and quite creative on stage, to the extent that their performances sometimes surprise the audience.

Adjacent to the school building beyond the school playground, there is a huge cycle shed facility that can accommodate more than 100 cycles, as most of the grown-up students commute to school by cycle. Further, it was also found that a large number of students travel to the school from home for more than 3 km as against the prescribed norm.

Autonomy and Accountability

Accountability and dedication are the topmost factors in running a school smoothly. The secretary explained about the dynamism one must possess while taking up such a huge responsibility of running a school successfully:

> I reside on the school premise itself. I fetch water from the pond, filter it and store it in the tank for drinking purpose. I clean the toilet and latrine used by children; help in constructing cycle shed, I also manage to maintain records. So I am an all-rounder. I work just like a clerk, a teacher, a manager and a fellow friend to my colleagues.

This again illustrates that there is a constant dialogue between the school and the parents. Consultation and discussion with parents is a routine programme for the school as the secretary expressed:

> Parents have lots of expectations from us, but we also expect them to share accountability for children. Last time a parent discussed about the shortage of toilets in the school. So I am planning to construct a toilet for male students. So, whenever we find

problems raised by parents, we try to solve them as soon as possible. We try to incorporate their suggestions, but everyday parents lodge lots of complaints.

In the absence of school funds and any assistance from the state government, the entire expenditure is borne by the students collected in the form of school fees. The amount of monthly fee paid varies from class to class. Children of class I and II pay an amount of ₹ 120 per month, while it is ₹ 130 for classes III, VI and V. The amount increases to ₹ 150 for students studying in class VI, VII and VIII. It is almost thirteen times higher than the fees charged in a government school.

The fee structure also reveals the economic position of the students. As many as 55 per cent of the students belong to salaried families as against the 40 per cent whose parents are engaged in both farming and cultivation, while 5 per cent have their parents engaged in low income business. This indicates that a little more than half of the children come from relatively better off families and a little less than half of them belong to low income families. It was also found that 30 per cent of these children live in relatively comfortable houses, as against the 70 per cent living in *kuccha* houses. Yet, 65 per cent of the students were privileged to have a separate room for study purpose, as against 30 per cent who were found deprived of such facility.

In addition to payment of such high tuition fees, all teachers interviewed agree that almost all children, at least 95 per cent of them, hired private tutors, most of whom are their own school teachers. This is despite the awareness created by the school secretary on the harmful effect of tuition system in society as a whole. He showed his concerns and worry over the rising popularity of the tuition system, not just in his own school, but in Manipur as a whole as he thoughtfully expressed that it is high time to sensitise both teachers and students about the mass tuition system that does not produce good grades.

Nevertheless, Bethel school is an enterprising school, where the limited resources, when utilised judiciously, can transform the school environment into a more vibrant and motivating place for children. The school, despite its rough and humble journey, has become one of the most famous and sought after schools in the locality, providing schooling to an estimated 1,800 children in and around the locality. Every year the school produces ranked students besides many first class students which is a matter of honour for it. Besides honouring the school as one of the best performers in terms of examination results by state government in 2006, the school was also recognised as the best performing school in the year 2007 by the All Manipur Private School Association.

From the foregoing discourse, it is clear that both Don Bosco and Bethel schools have made significant contributions in providing education in the state. In the initial stage, the aim of establishing both these schools was similar in purpose and spirit, i.e., providing educational facilities to the unreached, neglected and marginalised village children, who are deprived of basic literacy facility. Gradually these schools became very successful. In the course of their journey, both schools flourished due to the overwhelming demand of parents, most of whom are well-to-do. As the schools became successful in their performance, there was a steady process of exclusion of the marginalised children, as observed in the present study. Today, both the schools have no room for the marginalised, neglected, illiterate village children of poor families. This is due to the fact that the cost for the continuation, maintenance and running the schools is borne by the students in the form of fees and school development funds contributed by these children from time to time. This becomes unaffordable for poor families and, hence, a large chunk of children from poor households became steadily excluded from gaining access to such schooling facility. The case of Bosco Mangaal is similar. As the NGO became extremely successful in its literacy campaign and education mission for the most neglected children in far-flung villages of the state, it began to impose restrictions on the eligibility criteria for entry of children. This was noticed even in the selection and recruitment of teachers who come forward to volunteer in the mission. In the light of these observations, it can be rightly argued that the educational contribution made by civil society alone is not sufficient enough to realise the educational right of all children. Furthermore, the operation of these civil society organisations is not free from the structural logic of social inequality.

Notes

1. The Burmese forces occupied Manipur in 1819, during the reign of King Gambhir Singh, who sought help from the British against the Burmese incursions. Finally, with the help of the British, the Burmese were driven out of Manipur during the Anglo-Burmese war in 1824. The war between Burma and Manipur came to an end with the treaty of Yandaboo on 24 February 1826. King Gambhir Singh was restored to the throne of Manipur. Successive Burmese invasions on Manipur for the last 60 years thus came to an end with the termination of the first Anglo-Burmese war (Roy, 1958).
2. One major social factor that influenced Durkheim's contribution to moral education was the surrender of two provinces of France to Germany, Lorraine and Alsace, during the German-Franco war of 1870. Durkheim critically reflected on the surrender of the two provinces of France to Germany. He felt that France was defeated in the war due to declining moral order among the youth. It was a period when the third republic was formed in France. The new republic opened new schools, which competed with schools run by churches. The attempt was to revamp the new education system with a new social philosophy for which Durkheim seized the opportunity by being a major player.
3. DESAM was established in 2002 as a student frontal organisation of KYKL, a banned insurgent outfit actively operating in the state of Manipur. DESAM's main office is based in Imphal. Its main aim is to address educational issues in a radical way and make education a free zone.
4. Nambol *Keithel*, a town market centre is situated on the bank of the Nambol river, about 14 km southwest of Imphal on National Highway 150, popularly known as Tidim road.
5. About one third of a mile away from Nambol, *Keithel* stands at the famous *Khoriphaba* hillock, where the famous temple of the ancient traditional Meitei *Umang Lai* (Animistic God), popularly known as *Khoriphaba Lainingthou Ibungo* (King of Gods), is worshipped by all communities such as the Meitei Hindus and the tribes who reside in the *Khoriphaba* hillock.

CHAPTER 7

Conclusion

Right to Education – Challenges Ahead

Households and Schooling of Children: High Social Motivation

The household is a critical locus for decision-making regarding sending children to school. Children's participation in school education, therefore, is the natural outcome of a household's decision, which is often influenced by the other households in one's neighbourhood in the state of Manipur, where most parents consider that schooling for children is a social norm. Every parent has high aspirations of enriching their child's life through education. Apparently, the study has also shown that there is no gender bias in the decision of sending children to school. It further reveals an important value of social norms that the passion of educating every child is commonly shared by parents among the Manipuri households. Therefore, factors such as household poverty, being busy with economic engagement, poor infrastructure facilities, lack of commutation facilities, etc., do not conspire against parents' decisions to send children to school. Children equally respond to school participation, despite their engagement in household chores ranging from sibling care, cooking, fetching water and firewood to cattle rearing, poverty issues, etc. These observations suggest that aspiration for children's schooling in the state of Manipur has deep social roots.

As observed during the field observations, even the poorest parents are clear about the goals and vision for their children's education and are able to make judgements about its relevance and quality of schooling. These parents are convinced that the unresponsive, failed education system in the state has pushed them into a big dilemma, accompanied by a sense of shock, frustration and helplessness that today's education has failed to provide the kind of education they had aspired for. These parents have a unique sense of valuing education. For these parents, equating education with employment opportunities and economic returns are only half truths. Rather, the true meaning of education and its significance cannot be measured in terms of any quantifiable value, in that education is not only a means to an end but an end in itself. Such parental vision of education was uniformly shared across all economic strata of parents: educated, uneducated, salaried, daily wage labourers, etc.

Government Schools Doomed to Fail

While choosing a school for their children, almost all parents have abandoned the state-run schools, since these schools have fallen well below their expectations. In fact, for all these parents, government schools in the state are dead. The same feeling has been filtered into the hearts and minds of young children to the extent they themselves decide about which particular school they wish to attend, while treating their fellow friends in government schools with a fatalistic attitude. According to the findings of the present study, 80 per cent parents send their children to private schools of varying standards, as against to only 15 per cent parents sending children to government schools. The overwhelming parental choice of private school over government school is due to the availability of 'whole package', i.e., the feel-good factor of the school, discipline and morality, good habit formation, school uniforms, emphasis on English language learning, commitment of teachers, appropriate examination system, homework assignments, performance, accountability of management over school affairs, etc. The increasing phenomenon of the parental liberty of school choice has further empowered private schools, while leaving government schools impoverished and to be experienced only by those children, whose parents are either subsistent survivors or intermittent income earners, with the constant fear that the future prospect of their children is most likely to disappear into a void. The potential danger is that politicians, bureaucrats and government teachers have shifted their allegiance to private schools by ignoring the crucial issue of making government schools accountable. It is outrageous to learn about the process of snatching school resources among different layers of school authority, while the poor parents, unable to join the rat race of sending children to private schools, helplessly leave their presumed failure to their own fate.

Emerging from the parental accounts and the observation of the sample government school, non-implementation of major schemes, scholarship facilities for girls, free uniform, alongside the chaotic implementation of other schemes, an absence of an inspection system, lack of transparency, corruption, teachers' inertia and feminisation of teaching profession are cited as some of the silent features that continue to plague the functioning of government schools. In the present study, it is shown that mid-day meal distribution is in complete contrast to the prescribed norm. Similar cases of malpractice also exist in the purchase of stationery items and other forms of state apathy. In the government school, children were found to be underfed, undernourished and suffering from anaemia. The narrations of the school teachers reveal that they are visibly upset about the departmental failure and state apathy in school management. The height of state apathy is apparently reflected by the extent of impoverishment of the school under study: the walls of the school building are systematically broken; there are holes in the roof of the school building, classrooms are dark and dingy; benches and desks are shaky; toilet and latrine facilities are pathetic in the absence of water; and there is no separate toilet facility for boys and girls. It is equally outrageous that children fetch drinking water from neighbouring village in the absence of such basic facilities in the school. This demonstrates how state-run schools fail to serve children in poverty. This strongly suggests reasons why children, even after having completed basic education, could not attain much functional literacy as observed among the children of the sample school during the present study. When accountability in such provisioning of school fails, children of poor households are the hardest hit, by stripping them of reasonable school facilities that are there for their social mobility. This also defeats the hopes and dreams of parents and eventually children themselves, who regard schooling as perhaps the only key to earning a better income and status. Given this observation, the dampening teaching/learning environment of the sample government school could have sapped the morale of both the teachers and the students, had it not been for the sincerity and dedication of a few teachers to their profession and the welfare of the students.

Most teachers were honest in sharing the ground realities of their experience with state government officials, who have abandoned their responsibilities of improving government schools. In the sample school, it is the teachers who, through their collective efforts, maintain school infrastructure and basic conveniences such as benches, desks, toilets, electricity and medical facilities for children. It is also noticed that teachers in the sample school possess a high sense of humility and show great empathy to the fabric of social life and the poverty of their students. Thus, teachers' contribution in the non-academic sphere, as observed in the sample government school, is also an example of where education and sense of social justice condense when state accountability fails. In fact, the survival of the sample school as one of the rarest functioning government schools in the area is no doubt a pride of the local community.

Hard Choices for Parents

Notwithstanding the above observations, it would be wrong to assume that parents who send their children to private schools are all happy and satisfied; they more or less have hard choices. While the failure of government schools has virtually pushed children to desert government schools. The situation has caused overcrowding in private schools. A majority of the parents, being well aware of the development, are in fact worried about their children's inability to comprehend what is taught in the class. This has necessitated them to hire a private tutor that has become a norm, particularly among children attending private schools.

Considering these facts, private schools too fall short of parental expectations in terms of scholastic achievements and learning abilities of children. Another common concern is that private schools and the hiring of private tutors are concerned with examinations and performance, while neglecting other values to be instilled in children. The whole business of the private tuition system, therefore, is oriented towards competition and examinations, by cramming the tender heads of young children so that they pass the relevant examinations and, if possible, get rankings, through which the reputation of the school can be elevated. On the other hand, this has proved to be an extremely terrifying and horrendous experience for both children and parents. Furthermore, conscientious parents are equally aware that private schools are able to make a good impression in terms of provision of infrastructural facilities, discipline, morality, clean habit formations, school uniforms, etc., without necessarily meaning that they provide a high quality of education. Another important concern is that the pedagogic teaching is largely ill-equipped to socialise children to make education relevant to the larger social context of their own lives. Too much memorisation and the unnecessary regimental rules over the behaviour of children have frustrated the parents equally. Parents also blame the unqualified, untrained private school teachers who are capable of uttering only a few words of English, and join private schools randomly for earning some extra cash each month. This observation is particularly true in the case of Bethel school. However, as observed in the present study, parents are convinced that some amount of teaching and learning takes place in private schools. Moreover, not all of the children in private schools are rich, rather, poor parents also make enormous sacrifice, just to send their children to private schools due to their high motivation and aspirations for educating their children. Sometimes, highly motivated parents, despite their poverty, send children to private schools on their children's demand. Thus, as revealed in the present study, even children influence parents' decision-making of school choice for them.

Civil Society at Work

What emerges from the present study indicates that there is strong civil society involvement and contribution in the education sector in the state of Manipur. The dedication and commitment of civil society organisations towards education in the state is a great attraction for parents and the community at large. Don Bosco School, for example, stands out as one such ideal school in the state. The school under the control and management of the Salesian Catholic Fathers is rated as one of the most successful schools in the state, not only in terms of examination results of children, but also in rendering youth focus programmes, since the teachings of Don Bosco emphasises on the preparation of youth as the most incalculable through educational programmes.

Besides being commodious, the school provides good physical infrastructural facilities. The walls are neatly painted with interesting pictures hung; classrooms are well ventilated and large enough to accommodate sixty to seventy students, etc. The school has various physical facilities that are also efficiently utilised. Basic requirements of teaching/learning material aids such as globes, charts, maps, demonstrative materials, science kits, mathematic kits and audio-visual aids are not only available but regularly utilised in the classroom teaching as and when required. There is also a book bank and various journals kept in a library hall. Desks, benches, tables and chairs are painted to sustain longevity. Every corner of the school provides motivation and learning environment for children. These are sufficiently highlighted from the findings of the present study. Interesting pictures and writings about discipline, practical moral science are hung on the walls of almost every corner of the stair case of the school building. These writings and pictures are highlighted in bright colour to capture the attention of students. The displays are oriented to disciplining and sensitising students about habits of cleanliness, punctuality, discipline, important announcements and important news or events of the school. The school demonstrates how limited available school resources, when judiciously utilised, can make the learning environment truly empowering for children. The richness of the school environment could be further enhanced by the active engagement of the dedicated teachers, who have taken up the teaching profession as a serious vocation. Their spirit of nobility, jest for life, flexibility of mind, farsightedness and dedication to children's welfare was apparently noticed among teachers in their unique ways of teaching methods used inside and outside classroom, assignment undertaking during normal holidays, working for days and hours at a stretch, solely for the sake of the welfare of their students.

In fact, one can argue that the methods of teaching/learning and overall pedagogy adopted by these teachers are child-centred and quite empowering for children. While examining the pedagogy adopted by the teachers, the method was found to be truly joyful and successful in provoking children's curiosity and inquisitiveness. The method encourages both the teachers and the taught to be creatively engaged. Such methods could be seen adopted in the art of teaching for all types of disciplines – be it History, Geography, Literature and so on. These teachers are well aware of what works best for the children. They try their best to engage children emotionally, cognitively and physically while learning through observation and demonstrative methods of teaching. Children of Don Bosco School are regularly taken to the field and to the objects of their study. The method, in another sense, tries to nurture and extract the uniqueness in each child. For example, when children were taken to the site of Dzuko valley in Senapati district, some might enjoy the beautiful sight of the mountain, some might enjoy studying the beautiful flowers grown there, while some wonder about the mystery of the creator while watching the vastness of the beautiful layers of the blue mountain peak disappearing in the smoky clouds of the sky. There is no room for rote memory in such a process of learning.

Apart from these, the Salesian Fathers, particularly Father M.C. George, has taken extra effort to make learning extremely relevant and useful by relating it to the immediate environment of these children. This was noticed when he makes lesson plans and preparation for practical moral science and peace education by documenting the life stories of those youths trapped by illicit trafficking of drugs and arms published in local newspapers in the state of Manipur. This awakens the conscience of innocent children, prevents them from entrapment by the current pathological social order of drugs and substance abuse and trains them to grow as responsible adults. It is hard to believe that children, when given such an opportunity of learning, would result in gaining superficial knowledge. Pursuing an education agenda of this kind can be truly exciting, enriching and empowering for children.

All-Round Dependence

The successful performance of Don Bosco School is mainly due to the synergy among various resources of school dimensions – the physical setting, the head teacher, the teachers and the Salesian Fathers – who manage and control school affairs. In a way, the truly remarkable and inspiring teachers in the school and their commitment to children can be attributed to the autonomy and accountability of the school organisational structure directed by the Salesian Fathers. The Salesian Fathers can realise their vision as they are relatively free from the myriad of bureaucratic and political interference that perpetually beset government schools. This way, they successfully accomplish their goals with minimum interference and misuse of school resources. By adopting its own internal mechanisms with inward focus, the school establishes its own goals and accomplishes its vision. Maximum energy from the teachers was fully directed to the welfare of children. Not even a single teacher was found involved in activities outside school, such as assignment for survey, election duty, census collection or any other assignment given by the government department as is rampantly prevalent among government school teachers. Secondly, unlike the various layers of administration governing government schools, more often than not, the major task of responsibility is carried out by the school head teacher in consultation with Fathers who are readily available on the school premises. The head teacher, apart from playing a watchdog role, is also an instructional leader. All the teachers of Don Bosco are also privileged to attend suitable teacher training programmes and other education-related activities, such as workshops, seminars occasionally arranged by the Fathers. As revealed by these teachers, the training they received was quite useful not only in classroom teaching for particular discipline, but also in psychologically dealing with students of different personality traits. Discipline, morality and good habit formation remain core issues of teaching and are non-negotiable as principles of the Catholic education system. The thriving and promotion of these values remain a basic foundation of the school, which are well accepted by the parent community as well. There are pressures from parents for raising high quality standards along with traditional value systems within the school and teachers have responded to this demand. Parents come forward to cooperate in striving to achieve the same goal concentrating on their children's effort to achieve cognitive learning and disciplining their lives, which parents consider as supremely important for a society passing through intense political turmoil with its greatest impact on youths.

The success story of Don Bosco School demonstrates an excellent illustration wherein the organic relationship between the physical and human dimensions of school resources, when mutually articulate and consistent, can indeed harness maximum propensity of growth in children and youths.

In the case of Bethel, the school is not as developed, modern or commodious as Don Bosco. Yet, its modest facilities, such as the school premises, teaching/learning facilities, classrooms, basic conveniences, etc., are effectively utilised and maintained. Though majority of them are untrained, teachers with average qualifications are made more accountable for their performance and even if they use simple conventional methods of teaching in the classroom, they closely monitor the students not only in their academic performance but also in terms of overall good habit formation. Norms of obedience and discipline are strictly followed and non-negotiable. This host of factors attract parents and guardians of lower middle class families, who can afford to pay average fees. Hence, the school is better able to maintain a good teacher-pupil ratio. Being locals and from the same ethnic community, the rapport between parents and teachers is more open and constructive, as they can meet each other frequently to discuss about children. As observed in the present study, parents of private school children are able to create some kind of impact on school management and teachers. For example, some parents of children studying in Bethel school demanded to build more toilets and even shift the toilet to a more suitable place to which the school secretary had responded positively.

The school secretary, who is also the principal of the school, has made every possible effort of keeping the school in the good books of parents, by turning the modest school infrastructural facilities into a lively and stimulating environment of learning for children. The commitment, sincerity and its management with limited resources are reflected in producing students scoring good ranks during examinations every year. The examination results appear to be the testimony of commanding confidence and faith of parents by the school. In 2006, the school was honoured by the state government as the best performing school in terms of examination results. The school had also been recognised as the best performing school in 2007 by the All Manipur Private School Association. This has further elevated the status of the school and helped to command overwhelming support from the local parents.

Civil Society: Its Possibilities and Limitations

Undoubtedly both Don Bosco and Bethel schools were established for providing education to illiterate village children of destitute families. In the initial stages, the aim of establishing both the schools was similar in purpose and in spirit, i.e., providing education to the unreached and marginalised village children, who are deprived of basic education. Steadily, there was expansion of both the schools in varying degrees. In the course of its journey, both the schools became successful due to the overwhelming demand of parents, most of whom are well-to-do ones. Yet, as the schools became successful in their performance, there was a steady process of exclusion of the marginalised children as observed in the present study. Today, both the schools have become exclusive for the children of affluent and middle class parents, leaving no room for the marginalised village illiterate children of poor families. Therefore, the poor and the marginalised children, without the means and the capacities, are often excluded. The biggest challenge confronting both the schools is that expenditure and resources utilised in running and maintaining the schools are generated from the student community in the form of fees and funds collected from time to time. Therefore, participation in both the schools does not merely depend on merit alone, but also on the income and capacity of participating households. For example, if one simply compares the fee structures, it is extremely high in the case of

Don Bosco School, while it is relatively lower in the case of Bethel school, yet quite high when compared with the fee structure in government school. A student studying in Don Bosco School spends 24 times more than the amount paid by a student studying in government school, while it is almost 13 times bigger as in case of Bethel school. The expenditure is calculated absolutely in terms of fee structure and hence it could be much higher if one calculates the cumulative expenditure, such as expenditure for stationery items, uniform, transport charges, fees for private tutors, etc.

The above experience clearly demonstrates that the economic status of a family determines the success and schooling destination of a child. Secondly, good quality schools starting with the goal of providing education to the disadvantaged children steadily turned into the abode of children of the upper and middle classes, by systematically excluding the disadvantaged children over a period of time. As Karl Marx rightly observed, the poor and the underprivileged are excluded from the encirclement of civil society. Being an essentially middle class entity, the mindset of civil society institutions is influenced by market forces such as introduction of new computer courses by charging additional fees, expansion of internet facilities and ultimately an increase in fee structure. Managers of private schools, being well aware of the middle class mindset, can also be cunning to the extent that they may not even wish the government schools to improve, so that the vulnerable parents can ultimately fall back on their services and parental acceptance is what legitimises their existence and expansion. This observation points to the irrefutable fact that the operation of civil society is not free from the structural logic of social stratification.

Notwithstanding these limitations, on the other hand, civil society institutions, by virtue of their relative independence in ideology and philosophy, can perhaps be in solidarity with the poor as well. The options are well within their hands, though limited. This finding can be observed in the present study, as the case of Bosco Mangaal illustrates. Father M.C. George, Director of Don Bosco School established Bosco Mangaal, an NGO to extend literacy campaign for the unreached, marginalised children of destitute families in the villages of Manipur by identifying the needy villages for opening literacy centres through micro planning and school mapping with the help of *leikai* members. Apart from involving the villagers, the use of most innovative, interesting and pragmatic methods of teaching/learning, such as study of concrete objects that children can easily identify with and the joyful learning for children including songs, citing of rhymes, dance, body movements, etc., have been proved to be extremely successful for motivating children to learn. Teaching/learning in all the literacy centres has been made child-centred, activity-based and quite flexible. The method motivates and arouses keen interest in children to the extent that they look forward to going to classes held in open spaces, where only reed mats are spread for their sitting arrangement. It was surprisingly pleasant to observe the zest and interest in these children for learning that was often reflected in their interaction with me. Children at literacy centres were amazingly enthusiastic, readily smiling, reciprocate and quite articulate.

Today, Bosco Mangaal has become extremely successful and popular among many poor households of all communities such as Christians, Muslims, Hindus, etc. It has played a crucial role in enabling children of destitute families to pick up literacy skills, while some of them have become truly educated. By the time the research about Bosco Mangaal was conducted in 2009, there were as many as 2,344 children who got enrolled in regular schools, while some of them were found to be doing well by coping up in regular schools, even outperforming those children already enrolled in regular schools. Through the network of Catholic missionary schools in the state, some of them are successfully admitted to Catholic schools for furthering their education. Yet, as Bosco Mangaal became successful in its literacy campaign and education mission for the most neglected children in far flung villages of the state, there were new rules created. For example, restrictions on the eligibility criteria of entry for children were introduced. This was noticed even in the selection and recruitment of teachers, who come forward to volunteer in the education mission.

Education Emergencies

One common persistent observation that has emerged in the present study is the perennial destabilisation of schooling of children due to sporadic violence caused by ethnic clashes, economic blockades, bloody killings, disappearance of individuals (suspected to be insurgents), students, illegal detention and counter-insurgency movement by armed forces. These violent incidents critically sabotage school education in a variety of ways. School teachers, parents and children unanimously agree on the frequent disruption of school education by occasional and sporadic violence. During such periods, school children are forced to join protest demonstrations. For example, in the most infamous ceasefire incident in 2001, children were forced to join a protest demonstration against ceasefire extension in the state of Manipur. During the incident, school textbooks and reading materials were burnt and destroyed and innocent and tender children were compelled to be a part of societal crisis management. When violence occurs, schools remain closed, forcing children and teachers to experience an educational emergency in which the operation of schools is temporarily shut. As found in the present study, educational emergency is cited as the most frequent phenomena in the state.

True, educational emergency destabilises regular school activity and is damaging for all children, but most damaging for children of poor households in unique ways. Firstly, when school is perhaps the only hope for the child to pick up certain skills of learning, school closure crashes this hope. Secondly, since the child is temporarily prevented from learning, it becomes difficult for him/her to pick up afresh when he/she joins school after a time gap and making it a rather difficult and challenging task for teachers. Parents unanimously grieve about the fact that occasional stoppage of school functioning encourages the private tuition system to flourish at a fast speed, which only children of rich families can afford. Occasional violence in public space regularly uproots everyday economic engagement of parents. For example, during violence and conflict, operation of *keithels,* which is the mainstay of everyday livelihoods, is disturbed. During such periods, there is crisis of hunger among households due to disruption in livelihood engagements and other economic activity that partly supports the education of their children. Therefore, during such emergencies, the hardest hit is the poor households for they are unable to market their home-based products. Economic blockades often give rise to shooting up of prices of essential commodities and poor households are again hit the hardest. As observed in the present study, conflicts, instability and political violence in the state take their toll on education and pose one of the greatest challenges to realising the goal of educational right for all children.

Right to Education: A Continuing Journey

Given the above experience, it can be rightly argued that the educational right for children is to be understood in the social, political economic reality of a people. It is straddled among civil, political, economic and social rights. The rights agenda to education is, therefore, rooted in the successful implementation of each of these complementary rights in as much as the educational right is an associational right that can be achieved through strong positive state action. This further suggests that there is no place for poverty, hunger, disease, conflict and violence in a society striving to realise the educational right for children. Secondly, the state, unlike the civil society sector, cannot pursue the 'hands off' policy in its efforts in ensuring the educational right for every child, including the poorest of the poor and children living in isolated villages. Removing various obstacles is indeed a journey of institutional reforms in a multi pronged strategy, by suitably harnessing the local resources – both human and material.

Accountability

The state must restrain from pursuing self-interested, publicly harmful, short-term goals, such as corruption as practised in myriad forms during the recruitment of teachers, the non-implementation or patchy implementation of schemes and the shunting of teachers from one place to another on personal whims and fancies. Parents showed concerns against the callousness of government school teachers, engaging in many irregularities and pastime activities during school hours. Such callousness was not at all noticeable up to the late 1970s and early 1980s in the state-run schools, due to the effective functioning of the inspection system. Inspection systems matter for a variety of reasons. An inspection system is directly accountable to teachers, who are most visibly identified with the schools they serve. Through an effective inspection system, a teacher's teaching responsibility is called for examination in the form of testing classroom teaching/learning process. Monitoring through an inspection system also extends beyond inspecting teachers' and students' level of understanding alone. The inspector also gathers a fair knowledge of any major handicaps the school faces. An inspector, by registering all these conditions of a school, can put forward the matter to the higher authorities for removing such handicaps. Apart from these, through inspection system, teachers are better linked to the education policy makers and education managers at the top. In this way, the chasm between higher authorities and school teachers and the level of misunderstanding between the two can be greatly minimised. In short, through an effective inspection system, education policy makers, planners and managers can be accountable to teachers and school children indirectly.

As narrated by the government school teachers, the school facilities and the schemes are implemented on a piecemeal basis and in an erratic manner. This has shocked the conscience of the teaching community. Teachers can raise their voice against such irregularities, provided they are safeguarded, but there is a consistent culture of silence among school teachers, as found in the government school under study, since teachers readily compromise with such irregularities due to fear of transfer. Under the SSA policy, there is the scheme of free distribution of school bags and uniform for students, but it was found missing in the sample government school. Resources meant for these facilities have been directed elsewhere. Further, the state government has gone beyond the limit when it asked the private schools to sign forged expenditure paper under the SSA programme. The case was narrated by the secretary of Bethel school, as he lamented in vain that the school did not receive any amount of money from the state education department.

Regarding teachers' training and orientation programmes, despite all their good intentions, there is no uniformly prepared training course for teachers. A simple example will lend support to this argument. As per the provisions of teachers' training under SSA, a teacher must be trained for 20 days each year, with a 60-day refresher course being compulsory for untrained teachers who are already employed as teachers and 30 days' orientation course for freshly trained recruits. Despite such prescribed norms, not a single teacher of the government school under study was provided a refresher course under SSA. Further, the course content of training was not only patchy but also irrelevant, as teachers themselves complained. For example, it is absolutely pointless to train a teacher teaching children of class VI or VII by making him/her recite rhythms in which the skills can be utilised for teaching nursery students, as was found in the case of a teacher from the sample government school. Therefore, teachers who genuinely desire to learn something innovative through training must be encouraged. The problem can be overcome by providing suitable resources for training teachers, by taking stock of the existing socio-economic political dynamics of the state.

Almost a decade has already passed since SSA was first initiated in 2000 to realise the dream of the educational right for all children in India. SSA was pursued in different states of the country as a follow-up vision of achieving education for all children as per the Dakar framework of action. Despite all its good intentions, not much visible quality output has been achieved in schools; rather it is noticed that children left government schools in hordes. The situation has created a kind of fear among teachers and an uncertainty about their future as their employability as teachers in the absence of a satisfactory number of students in schools. This is despite the fact that there are dedicated, well-qualified teachers available in government schools. Therefore, the state must correct its own blunder by encouraging dedicated teachers, but also to generally arouse faith in the teaching community, who are directly accountable to children. Assigning duties of election, census and household survey to the teachers must be done away with, since their engagement in non-teaching activity hampers the regular teaching/learning process for children. Instead, the state must empower the teacher community by giving due honour to the job of a teacher as one of the most challenging tasks.

Synergy between State and Society

Understanding the dynamics of the social fabric of Manipuri society, there is every possibility that strong state action on improving school education can be reinforced by the accountability of civic bodies to the efforts of the state. This is due to the existence of a favourable socio-cultural milieu of the society, which has not experienced violence and atrocities based on casteism, communalism, highly stratified class hierarchy, impinging patriarchy, as is rampantly existent in majority societies of India. In the state of Manipur, neither the state nor the civil society faces the challenges of such stubborn social mores and norms, while bringing children, including girls, to schools. The state must fully seize this favourable socio-cultural milieu as an opportunity while pursuing the goal of educational right for all children, by removing all other possible obstacles faced by its people. There is also immense possibility that strong solidarity can be created between teachers, parents and the community at large for a common goal of making government schools accountable to children, in which the attempt is much more likely to be successful in Manipuri society since there is a strong sense of belonging to a common ethnic group. Further, as it emerges from the present study, achieving these targets may not be a difficult task, since there is high social motivation for the education of children as a matter of social norm.

Creating an Enabling Environment

No social condition is inevitable; these social conditions are created by people and, therefore, what people create can also change. While pursuing the above goals, the state must provide sufficient space and every possible opportunity for various civil society organisations to actively participate in educational activities on a large scale across the state. This is possible by breaking the historical mistrust between the state and civil society, by finding common methods of mutual collaboration. As seen in the present study, the role of NGOs and other civil society organs, except religious organisations and few private individuals in education, is practically negligible, since the majority of civil society organisations are channelled in issues related to human rights violations, insurgency and counter-insurgency, illicit trafficking of drugs and HIV/AIDS, etc. Educational services of civil society need not necessarily be confined to private schools or religious organisations alone, but also extend to other civil society sectors, including media – print, electronic, radio – and organisations such as local youth clubs, student organisations, self-help groups and even *Ima Meira Paibis,* which can make one not only 'education aware' but also 'education right aware'.

Civil society involvement can be further strengthened by active parental participation, through village education committees, which can play an active role in linking parents to teachers and schools. As seen in private schools, the open and constructive dialogue between parents and teachers ensures a certain amount of accountability to children. The same can be followed in government schools as well. However, the strategy of involving parents in the schooling of their children requires providing sustainable income to economically poor parents to enable them to be a part of their schooling, since majority of the poor parents are daily wage labourers and do not find sufficient time for their children. To partly overcome the financial constraints faced by parents, to provide viable financial assistance, the state can initially start off by establishing micro-credit cooperatives and self-help groups to generate income for households. The same strategy is adopted by NGO members of Bosco Mangaal.

Another crucial issue is the intensity of exclusion experienced by the marginalised tribal communities in educational participation. Tribal children travel long distance to reach a functioning government school, as seen in the case of the sample government school. These children commute to school without any public transport facility. Therefore, while addressing the issue of access and equity for all children, the state is morally bound to ensure that such constraints do not pose any obstacle for these children. The fact that tribal children commute to school by travelling long distances further suggests that there is no ashram school available for them or other school facilities within their own village, suggesting that opening of schools in tribal villages is inevitable.

As repeatedly captured in all the chapters of the book, conflict, instability and political violence have taken a high toll on education in myriad ways. School children and the teaching community have been facing educational emergency due to occasional conflict and violence in the state. The state and civil society must create continuous teaching/learning opportunities for children in a secure and peaceful environment during and post-conflict period so that they can continue learning without a time gap. Making school education a free zone will drastically reduce the loss of learning opportunities by children during and post conflict period.

Addressing the crucial issue of the educational right as fundamental for children cannot be treated in isolation. Striving for the educational right is conceived not only as a vision, but a movement and a framework for actions to be rigorously pursued. Facilities provided in NEP (1986), POA (1992), EFA (2000), mobile school/residential school facilities, ECCE and ICDS facilities, adult education programmes, total literacy drives, adequate representation of SC/ST teachers, etc., must be implemented in full measure. This should be addressed urgently by taking specific local experience, needs and target groups. Revamping of the functioning of DIET and DEOs must be ensured while DIET must be established in backward districts.

The state, while simultaneously revamping the above schemes, projects and educational institutions, must make the education system organically linked with the immediate community and society of children. For example, take the case of growing *leihao,* the joy perfume as explained by the English teacher in the government sample school. *Leihao* is a conspicuous plant, yet every household can afford to grow it and hence generate income in a much easier way. The concept of planting and growing *leihao* as explained by the teacher was so amazingly beautiful that every child became engrossed in the classroom because, at that moment, the child's classroom experience was not boring. Likewise, in Don Bosco School, every child is made to creatively engage by letting children study the natural beauty, such as hills, flowers, historical sites, etc. By directly relating children to these objects, these sites become a part of their own living and history. Even classroom teaching was full of demonstrative methods. Each way of learning can be made uniquely interesting for children. The method trains children to learn about certain objects and go beyond preconceived notions, hence broadening their understanding of the world they constantly interact with. Meaningful and joyous learning is also a way of learning by doing. This is amply illustrated in the learning methods adopted by children in Bosco Mangaal. Children were given objects such as stones, leaves, pots and flowers. By identifying these objects in concrete forms, they learnt the various dimensions and facets of these objects. Secondly, this form of teaching/learning not only infuses jest and life in them, a number of recreation activities like singing, prayers, dance and body rhythms fascinate children and make them look forward to attend the class on the following day. Most importantly, teachers of Bosco Mangaal treat their children with love, affection and tenderness. In turn, this empowers children to be morally and emotionally bonding to the teachers they often interact with. This provides some of the reasons why Bosco Mangaal has become uniquely successful, despite mounting constraints like limited financial resources and extremely challenging physical circumstances of teaching/learning activity.

The state must ensure that the capacity of the government to revamp the education system is not eroded by budgetary constraints, as spending on military and police forces crowds out social spending in the state. Furthermore, the state must guarantee that civil society organisations are given safe and sufficient space and their operations remain unhindered by the harmful activities of both the state and the insurgent outfits. By gaining the faith of its people, the state can counter any unwanted elements including extortion, threat by insurgents and other obstacles that come in the way of implementing EFA programme. This is possible only if the state falls back on its people. The possibility of generating a dialogue with its own people based on faith and love is feasible only if the state restrains itself from engaging in the accumulation of free floating public resources and barbaric acts of misusing heavily armed state commandos, police and paramilitary forces against its own people, while shielding their criminal acts from the very people who balloted them to power. Without winning faith, confidence and love from the people, who can be the strongest weapon for the state in bringing about societal reforms, any effort towards educational reforms cannot take its roots. However, as things stand today, the state continues with its baffling refusal to come up with reforms. In the given scenario, the realisation of the educational right for all children will continue to be out of reach and remain a long continuous journey.

Bibliography

Agarwal, S.P. and A. Biswas (eds) 1986. *Development of Education in India: A Historical Survey of Educational Developments*. New Delhi: Concept Publishing Company.

Aggarwal, Kailash S. (ed.) 1999. *Dynamics of Identity and Intergroup Relations in North-East India*. Shimla: Indian Institute of Advanced Study.

Alexander, John W. and Truman A. Hartshorn. 1988. *Economic Geography*. New Delhi: Prentice Hall of India Private Limited.

Ansari, S.A. 1986. *Socio-Economic Development in Tribal Areas of Manipur*. New Delhi: B.R. Publishing Corporation.

——. 1985. *Some Aspects of the Geography of Manipur*. New Delhi: B.R. Publishing Corporation.

Apple, M.W. and Jules. 1995. 'The State and Educational Reform' in Pink and Noblit (eds), *Continuity and Contraction: The Futures of the Sociology of Education*. New Jersey: Hampton Press, Inc.

Apple, M.W. 1982. *Education and Power*. Boston: Routledge & Kegan Paul.

——. 2001. *Educating the Right Way. Markets, Standards, God, and Inequality*. New York & London: Routlege Falmer.

Barry, Norman. 2002. *Concepts in Social Thought: The Welfare State*. New Delhi: Viva Books Pvt. Ltd.

Baruah, Sanjib. 2005. *Durable Disorder: Understanding the Politics of Northeast India*. New Delhi: Oxford University Press.

Bass, Jossy. 1976. *The Craft of Teaching: A Guide to Mastering the Professor's Art*. London: Chapman and Hall.

Basu, D.D. 2000. *Introduction to the Constitution of India*. New Delhi: Wadhwa and Company Law Publishers.

Bhattarjee, J.B. (ed.) 2010. *State and Economy in Pre-Colonial Manipur*. New Delhi: Akansha Publishing House.

Bhatty, Kiran. 1998. 'Educational Deprivation in India: A Survey of Field Investigators'. *EPW*, Vol. xxxiii, No. 27, 4–10 July.

Bhola, S. Harbans and Akpovire Oduran (eds) 2006. *Widening Access to Education as Social Justice: Essays in Honour of Michael Omolawa*. Netherlands: Springer.

Biesta, Girt J.J. and Denise Egea-Kuehne (eds) 2001. *Derrida and Education*. London: Routledge.

Bino, Devi L. 2002. *The Lois of Manipur*. New Delhi: Mittal Publications.

Blackage, David and Barry Hunt. 2001. *Sociological Interpretations of Education*. Sydney: Croom Helm.

Bourdieu, Pierre. 1972. *Outline of a Theory of Practice*. London, New York and Melbourne: Cambridge University Press.

Brara, N. Vijaylakshmi. 1998. *Politics, Society and Cosmology in India's North East*. New Delhi: Oxford University Press.

Briddle, J. Bruce. 2001. *Social Class, Poverty and Education: Policy and Practice*. London: Routledge Falmer.

Brown, R. 1873. *Statistical Account of the Native State of Manipur and the Hill Territory under its Rule*. Delhi: Sanskaran Prakashak.

Byrne, David. 2005. *Social Exclusion*. UK: Open University Press.

Census of India. 2001. 'Provisional Population Totals'. Manipur Series 14, Paper 1 of 2001.

——. 2001. 'Provisional Population Totals'. Manipur Series 14, Paper 3 of 2001, April.

——. 2001. 'Provisional Population Totals'. Manipur Series 15, Paper 3 of 2001.

Chandhok, Neera. 1995. *State and Civil Society: Exploration in Political Theory*. New Delhi: Sage Publications.

Chandrashekhar Panchani. 1987. *Manipur: Religion, Culture and Society*. New Delhi: Konark Publishers.

Chapman, Karen. 1986. *Sociology of Schools*. London and New York: Tavistock Publications.

Constantine, R. 1981. *Manipur: Maid of the Mountains*. New Delhi: Law Publishers.

Coser, Lewis A. 2007. *Masters of Sociological Thought*. Jaipur and New Delhi: Rawat Publications.

Cosin, B.R. (ed.) 1972. *Education: Structure and Society*. United Kingdom: Penguin.

Das, Veena (ed.) 2003. *The Oxford India: Companion to Sociology and Social Anthropology*. New Delhi: Oxford University Press.

Datta, Sreeradha. 2001. 'What Ails the Northeast: An Enquiry into the Economic Factors'. *Strategic Analysis*, Vol. XXV, No. 1.

Dena, Lal (ed.) 1988. *Christian Missions and Colonialism*. Shillong: Vanderam Institute.

Devi, Jamini. 1989. *Education in Manipur*. Imphal: Rai Pravina Press.

Directorate of Economics & Statistics. 2005. 'Statistical Abstract: Manipur'. Imphal: Government of Manipur.

Downs, Frederick S. 1992. *History of Christianity in India, Vol. 5, Part 5: North East India in the Nineteenth and Twentieth Centuries*. Bangalore: The Church History Association of India.

Dreze, Jean and Amartya Sen. 1998. *Indian Development: Selected Regional Perspectives*. New Delhi: Oxford India Paperbacks.

——. 2002. *India: Development and Participation*. New Delhi: Oxford University Press.

Dubey, S.M. 1978. *North East India: Sociological Study*. New Delhi: Concept Publishing Company.

Durkheim, Emile. 1961. *Moral Education: A Study in the Theory and Application of the Sociology of Education*. New York: The Free Press.

——. 1912. *The Elementary Forms of Religious Life*. London: Allen and Unwin.

——. 1957. *Education and Sociology*. New York: The Free Press.

——. 1982. *The Rules of Sociological Method*. London: Macmillan.

Economic Survey of Manipur. 2007–08. Imphal: Directorate of Economics and Statistics.

EFA Global Monitoring Report. 2002. Paris: UNESCO.

Foucault, Michel. 1977. *Discipline and Punish: The Birth of the Prison*. England: Penguin Books.

Free and Compulsory Education Bill. 2004. New Delhi: MHRD, Government of India.

Freire, Paulo. 1972. *Pedagogy of the Oppressed*. Baltimore, MD: Penguin Books.

Fromm, Erich. 1956. *The Art of Loving*. New York: Harper & Row, Inc.

Gennep Van, Arnord. 1960. *The Rights of Passage*. London : Routledge and Kegan Paul.

Gewirtz, Sharon. 2001. 'Rethinking Social Justice: A Conceptual Analysis', in J. Demaine (ed.), *Sociology of Education Today*. New York: Palgrave, pp. 49–64.

Ghathia, Joseph. 2000. *Child Labour in Marginalized Communities*. Delhi: Centre of Concern for Child Labour.

Ghurye, G.S. 1950. *Caste and Race in India*. New Delhi: Popular Prakashan.

Giddens, Anthony. 1998. *Sociology*. UK: Blackwell Publications.

Goffman, Erving. 1959. *The Presentation of Self in Everyday Life*. England: Penguin Books.

Govinda, R. and Reshmi Dewan (eds) 2003. *Community Participation and Empowerment in Primary Education*. New Delhi: Sage Publications.

Goyal, Aparajita and Jean Dreze. 2003. 'Future of Mid-Day Meals'. *EPW*, Vol. XXXVIII, No. 43.

Halsey, A.H. (ed.) 1997. *Education: Culture, Economy and Society*. Oxford: Oxford University Press.

Higgins, J.C. (ICS). 1998. 'Notes on Meithei (Manipuri Beliefs and Customs)'. Imphal: Manipur State Archive, Directorate of Art and Culture, Government of Manipur.

Hodgson, Douglas. 1998. *The Human Right to Education*. Ashgate: Darmouth Publishing Company Ltd.

Homen, Th. 2005. 'Armed Conflict and Women's Well in Manipur in Modernity, Tradition & Contested Space', *Eastern Quarterly*, Vol. 3, Issue 11, July–September.

Hudson, T.C. 1908. *The Meitheis*. New Delhi: Low Price Publications.

Jalali, Jayashree Roy. 2003. 'Decentralisation of Primary Education in the Autonomous District Council of Karbi Anglong-Assam'. Unpublished report submitted to NIEPA, New Delhi.

Johnstone, James. 1896. *My Experiences in Manipur and the Naga Hills*. London: Marston and Company Limited.

Jordan, Bill. 1985. *The State: Authority and Autonomy*. Oxford: Blackwell.

Josephine, Yazali. 2005. *School Resource Planning and Management*. New Delhi: Shipra Publications.

Joychandra, L. 1995. *The Lost Kingdom: Royal Chronicle of Manipur*. Imphal: Prajatantra Publishing House.

Juneja, Nalini. 2003. 'Constitutional Amendment to Make Education a Fundamental Right: Issue for a Follow-up Legislation'. Occasional Paper No. 33, New Delhi: NIEPA.

Karna, M.N. (ed.) 1998. *Social Movements in North-East India*. New Delhi: Indus Publishing House.

Kate, Nash (ed.) 2000. *Readings in Contemporary Political Sociology*. Oxford: Blackwell Publishers.

Keane, John. 1988. *Civil Society and the Sate: New European Perspectives*. New York: Verso.

Khilnani, Sunil and Sudipta Kaviraj (eds) 2001. *Civil Society: History and Possibilities*. New Delhi: Cambridge University Press.

Kohli, Atul. 1987. *State and Poverty in India: The Politics of Reforms*. Cambridge: Cambridge University Press.

Kothari, C.R. 2006. *Research Methodology: Methods and Techniques*. Delhi: New Age International (P) Ltd. Publishers.

Kothari, Rajni. 1976. *Democratic Polity and Social Change in India: Crisis and Opportunities*. Calcutta: Allied Publications.

——. 1988. *State Against Democracy: In Search of Human Governance*. New Delhi: Ajanta Publications.

Kumar, Krishna. 1991. *Political Agenda of Education: A Study of Colonialist and Nationalist Ideas*. New Delhi: Sage Publications.

Laiba, M.T. 1992. *The Geography of Manipur*. Imphal: Public Book Store.

Lemert, Charles C. 1990. *Sociology and Twilight of Man*. USA: Heritage Publishers.

Levitas, Maurice. 1974. *Marxist Perspectives on the Sociology of Education.* London: Routledge and Kegan Paul.

Livingstone, David W. 1987. *Critical Pedagogy and Cultural Power*. London: Macmillan.

Louis, Prakash and R. Vashum (eds) 2002. *State, Development and Identity in South Asia: A Search for Alternative Paradigms*. New Delhi: Indian Social Institute.

Lyndem, Biloris and Utpal Kumar De (eds) 2004. *Education in North East India*. New Delhi: Concept Publishing Company.

Mackenzie, Alexander. 1884. *History of the Relations of the Government with the Hill Tribes of the North-East Frontier of Bengal*. Calcutta: Home Department.

Mandelbaum, G. 1972. *Society in India: Continuity and Change*. Vol. 1, Bombay: Popular Prakashan.

Manheim, Karl. 1952. *Essays on the Sociology of Knowledge*. London: Routledge & Kegan Paul Ltd.

Marx, K. and F. Engels. 1968. *Selected Works*. Moscow: Progress Publishers.

McCulloch, W. 1980. *An Account of the Valley of Manipur*. New Delhi: Gyan Publishing House.

Mclaren, P. and Henry A. Giroux (eds) 1989. *Critical Pedagogy, the State and Cultural Struggle*. Albany: University of New York Press.

Mehta, Arun. C. 2004. *Elementary Education in India: Where Do We Stand?* New Delhi: NIEPA.

Menamparampil, S.D.B. and M.C. George (eds) 2007. *Golden Memoirs*. Imphal: Don Bosco.

Miller, David. 2002. *Social Justice*. Oxford: Clarendon Press.

Milliband, Ralph. 1976. *The State in Capitalist Society*. London: Quartet Books.

Mishra, Jayshree. 2000. *The Girl Child in a Scavenging Community*. New Delhi: Nanak Publications.

Mohammed, A. and M. Harsh. 2004. *Good Governance*. Bangalore: ActionAid.

Morrow, Raymond Allen and Carlo Alberto Torres (eds) 1995. *Social Theory and Education: A Critique of Theories of Social and Cultural Reproduction*. New York: State University of New York Press.

Myrdal, Gunnar. 1967. *Asian Drama: An Enquiry into the Poverty of Nations*. Vol. 111, New York: Penguin.

——. 1970. *The Challenge of World Poverty*. New York: Penguin International Edition.

Nambissan, B. Geetha. 1994. 'Language and Schooling of Tribal Children: Issues Related to Medium of Instruction'. *EPW*, Vol. XXIX, October.

National Education Policy. 1986. New Delhi: Ministry of Education, Government of India.

NIEPA and UNESCO. 2003. 'Different Approaches for Achieving EFA: Indian Experience'. New Delhi.

Parratt, John. 2005. *Wounded Land*. New Delhi: Mittal Publications.

Parratt, S.N. 1980. *The Religion of Manipur: Beliefs, Rituals and Historical Development*. Calcutta: Firma KLM Private Limited.

Parsons, Talcott and Edward Shills (eds) 1951. *Towards a General Theory of Action*. New York: Harper & Row Publishers.

Parsons, Talcott. 1968. 'The School Class as a Social System: Some of Its Functions in American Society' in Robert, R. Bell and Holger R. Stub (eds), *Sociology of Education*. Homewood, Illinois: The Dorsey Press.

Pathak, Avijit. 2004. *Social Implications of Schooling, Knowledge, Pedagogy and Consciousness*. New Delhi: Rainbow Publishers.

Pavalko, Ronald. 1968. *Sociology of Education*. Itasca: F.E. Peacock Publications, Inc.

Peters, Michael and James Marshall (eds) 1996. *Education Policy*. UK: Edward Elgar Publishing Ltd.

Phillips, David and Geoffrey Walford (eds) 2006. *Tracing Education Policy: Selections from the Oxford Review of Education*. London: Routledge.

Pink, W.T. and G.W. Noblit (eds) 1995. *Continuity and Contradiction: The Futures of the Sociology of Education*. New Jersey: Hampton Press, Inc.

Prime Mayek Mapi. Imphal: Department of Education, Government of Manipur.

Programme of Action. 1992. New Delhi: Ministry of Education, Government of India.

Public Report on Primary Education in India. 1999. New Delhi: Oxford University Press.

Rabinow, Paul (ed.) 1984. *Foucault Reader*. New York: Pantheon.

Report of the Education Commission. 1964–66. New Delhi: Ministry of Education, Government of India.

Report of the Education Commission. 1997. New Delhi: Ministry of Education, Govt. of India.

Roy, Jyotirmoy. 1973. *The History of Manipur*. Calcutta: Eastlight Book House.

Russell, Bertrand. 1977. *Education and Social Order*. London: Unwin Paperbacks.

Sadgopal, Anil. 2003. *Political Economy of Education in the Age of Globalisation*. New Delhi: Bharat Jan Vigyan Jatha.

Salam, Jeebanlata. 2004. *Social Exclusion and Education*. New Delhi: Indian Social Institute.

——. 2007. 'Millennium Development Goals and the Education Challenge'. *Social Action*, Vol. 57, No. 2, April–June.

Sanajaoba Naorem (ed.) 1991. *Manipur: Past and Present*. Vol. 2, New Delhi: Mittal Publications.

——. 1995. *Manipur: Past and Present*. Vol. 4, New Delhi: Mittal Publications.

Sarin, V.I.K. 1980. *India's North East in Flames*. New Delhi: Vikas Publishing House.

Sarva Shiksha Abhiyan. 2002. *Manual for Appraisal of Plans*. New Delhi: MHRD.

Scrase, Timothy J. 1993. *Image, Ideology and Inequality: Cultural Domination, Hegemony and Schooling in India*. New Delhi: Sage Publications.

Selected Educational Statistics. 2000–02. New Delhi: MHRD, Government of India.

Sethi, Harsh and Vimala Ramachandran. 2001. *Rajasthan Shiksa Karmi Project: An Overall Appraisal*. Stockholm: Swedish International Development Cooperation Agency.

Shanti, Maimom. 2001. *Development of Education in Manipur*. New Delhi: Rajesh Publications.

Sharma, Naresh K. 2010. 'Locating Civil Society in the Northeast'. *Eastern Quaterly*, Vol. 6, No. 111, Autumn, p. 110.

Shushila, Ramaswamy. 2003. *Political Theory: Ideas and Concepts*. New Delhi: Macmillan India Ltd.

Singh, Arun. 2001. 'Problem of Governance in North East India'. *Journal of Peace Studies*, Vol. 8, No. 4, July–August.

Singh, Jhaljit. 1975. 'Manipur'. Publications Division, Ministry of Information and Broadcasting, Government of India.

Singh, K.S. (ed.) 1998. *People of India: Manipur*. Vol. XXXI, Calcutta: Seagull Books.

Singh, M. Kirti. 1988. *Religion and Culture of Manipur*. Delhi: Manas Publications.

Singh, Mangoljao. 1967. *Western Education in Manipur*. Imphal: Student Store, Paona Bazzar.

Singh, N. Joykumar. 2005. *Social Movements in Manipur*. New Delhi: Mittal Publications.

Singh, N. Lokendra. 1998. *The Unquiet Valley: Society, Economy and Politics in Manipur* (1891-1950), New Delhi: Mittal Publications.

——. 1998. *The Unquiet Valley: Society, Economy and Politics in Manipur* (1891–1950).

Singh, Ravindra P. 1982. *Geography of Manipur*. New Delhi: M.B. Trust.

Singh, S.I. 1987. *Introduction to Manipur*. Imphal: Vivek Publishing House.

Singh, Surjan Kumar. 2009. *Situational Analysis of Children in Government Schools*. Imphal: Manipur Alliance for Child Rights.

Singh, Yogendra.1986. *Modernization of Indian Tradition*. Jaipur and Delhi: Rawat Publications.

Sircar, M. Chaki. 1984. *Feminism in Traditional Society: Women of Manipur Valley*. New Delhi: Shakti Books.

Srinivas, M.N. 1962. *Caste in Modern India and Other Essays*. Bombay: Media Promoters and Publishers Pvt. Ltd.

Srinivas, M.N., A.M. Shah and E.A. Ramaswamy (eds) 2004. *The Field and the Fieldworker: Problems and Challenges in Sociological Investigation*. New Delhi: Oxford University Press.

State Education Commission, Manipur. 1992. *Education in Manipur: Towards a New Education Order: Report 11*. New Delhi: National Publishing House.

Stephen, Ward (ed) 2004. *Education Studies: A Student's Guide*. London and New York: Taylor and Francis Group.

Sudhir, H. 2010. 'Touching Upon the Neglected: An Overview of the World of Women in Pre-Colonial Manipur' in Bhattarjee, J.B (ed) , *State and Economy in Pre -Colonial Manipur*. New Delhi: Akansha Publishing House.

Tandon, Rajesh and Ranjita Mohanty (eds) 2003. *Does Civil Society Matter? Governance in Contemporary India*. New Delhi: Sage Publications.

Tarapot, Phanjoubam. 2005. *Bleeding Manipur*. New Delhi: Har-Anand Publications.

The Right of Children to Free and Compulsory Education Act, 2009. New Delhi: Universal Law Publishing Co. Pvt. Ltd.

The Sangai Express. 2009. 'Operation Summer Storm Stumps Students'. Imphal, 20 April.

Thio, Alex. 1986. *Sociology: An Introduction*. New York: Harper and Row Publishers.

Torres, Carlos Alberto. 1995. 'State and Education Revisited: Why Researchers Should Think Politically about Education'. in Michael Peters and James Marshall (eds). 1996. *Education Policy*. UK: Edward Elgar Publishing Ltd.

Torres, Carlos Alberto and Morrow Raymond Allen (eds).1995. *Social Theory and Education: A Critique of Theories and Social and Cultural Reproduction*. New York: State University of New York Press.

Tyagi, O.S. et al. 2002. 'Shift from Farm to Non-Farm Sector and Rural Women'. Unpublished report submitted to Indian Social Institute, New Delhi.

UNICEF. 1994. 'The Right to be a Child'. New Delhi.

Unni Krishnan vs the State of Andhra Pradesh,1993.

Van Gennep, Arnold. 1960. *The Rites of Passage*. London: Routledge and Kegan Paul.

Verghese, N.V. 1995. *School Facilities and Learner Achievement: Towards a Methodology of Analysing School Facilities in India*. New Delhi: NIEPA.

Walford, Geoffrey and David Phillips (eds) 2006. *Tracing Education Policy: Selections from the Oxford Review of Education*. London: Routledge.

Wasserstrom, Jeffrey N., Lynn Hunt and Marlyn Young (eds) 2000. *Human Rights and Revolutions*. Lanham, MD: Rowman & Littlefield.

Wazir, Rekha (ed) 2000. *The Gender Gap in Basic Education: NGOs as Change Agents*. New Delhi: Sage Publications.

Weber, Max. 1920. *Economy and Society*. Berkeley: University of California Press.

Woods, P. and M. Hammersley (eds) 1976. *Process of Schooling: A Sociological Reader*. London: Routledge & Kegan Paul and Open University Press.

Young, Michael and Geoff Whitty. 1977. *Society, State and Schooling*. England: The Falmer Press.

Index